The Postwar World
General Editors: A.J. Nicholls and Martin S. Alexander

As distance puts events into perspective, and as evidence accumulates, it begins to be possible to form an objective historical view of our recent past. *The Postwar World* is an ambitious new series providing a scholarly but readable account of the way our world has been shaped in the crowded years since the Second World War. Some volumes will deal with regions, or even single nations, others with important themes; all will be written by expert historians drawing on the latest scholarship as well as their own research and judgements. The series should be particularly welcome to students, but it is designed also for the general reader with an interest in contemporary history.

The Community of Europe:
A History of European Integration since 1945

Derek W. Urwin

Longman
London and New York

Longman Group UK Limited,
Longman House, Burnt Mill, Harlow,
Essex CM20 2JE, England
and Associated Companies throughout the world.

*Published in the United States of America
by Longman Inc., New York*

© Longman Group UK Limited 1991

First published 1991

British Library Cataloguing in Publication Data
Urwin, Derek W. (Derek William) 1939 –
 The community of Europe : a history of European
 integration since 1945. – (The postwar world).
 1. Europe. Economic integration, history
 1. Title II. Series
337.14

ISBN 0–582–04530–4
ISBN 0–582–04531–2 pbk

Library of Congress Cataloging in Publication Data
Urwin, Derek W.
 The community of Europe : a history of European integration since
1945 / Derek W. Urwin.
 p. cm — (The Postwar world)
 Includes bibliographical references and index.
 ISBN 0–582–04530–4 (cased) : £19.95. — ISBN 0–582–04531–2 (paper)
£8.96
 1. Europe—Economic integration—History. 2. European Economic
Community—History. 3. Europe—Economic conditions—1945–
I. Title. II. Series.
HC241.U78 1991
337.1'4'09045—dc20   90–48619
                                                                              CIP

Set in 10pt Bembo

Produced by Longman Singapore Publishers (Pte) Ltd.
Printed in Singapore

Contents

Abbreviations and Acronyms

ACP	African, Caribbean and Pacific States
ASEAN	Association of South–East Asian Nations
CAP	Common Agricultural Policy
CFP	Common Fisheries Policy
COMECON	Council for Mutual Economic Assistance
COREPER	Council's Committee of Permanent Representatives
CSCE	Conference on Security & Cooperation in Europe
EAGGF	European Agricultural Guidance and Guarantee Fund
EC	European Communities
ECE	Economic Commission for Europe
ECSC	European Coal & Steel Community
ECU	European Currency Unit
EDC	European Defence Community
EEC	European Economic Community
EFTA	European Free Trade Association
EMCF	European Monetary Cooperation Fund
EMS	European Monetary System
EMU	Economic & Monetary Union
EP	European Parliament
EPC	European Political Cooperation
EPU	European Payments Union
ERM	Exchange Rate Mechanism
Euratom	European Atomic Energy Community
EUROFER	European Confederation of Iron & Steel Industries
GATT	General Agreement on Trade & Tariffs
IEA	International Energy Authority
MCA	Monetary Compensation Amount
MEP	Member of the European Parliament

MFA	Multifibre Agreement
MLF	Multilateral Force
NATO	North Atlantic Treaty Organisation
NORDEK	Nordic Economic Union
OCT	Overseas Countries & Territories
OECD	Organisation for Economic Cooperation and Development
OEEC	Organisation for European Economic Cooperation
OPEC	Organisation of Petroleum Exporting Countries
PASOK	Panhellenic Socialist Movement (Greece)
SAS	Scandinavian Air Lines
SEA	Single European Act
UN	United Nations
UNCTAD	United Nations Conference on Trade & Development
Unesco	United Nations Educational, Scientific & Cultural Organisation
VAT	Value–Added Tax
WEU	Western European Union

Editorial Foreword

The aim of this series is to describe and analyse the history of the world since 1945. History, like time, does not stand still. What seemed to many of us only recently to be 'current affairs' or the stuff of political speculation, has now become material for historians. The editors feel that it is time for a series of books which will offer the public judicious and scholarly, but at the same time readable, accounts of the way in which our present–day world was shaped by the years after the end of the Second World War. The period since 1945 has seen political events and socio–economic developments of enormous significance for the human race, as important as anything which happened before Hitler's death or the bombing of Hiroshima. Ideologies have waxed and waned, the industrialised economies have boomed and bust, empires have collapsed, new nations have emerged and sometimes themselves fallen into decline. Whilst we can be thankful that no major armed conflict has occurred between the so–called superpowers, there have been many other wars, and terrorism has become an international plague. Although the position of ethnic minorities has dramatically improved in some countries, it has worsened in others. Nearly everywhere the status of women has become an issue which politicians have been unable to avoid. These are only some of the developments we hope will be illuminated by this series as it unfolds.

The books in the series will not follow any set pattern; they will vary in length according to the needs of the subject. Some will deal with regions, or even single nations, and others with themes. Not all of them will begin in 1945, and the terminal date may similarly vary; once again, the time–span chosen will be appropriate to the question under discussion. All the books, however, will be written by expert historians drawing on the latest fruits of scholarship, as well as their own expertise and judgements. The series should be particularly welcome to students, but it is designed also for the general reader with an interest in contemporary history. We hope that the books will stimulate scholarly discussion and encourage specialists to look beyond their own particular interests to engage in wider controversies. History, and particularly the history of the recent past, is neither 'bunk' nor an intellectual form of stamp–collecting, but an indispensable part of an educated person's approach to life. If it is not written by historians it will be written by others of a less discriminating and more polemical disposition. The editors are confident that this series will help to ensure the victory of the historical approach, with consequential benefits for its readers.

A.J. Nicholls
Martin S. Alexander

CHAPTER ONE
The Persisting Idea of Europe

The story of European integration, as it is understood today, essentially begins and is conventionally dated as beginning in 1945. The titanic struggle of World War II was over, and amidst the widespread feelings of relief and exhaustion there was also the sense that a significant watershed in the history of the continent had been reached, that the ending of the war heralded the beginning of a new reality. Central to this changed atmosphere was the belief that the war had been a cleansing agent. The European economies were in ruins or at the least had been severely disrupted, and the old political systems had either been discredited for their inadequacies in coping with the economic conditions of the 1920s and 1930s, or destroyed by Hitler and his allies. Many people therefore thought and argued that Europe could start afresh, with a different political and economic order that rejected the tired doctrines of nationalism, political sovereignty and economic autarky upon which the old state system of the continent had been built. In its place they wanted some kind of political union or federation that would effectively put into practice the old symbolic concept of the harmony of European nations.

Yet while this ferment of the months surrounding the final cessation of hostilities may have provided the seed bed for the developments in European integration in the years since 1945, the idea of and the desire for unity had had a much more prolonged prologue. Across the centuries intellectuals and political leaders alike had dreamed of overcoming the unique historical characteristic of Europe: its extreme political fragmentation. Most obviously, the historical record is replete with attempts at conquest: political leaders from Charlemagne through the Habsburgs to Napoleon, and even perhaps Hitler, had sought to realise the dream through imperial domination of the continent.

Yet in the end all aspirations came to nought, defeated in part by the complex fragmented mosaic of the continent as well as by the inadequate technical resources of the would-be conquerors to establish and maintain effective control by force over large areas of territory against the wishes of the local populations.

But the dream of unity was not confined to would-be military conquest. Intellectuals and thinkers had also persistently returned to the theme; some of their ideas and views on the necessity of union proved to have some lasting effect on the history of European integration. The role model adopted by many writers was perhaps the old Roman Empire, which was perceived as having integrated the whole of civilised Europe. It was this civilising aspect which appealed to many, a united Christian Europe at peace with itself and better able to defend itself against depredations and invasions from outside. The greatest value of unity, in other words, was the maintenance of peace and the avoidance of war. This was the theme of early devotees of Europe such as Pierre Dubois, a jurist and diplomat for the courts of both France and England, and his proposal of 1306 for a permanent assembly of princes working to secure peace through the application of Christian principles, or Maximilien de Béthune, the Duc de Sully, who suggested a federation of states that would better be able to defend Europe against Turkish threats. Such early schemes and ideas were all universalist, as well as being directed towards achieving a greater political influence for some specific state or dynasty: they embraced all Christian Europe, accepted the rights of princes, and often saw ultimate authority, if any, residing with an emperor or pope.

As the Enlightenment and ideas on liberalism and democracy began to take firmer root, the focus of integrative schemes shifted away from the religious unity of Europe towards its intellectual unity, and away from the rights of princes and kings towards a broader institutional framework that explicitly or implicitly meant the end of independent territorial units. The prominent English Quaker, William Penn, was one of the first to argue, in 1693, for a European parliament and the end of the state mosaic in Europe. The theme was sustained by eighteenth century writers: Jeremy Bentham, for instance, reiterated the argument for a European assembly as well as urging the creation of a common army, while Jean-Jacques Rousseau was also in favour of a European federation.

All of these ideas and views fed into the even greater intellectual agitation of the nineteenth century, much of which acknowledged in particular its debt to the work of Henri Saint-Simon. In 1814 Saint-Simon advanced a stronger and more detailed scheme for institutional unity, embracing a European monarch, government and parliament. The links with thinkers of the past were preserved through what was the dominant motif for Saint-Simon and his followers: peace through a United States of Europe. The latter was a phrase well understood by nineteenth century intellectuals. It was the theme or catchphrase of the several peace movements that in the event were to be principal torch bearers of integration throughout the century. The French novelist and publicist, Victor Hugo, used it, for example, at the Paris Peace Congress of 1849, while eighteen years later a similar congress established a journal with that very title.

Yet these were but schemes advanced by people who were, at the most, only at the fringes of politics. They held little appeal or relevance for political leaders. The same, however, was not so true of the parallel development of ideas on some form of economic integration. Many political leaders could see potential political advantages in either a customs union or some form of free trade area. The distinction between these two forms of economic structure is important for it proved to be the fundamental dividing line in all debates on European integration and organisation through to the present. For that reason it may be useful to spell out the basic distinction at this point. Briefly, in a customs union the member states would belong to a single tariff area where, ideally, there would be no customs duties on goods circulating within the union, though the members would construct a common external boundary where a common tariff would be levied on all imports entering the union from outside. By contrast, a free trade area is a looser concept, with much more limited political implications. There would be no common external tariff, with each member state free to impose its own tariff levels on goods coming from non-members: the goal was merely to eliminate or reduce internal tariffs, but usually without any compulsion to do so.

Attempts to launch such economic schemes on a continental basis were not successful. Essays into free trade arrangements proved to be short-lived, while customs unions like the prototypic Zollverein of 1843 were region-specific, not European: as such they were protectionist and disliked by other states. In a sense, economic ideas on unity suffered the same fate as political ideas on the same theme. The nineteenth century witnessed an ever-increasing imperialist competition among states, an assertion of the supremacy of national autarky and intensification of competition that eventually culminated in World War I.

The war and its aftermath, in radically redrawing the political map of Europe and launching several new states on to the scene,

3

should ideally have made political and economic cooperation, if not integration, even more pressing. On the other hand, the war that was supposed to impose a durable peace upon Europe, the 'war to end war', had, in accepting the idea of national self-determination as the basic building block of the new Europe, actually increased the obstacles to cooperation and integration. With the disintegration of the old empires of Central and Eastern Europe, the continent had become even more fragmented, with an almost inevitable reinforcement of nationalism. In addition, the defeat of Germany imposed a further instability over and above fragmentation. The hope that in 1918 had been placed in the newly-established League of Nations also quickly evaporated. New states, jealous of their independence and giving governmental expression to historic national and ethnic rivalries, were not in a mood to accept any diminution of their political and economic freedom. Moreover, the economic problem had been made worse by a reduction of Europe's economic role in the world: the continent's foreign trade, as a share of the gross national product of the industrialised states of the world, had slumped dramatically.

THE INTER-WAR YEARS

In the highly charged postwar atmosphere it was almost inevitable that in the 1920s Europe would move towards more and higher tariff barriers. By the end of the decade the notion of countries imposing quota restrictions upon imports into their territory had become a popular theme. Insofar as support was given to a belief in economic cooperation, it was towards more limited structures, such as regional agreements or those like the International Steel Cartel of 1926 established by a number of independent steel companies and meant to control Europe's export market, in part through restrictions on trade.

Generally speaking, it was only the smaller states of Western Europe that expressed an interest in exploring new customs arrangements. Belgium and Luxembourg, for example, established a Belux economic union in 1922, though its practical effects were very limited. Perhaps the most important attempt was made through the Oslo Convention of 1930, in which the Low Countries and the Scandinavian states agreed to some limited measures to peg tariffs. While the Convention survived the decade, it was not particularly successful. Indeed, the attempt by the Low Countries in the Ouchy Convention of 1932, a follow-up to Oslo, to move further towards a cooperative lowering of tariffs proved too radical for the Scandinavian states to stomach. The larger states remained totally uninterested in such ventures, if not – like Britain – actively hostile to them. While Oslo and Ouchy, abortive though they were, perhaps offered a pointer to the future, of far more immediacy for the present, and symbolic of Europe's drift away from free trade, was Britain's decision in 1931 to abandon multilateral free trade, of which historically it had been the arch-proponent, and to establish under the Ottawa Agreement a system of imperial preference within its empire.

Despite, or perhaps because of, the seemingly parlous political and economic state of post-1918 Europe, the idea of integration and cooperation as the way forward to a better future continued to be expounded. Even in the early 1920s, the number of groups advocating this route were legion: however, the only one which has achieved any kind of lasting memory was the Pan-European Union, founded by the Austrian aristocrat, Count Richard Coudenhove-Kalergi, in 1923. Coudenhove-Kalergi was a tireless publicist, and through the Union and publications such as his *Paneuropa* of 1923 he argued forcefully for a European federation. His ideas were not new, but he did succeed in attracting to the Union several prominent politicians such as Eduard Benes, the foreign minister of Czechoslovakia, and Aristide Briand and Edouard Herriot, future premiers of France. Among the membership of the Pan-European Union could be found the names of people like Konrad Adenauer, Georges Pompidou and Carlos Sforza, men who were to figure strongly in the story of European integration after 1945.

The major aim of the Union followed in the footsteps of its nineteenth century predecessors: to prevent war and maintain the peace, but now not to guard Europe against alien hordes but to allow it to compete more effectively in the world's economic markets. But in setting out its objectives, the Union still detected an external enemy, and in so doing it marked the first contraction in the territorial definition of European unity. As a result of the Russian Revolution of 1917, Bolshevism was accused of being an enemy of peace, and hence the Soviet Union was not to be part of the proposed structure; nor incidentally, did Coudenhove-Kalergi seem to regard Britain as a potential participant.

The impressive list of politicians that stood in the ranks of the Union could not disguise the fact that, like its contemporaries and predecessors, it was unable to achieve any practical results. No government responded to its clarion call, though some government figures, like Briand and Herriot, advocated similar views outside the context of the Union. The first major statement by a leading politician was perhaps made by Edouard Herriot, the prime minister of France, who in a speech on European security, declared on 24 October 1924, 'Let us create, if it is possible, a United States of Europe', something to which he returned in subsequent years but without trying to set in motion anything that might enable the objective to be achieved. His compatriot, Aristide Briand, in signing the Locarno Pact in October 1925 on behalf of France, saw it as a first step towards the same goal.

It was Briand, however, who first attempted to advance the debate to a governmental level. At the League of Nations in Geneva, he proposed, in September 1929, a scheme of union which would involve a 'confederal' bond between European peoples. The following year he circulated a memorandum on the same theme to other European governments. The Briand Memorandum of 1 May 1930 represents the first official endorsement of ideas on integration, in a fairly specific political format.

In fact, the Memorandum was rather vague and a dilution of the implications of Briand's original proposal. While it did introduce the novel notion of a permanent political committee and secretariat, its objective was seemingly merely a union between governments within the framework of the League of Nations. Similarly, it said little about possibilities for an economic union beyond suggesting a 'rationalisation' of customs barriers. Briand's ideas, like those of Herriot before him, came perhaps more from the desire of France to ensure an effective security for itself, especially against Germany. Briand had been the architect of the 1925 Locarno Pact, whose signatories (Belgium, Britain, France, Germany and Italy) had guaranteed existing state frontiers and renounced war between themselves. The Briand Memorandum could be taken as being primarily another effort by France to ensure the perpetuation of the peace settlement imposed upon Germany in the Treaty of Versailles.

Even though the Briand Plan ultimately did not envisage the loss of sovereign rights by states, official responses to it were muted and, where favourable, couched in vague and circumspect language. To have succeeded, it would have required the endorsement of the other major states. However, Britain was deeply sceptical, while in Italy Mussolini was totally hostile to it. Attitudes in Germany were mixed, but with strongly expressed fears that it was little more than a stratagem to guarantee French hegemony on the continent. Although France tried to modify the plan, it had to all intents and purposes been abandoned even before Briand's death in March 1932. Its one organisational legacy was a 'Study Group on European Union' located in Geneva within the League of Nations secretariat, a body which, ironically, was itself out of sympathy with the whole idea.

With the collapse of Briand's efforts, the search for integration was returned to private organisations. While these continued to flourish, including some new ones like the Federal Union of 1938, the 1930s were a particularly barren time for the proponents of European unity. Economic depression, the rise of Fascism, and the lengthening shadow of Adolf Hitler led countries to look to their own defences. European integration, in any shape or form, was not to be a serious topic of discussion until the closing stages of World War II.

THE IMPACT OF WORLD WAR II

It was the war itself which was the catalyst for a new surge of interest in European unity, leading to negative assessments of the prewar political situation and economic practices. Once the tide of war had swung in their favour, the protagonists of the struggle against Hitler and his allies began to turn their attention towards the future and the reconstruction of Europe. The idea of unity resurfaced again, but this time as part of an argument that retention of the historic notion of the independent state as the foundation of political organisation had been discredited and that it should be abandoned, to be substituted by a concerted effort at unifying state practices that in time might lead to a comprehensive continental political community. The thrust of these arguments, however, was rarely to be found among the exiled or potential governments of the continent. It was among the Resistance movements of occupied Europe that the voice of unity was most strongly heard.

While in each occupied country the Resistance was essentially a loose amalgam of numerous factions, divided both regionally and by political affiliation and ideology, with each group jealous of its own autonomy, there was nevertheless something that might, with some license, be called the philosophy of the Resistance. It was a view of the future that extended a welcome to all those who felt that a new spirit should be injected into European reconstruction after the war. Brought together by the necessity of fighting a common enemy, men and women from all the political persuasions within the Resistance, and from all walks of life, seemed genuinely determined to forget their differences in the fight for a common, peaceful and harmonious future.

The Resistance dream was that the wartime camaraderie would persist into the postwar world to encompass the whole of society. And, because of their active role in the struggle against Nazism, many thought that the political leadership of postwar Europe would be drawn from the ranks of Resistance activists. The scenario for reconstruction was all-embracing; but central to that scenario was the concept of a united Europe. The new morality which the Resistance deemed necessary did not stop at national boundaries. Nationalism and national pride stood accused of being root causes of past European wars. Resistance views on the future therefore stressed the need to transcend historical national boundaries, dismissed as artificial and discredited, in order to rebuild a revitalised and genuine European community.

Declarations to this effect were made long before the end of the war, with statements on union being produced independently and more or less simultaneously by Resistance groups in Czechoslovakia, France, Italy, the Netherlands, Poland and Yugoslavia, as well as by underground groups in Germany. During 1944, for example, several French Resistance groups in both France and North Africa argued for some supranational structure in Europe, built along federal lines, to replace the old system of independent states. The most vociferous groups, perhaps, were to be found in Italy, with many insisting that constructing a new federal Europe should take priority even over economic reconstruction. It was, in fact, in Italy that the idea of postwar union was first set out, in the Ventotene Manifesto of July 1941, written in, and smuggled out of, jail by Altiero Spinelli (who was to be an ardent European federalist throughout his later life) and his associates. The Ventotene ideas were adopted by the Italian Resistance as a whole, and led eventually to the formation in August 1943 of a European Federalist Movement (Movimento Federalista Europeo) which pledged itself to contact and align itself with similar groups in other countries.

It was Italian activists who took the lead in organising a series of meetings in neutral Switzerland. These culminated in a major conference in Geneva in July 1944. The document that emerged from the conference, largely written by Spinelli, received wide circulation in Europe. It argued for a federal Europe with a written constitution, a supranational government directly responsible to the people of Europe and not national governments, along with an army under its control, with no other military forces being permitted. The government would be supplemented by a judicial tribunal which would have the sole authority to interpret the constitution and to arbitrate in conflicts between the federation and its constituent states. Apart apparently from the representatives from Denmark and Norway, all the delegates endorsed the declaration of the necessity for a completely new federal Europe and democratic governmental structure for the whole of Europe.

The Geneva statement and other documents expressing similar sentiments were widely publicised in Resistance circles. They helped reinforce the belief of many Resistance leaders that nothing short of total political reconstruction would be acceptable. In the eyes of the Resistance, the prewar political and social systems, and their political leaders had been found wanting. The wholesale victories of the Nazi juggernaut, it was believed, had provided an outstanding opportunity to recast Europe in an entirely new guise.

There did seem, however, to be other supporters of European union, supporters whose decisive role in the future of European affairs was only dimly beginning to be perceived. The Soviet Union did not seem to be averse to the notion of union, and within the Resistance national Communist parties were following orders from Moscow to cooperate politically as well as militarily with their fellow fighters. Across the Atlantic, official American opinion, insofar as it had thought about the future, looked rather favourably upon European union. Itself a continental federation, the United States did not see anything strange about a similar structure in Europe. To some extent, some of the credit might go to Coudenhove-Kalergi who, in exile in the United States, continued his crusade for union by seeking to convince the American authorities and public of its value.

But for much of the Resistance the key to the future lay with Britain. Standing alone against Hitler and serving as a floating fortress and supply base, Britain was the symbol of Resistance and the future. All that was needed was for Britain to take the lead. On the continent Britain was also seen as a sympathetic supporter of European union. Not being able to foretell the result of the 1945 British general election, many simply assumed that the great prestige of Winston Churchill would be acknowledged, and that he would continue in office after the war. The pan-Europeans assumed that with the war behind him, Churchill would pursue an expanded policy along the lines of his dramatic offer to France in 1940 that 'there shall no longer be two nations, but one Franco–British union'. That plea had not been just rhetoric. Behind it lay efforts made during the early months of the war to draw up a detailed blueprint for economic and political as well as military cooperation. Some of those involved in these discussions, including Jean Monnet, who was to play such a decisive role in later European developments, had already begun to consider this potential union as the nucleus of a wider European integration to be launched once the war was over. Churchill's plea, however, had been rejected by a beleaguered French government, and all ideas had been simply scrapped in June with the military collapse and surrender of France.

But all these events led many in the Resistance to believe that they had the blessing, tacit or explicit, of the major Allies; and confident that because of their leadership and sacrifices in the fight for liberation they would gain massive electoral support, men of the Resistance looked towards the postwar world with increasing optimism. The next step in the Resistance script, however, was never reached. It would have been taken, it had been believed, when the Resistance movements became the governments of their respective countries. That hope was ended by the return of former political party leaders from exile or imprisonment: with them came also the return of old political attitudes and identities whose consensus on the future did not extend beyond giving first priority to repairing economic dislocation and to economic reconstruction.

Many Resistance activists, in fact, proved incapable of being effective politicians. Once the war was over, old historical divisions and hostilities, such as those between Communists, Socialists and Catholics, returned to drive wedges between the various segments of the Resistance. Simultaneously, the deteriorating relationship between the wartime Allies was also having an effect upon Resistance hopes. The gulf that was opening up between the Soviet Union and the Western Allies had a particular impact upon the national Communist parties. Men like Maurice Thorez in France and Palmiro Togliatti in Italy returned from exile in Moscow to impose a more rigorous discipline upon their native parties. While perhaps not averse to European unity, that would have to be on Moscow's terms: in short, European union would be acceptable only if the Communists could control and direct it.

On a broader front, the rift between the Allies was to lead to the Cold War, of which Europe, at least in the late 1940s, would be the cockpit. The continent was to be divided into two armed camps, decisively separated by Churchill's symbolic iron curtain. If integration was to occur, it would come as two separate developments: one in the west sheltering under American protection, the other under Soviet auspices in the east. Not until the momentous events of 1989 shattered Communist hegemony across the whole of Eastern Europe was it even possible to entertain the thought of continental unity.

In Western Europe there was a rapid return to traditional political and parliamentary life. Resistance unity of purpose fragmented, and unless a majority of the political parties in a country were agreed, not only upon the goal, but also upon its details and the methods necessary to achieve it, the likely outcome would be deadlock and the shelving or abandonment of the Resistance dream. In any case, the federal commitment had varied from country to country: in Denmark and Norway, for instance, the Resistance movements had always been at best lukewarm about the idea. There was to be no resurrection of Churchill's 1940 proposal, and the preliminary plans of Jean Monnet and others for a union built around an Anglo–French core remained unutilised. The new Labour Party government elected in Britain in 1945 was suspicious of European ideas and involvement, and wished not to be distracted from its major objective of social and economic reconstruction in Britain. But even if Churchill had remained at the helm in London, a strong British lead on union would probably not have been forthcoming. At least as far as Churchill himself was concerned, that 1940 idea had not been a serious proposal that might serve as a core for some distant future, but rather a stratagem, as Churchill himself later confessed, that might persuade a wavering French government to continue as a belligerent in the war against Nazi Germany.

Pushed to the political sidelines, some Resistance activists did attempt to persist with a concerted campaign for European integration. A further international conference was held in Paris in March 1945, organised by the French Committee for a European Federation. It simply reiterated previous resolutions, again in a document drafted by Altiero Spinelli. This and similar efforts barely caused a political eyelid to flutter during the first postwar months, as the Resistance ideal of a federal union faded from the scene. The idea returned to the province of private associations, which seemed not to be able to make an impact upon the new governments of Western Europe. The latter found and believed that bread and butter issues, such as supplies of food, fuel and shelter, were more urgent and the issues upon the electorates were demanding action.

It was perhaps inevitable that economic rebuilding would take precedence over plans for European union. The economic cost of the war, in both material and human losses, had been enormous. In addition, if Europe was to have a future, in those first uneasy months of peace the escalating tension between the two emerging superpowers and true victors of the war, the Soviet Union and the

United States, meant that they too would have something to say about that future. For the Soviet Union that clearly meant at the very least implementation of the spheres of influence policy which it had advocated at the wartime Allied summit meetings. Eastern Europe, where expressions of interest in integration had in any case been relatively weaker, was to be part of the Soviet orbit and to be subordinated to Soviet security interests. Before the war advocates of union had taken for granted that it would embrace a territory stretching from the Atlantic to the border of the Soviet Union – and even perhaps beyond. But with the new reality of the Cold War, any moves towards a federation or some other form of union would in effect be confined to the western half of the continent where it seemed in late 1945 that its sponsorship would once more be confined to private associations.

Yet the situation was not quite the same as in the 1920s. The integrationist lobby may not have been any more active, but it did enjoy links with, and the support of, many more politicians. While a federal union may still have been the dream of many, others began to argue for a more functional approach, one which stressed economic cooperation and integration with a minimum level of political institutionalisation. The functional approach was the one that gained added momentum in the late 1940s, not least because many of its leading exponents were from France, a country which was seeking to restore itself as a leading European power. More generally, despite their economic problems – or perhaps because of them – Western European governments were soon obliged to consider some form of both political and economic cooperation because of the worsening international environment. Europe's diminished role in the world economy, the dominating financial and economic strength of the United States, fears of the Soviet Union and Communism, as well as of a revived Germany, along with increasing pressure from the United States for more collective European action, all combined with the severe domestic economic problems to force governments to consider new forms of cooperation. It was this changed atmosphere which, despite the failure of the Resistance, gave the protagonists of unity an opportunity to sell their ideas to governments. Before describing the re-emergence of European moves towards integration in the late 1940s, it would be useful to give a brief account of the parallel developments that were decisively influenced by the Cold War and American foreign policy.

CHAPTER TWO
The Cold War, the United States and Europe

The United States emerged from the war as undisputedly the strongest military and economic power. Its leaders had come to accept that it had, even if only for the sake of its own security and prosperity, global responsibilities which could not be evaded. But as the American government in 1945 viewed the future world and its own input, it was adamant that there were to be finite limits on how far those responsibilities were to extend. There would be collaboration with the Soviet Union within both the newly formed United Nations (UN) and broad spheres of influence policy in which the European victors would also participate. The Allies would share in the task of watching over and reconstructing Germany, and that process would provide the core of a peace settlement that would secure normality on the continent. But by 1947, under pressure from Western Europe which like itself was fearful of a Soviet Union that was believed to have embarked upon a crusade of Communist expansion across the continent, the United States was locked into an enduring European involvement, within which it had a decisive influence upon West European moves towards closer collaboration and integration.

American policy for the future had been based on two erroneous assumptions, both of which had serious consequences for Europe. The first was that the Allies would continue to collaborate in the postwar world. The first indication that this would not be so came in disagreements over the occupation of Germany. The country had been divided into four zones of military occupation: American, British, French and Soviet. These very quickly came to resemble four distinct areas with four distinct policies. While the three Western Allies did move towards collaboration, France albeit reluctantly, Germany was to be merely a microcosm of the new world alignment of political power. The Allied Control Authority, the supreme body where political and economic policy across the occupation zones was to be coordinated, was never entirely successful. In western eyes the Soviet Union was pursuing an increasingly obstructionist course. Ultimately, with the Soviet withdrawal from the Authority in March 1948, any pretence at Allied coordination in Germany was at an end. The Western Allies had in any case already decided that it would be futile to await Soviet collaboration on German reconstruction. Germany was to be divided between east and west, as was the whole of Europe, with two independent German states, the western Federal Republic and the eastern Democratic Republic, being established in 1949.

As with Germany, so with the United Nations, the major symbol of the new moral order. The UN never operated in the way it had originally been conceived, rapidly turning itself into a battleground of stylised verbal warfare between American and Soviet representatives. While the UN over time has proved to have some value, it found itself powerless to intervene or arbitrate effectively in matters intimately affecting the security of the two superpowers; the European continent fell unambiguously into this category of exclusion. Outside the main forum of the UN, some limited collaboration between east and west did take place within UN agencies such as Unesco, and also after 1947 within the Economic Commission for Europe (ECE), a regional branch of the UN's Economic and Social Council based in Geneva, which was charged with the task of helping economic reconstruction. But while the ECE remained virtually the only arena in which Eastern and Western Europe met to discuss European affairs, its effect and impact were necessarily severely constrained by the iron curtain.

The second false assumption made by the United States arose from an over-estimation of the strength of its major European allies. The toll of the war on the resources of Britain and France had been severe, and neither was able to fulfil the military and security role assigned to it in American thinking. Both were stretched by their economic problems and the challenges that were directed against their retention of an empire. France also had problems of political stability and the challenge of a large and hostile Communist Party. American conceptions became illusions. With Britain and France greatly weakened, and Germany prostrate, a power vacuum had opened between the United States and the Soviet Union. If America did not wish to become isolated and confined to its own continent, steps had to be taken to consolidate its presence in Europe. Whatever wartime camaraderie that still survived had definitely evaporated by the early months of 1947. A sequence of events and crises over the next two years, all following swiftly upon one another's heels, hardened western suspicions of the Soviet Union, and reluctantly and inexorably the United States was sucked further into European affairs with a consequent stress upon European cooperation.

TRUMAN DOCTRINE AND MARSHALL PLAN

The catalyst which may be said to have finally provoked America into positive political action was Communist activity in the Eastern Mediterranean, most specifically the attempt by Communist guerillas to seize control of Greece. Under the spheres of influence policy Greece had fallen within the British ambit. It soon became clear that British military support was the major prop of a weak Greek government. On the other hand, Britain was itself exhausted and incapable of diverting sufficient resources to bring the war to a speedy end. Early in 1947 an assessment of its own economic problems and its other overseas commitments led the Labour government to inform the United States that it could no longer fulfil its obligations in Greece no matter what the consequences might be. Since only the United States was capable of filling the vacuum that would be created by the British withdrawal, it had to accept responsibility for the area or risk seeing its influence and prestige in Europe suffer a damaging defeat.

In March 1947 President Harry Truman outlined what was to be known as the Truman Doctrine. The American commitment to the governmental cause in Greece marked a fundamental re-evaluation of American foreign policy, most particularly in terms of its commitment to Western Europe. The Truman Doctrine was a pledge of American support for 'free peoples who are resisting subjugation by armed minorities or by outside pressures'. Stressing the interrelatedness of the democratic world, it emphasised that such subjugation did concern the United States, that world peace was necessary for American security. The Truman Doctrine marked the opening of a more aggressive phase in American foreign policy, giving it a new purpose and crusade. Its immediate target and beneficiary was Western Europe where hitherto, despite its words, the United States had been somewhat hesitant, even reluctant, to intervene.

The most immediate consequence of the new American attitude was the despatch of military aid to Greece and the Eastern Mediterranean. More importantly, however, the Truman Doctrine was above all a pledge of a firm political relationship between the United States and Western Europe, one that was deeply welcome to the latter's governments. But that relationship would be much better and the pledge of support more certain of success if the European democracies were themselves on a sound economic footing and able to contribute more decisively to their own defence. But the Truman Doctrine did not set out to do this. It was these factors, however, which contributed to the American announcement of the Marshall Plan later in 1947. While a plan for economic aid that was open to all European states, including the Soviet Union, the Marshall Plan was clearly politically as well as economically motivated: the United States must have taken into account that the offer would be rejected by Moscow and its satellites, as indeed it was. The Marshall Plan would be primarily something that more firmly linked Western Europe with the United States, and in so doing would also foster habits of closer collaboration.

The shift in American policy that led to economic aid for Europe is conventionally dated to a report prepared in May 1947 by an American official, who wrote upon his return from Europe that 'Europe is steadily deteriorating. The political position reflects the economic. One political crisis after another merely denotes the existence of economic distress. Millions of people in the cities are slowly starving.' A few weeks later the American Secretary of State, George Marshall, reinforced the message with his statement that 'the truth of the matter is that Europe's requirements for the next three or four years of foreign food and other essential products – principally from America – are so much greater than her present ability to pay that she must have substantial additional help or face economic, social and political deterioration of a very grave character.'

There may, in 1947, have been severe political problems in some Western European states – France, Greece and Italy, for example – but overall there was little that one could identify as approximating a revolutionary situation. Similarly, rationing may have been endemic on the continent, but that was not the same as starvation. It was true that in 1945 assessments of the state of the European economies had been extremely gloomy, based upon evaluations of industrial and agricultural damage, lack of machinery, disruptions to communications and transport infrastructures, and the drain on human resources during the war. The general gloom seemed to give credence to the pessimistic assertion that European recovery would take the best part of 20 to 25 years.

In the event, recovery occurred at a rapid and surprising rate. It was the rate of recovery, and governmental anxiety to push hard for even more economic growth, that was causing the economic problem, one related to the place of Europe in the world economy. The war had disrupted international trade and payments, and had confirmed the economic dominance of the United States, which by war's end held some two-thirds of the world's gold stock. During the war American aid had taken the form of the Lend–Lease programme initiated in 1941 by President Franklin Roosevelt. Under its terms several governments had signed the Mutual Aid Agreement of 1942, which among other things reflected the American objection to trade barriers of any kind, including protectionism and Britain's system of imperial preference: the signatories agreed to 'the elimination of all forms of discriminating treatment in international commerce, and to the reduction of tariffs and other trade barriers'. This attitude was carried forward by the United States into its postwar policy, ultimately to be expressed in the General Agreement on Trade and Tariffs (GATT), signed in Geneva in October 1947 by 23 states, and which immediately began negotiations on well over 100 bilateral treaties affecting one half of the world's trade. In addition, at a conference held at Bretton Woods in America in 1944, 44 countries had agreed upon a new monetary system based upon fixed exchange rates and backed by two reserve currencies, the dollar and sterling. The idea was to make currencies convertible for payments on current account, something that would greatly assist multilateral trade between countries, while stable exchange rates would also avoid the need for devaluation.

Insofar as Western Europe had a serious economic problem in 1947, it was related to foreign trade, to the new freer trade commitment, currency convertibility, and cash reserves. The economic domination of the United States meant that it had a huge export surplus, but very low import needs. On the other hand, European countries found it difficult to provide the necessary credit or cash for American purchases. By 1947 the Bretton Woods agreement was badly out of kilter. Its assumptions about a swift realisation of a pattern of multilateral trade and payments buttressed by a system of fixed exchange rates had been far too optimistic. Western Europe was experiencing a massive outflow of capital, so jeopardising its own domestic economies.

It may well have been the case that a massive injection of American economic aid would have had to come anyway: certainly, in governmental circles in Britain and France there was a tacit assumption that this would have to occur. In the end, however, the United States had to make a decisive move in order to ensure export outlets for its own hugely increased economy. The political revaluation of its world role undertaken by the United States in 1947 gave further ammunition to those officials seeking to convert domestic American opinion to their side. The argument that Europe was in grave economic crisis was designed for American consumption, that help was necessary not just to halt a breakdown in international trade that would damage the American economy, but also to prevent possible Communist hegemony on the continent. In other words, the United States came to Western Europe's assistance in part as a result of its own economic and strategic interests. But in so doing, however, it forced European countries into a closer pattern of economic cooperation which in turn provided an invaluable experience out of which further developments could emerge.

The intention of the plan announced by George Marshall in June 1947, or the European Recovery Programme to give it its formal title, was couched in humanitarian terms. Aid was offered to all states: it was to be 'directed not against country or doctrine, but against hunger, poverty, desperation and chaos'. Believing the United States to have ulterior motives, the Soviet Union and its supporters rejected the offer. They were perhaps correct. The Marshall Plan was clearly politically rather than economically motivated, and its net effect was to escalate superpower tension and heighten the gulf between east and west on the continent. Only 16 countries agreed to meet as a Committee of European Economic Cooperation in 1947 to draft a report on Marshall's proposals; and when financial aid first appeared in Europe under the Plan's auspices the following year, it was apparent that to all intents and purposes the programme was the economic complement of President Truman's expressed political intent to organise Western Europe in an ideological alliance against the Soviet Union and Communism. The United States, therefore, had an alliance in political and economic terms: the military component was to appear later in the North Atlantic Treaty Organisation.

Marshall Aid had a particularly important impact upon possibilities of European integration: indeed, by 1948 the United States seemed to be in favour of financial aid being paralleled by some kind of federation. While reluctant, for obvious reasons, to issue any kind of diktat, it did incorporate this view in the final version of the Foreign Assistance Act of 1948, which released the funds for Western Europe. In addition, America decided that while it did not wish to impose its own directives upon how the money should be spent, the programme should not nevertheless be an open-ended offer. The important proviso was that Marshall Aid would not come as a series of separate bilateral arrangements, but that the recipient states should coordinate their economic activities and planning to achieve the maximum benefit from the programme. The United States insisted that the Committee of European Economic Cooperation should become a permanent organisation which would administer the programme. This was the origin of the Organisation for European Economic Cooperation (OEEC), which was to be one link in the intermeshing chain of obligations that Western European governments accepted in these first postwar years. As such it is part of the story of European integration.

ECONOMIC COOPERATION: OEEC

OEEC came into being in April 1948. Its first and immediate preocupation was the European Recovery Programme, to identify a method of allocating American aid among the recipients. OEEC was reluctant to undertake this chore, since no matter what was decided some members would receive less than others. Nevertheless, a decision had to be made: the responsibility had to be Western Europe's since the United States had made it clear that it did not wish to draw up the details itself. Under persistent American pressure, the states eventually found a formula which all, some albeit reluctantly, could accept: aid was to be distributed among the OEEC members according to their trade and payments deficits. Those states which possessed a lower standard of living, but had very small deficits, suffered most by the arrangements. But OEEC, with American encouragement, survived this first hurdle, even though the level of coordination that emerged fell short of what had originally been intended, to pass on to a wider area of activity.

The basic responsibility for the successful operation of OEEC belonged to the member states: the organisation itself was primarily concerned with questions of cooperation and coordination. It did not mark or attempt any advance towards any kind of union beyond making vague commitments to study possibilities of, for instance, customs unions. It remained essentially an intergovernmental body. However, the nature of its task, and those it subsequently undertook later, necessarily demanded some permanent institutional organs to enable it to perform its functions satisfactorily. The focus of OEEC and its governing body was the Council of Ministers, where each member state had one representative. This body had the power to determine questions of general policy and administration. Its decisions were obligatory on the members, but not because it was, as France for instance had wished, a supranational authority with the ability to control national economies. They were obligatory only because a proposal became a decision when all had participated in its formulation and had already agreed to adhere to it. Britain, supported by the Low Countries and the Nordic members, had insisted that OEEC decisions had to be reached by unanimous vote. OEEC could not force anything upon a recalcitrant member: any state could go its own way on any one issue by ignoring or vetoing OEEC suggestions, or by pleading special circumstances of national importance.

The OEEC Council could not hope to function in a vacuum. It constructed a complex structure of subordinate committees and boards, usually composed of experts, which performed specialised functions. Council recommendations were nearly always based upon reports prepared by these specialist groups. As the workload of OEEC grew, it was forced to decentralise. The result was the establishment of several separate but related agencies. For example, in 1953 it established a European Productivity Agency to aid the flow of technical information and new technology between states. In the same year it also set up a permanent Conference of Ministers of Transport. The best known and perhaps the most successful agency was the European Payments Union (EPU) of 1950. In 1949 most OEEC currencies had been devalued against the dollar. The EPU, building upon earlier agreements, was intended to tackle the problem of reciprocal credits and facilitate multilateral trade once Marshall Aid came to an end. It was essentially a central bank and clearing house processing multilateral intra-European trade and payments, but with the major drawback that its financial settlements discriminated against the dollar. This was contrary to the Bretton Woods agreement, to which the OEEC states were signatories, and so something that could not be allowed to continue indefinitely.

On paper, the OEEC structure did not appear to possess a great number of possibilities. Undoubtedly it had its drawbacks and liabilities, including the initial failure to develop, as the United States had wished, a comprehensive European Recovery Programme. But on a wider front it succeeded in liberalising trade and payments far beyond what a first glance might suggest. As an example of mutual cooperation it could hardly be bettered. The right of veto, for instance, was rarely exercised, and not just because contentious issues were avoided. It was unusual for a member to go against the weight of expertise which the OEEC came to command.

Acceptance of the principle of voluntary cooperation undoubtedly helped OEEC to sidestep some of the economic difficulties with which it might have been confronted, especially at a time when many states and governments were relatively unfamiliar with, and indeed suspicious of, collaboration. Partly because in its formative years it developed a valuable relationship with other emerging European bodies, OEEC did inspire some people to consider other ways of achieving closer integration. The founders of the European Communities in the 1950s undoubtedly learnt some important lessons from the OEEC.

The problem for integrationists was that OEEC not only had no political implications; it also had clear economic limitations. Its work was mostly concerned with the removal or reduction of quota restrictions on European trade. While it did achieve some important liberalising effects, working in conjunction with the efforts of GATT to lower tariff barriers, it could not totally prevent distortions or discrimination in trading patterns. Furthermore, it concentrated, not surprisingly, on easier problems, which meant that progress became increasingly slower as only more difficult questions remained. Again, it concerned itself more with short-term issues rather than the long-term difficulty of attempting to settle problems of economic growth and development.

These are some of the reasons why the founders of the European Coal and Steel Community and Common Market preferred to do just that rather than work through OEEC. It did not match up with the demands of federalists; nor did it satisfy those like Jean Monnet who wanted a closer functional integration in targetted policy areas. OEEC was too non-political and worked on too broad a canvas to satisfy either federalists or functionalists. Though OEEC did work reasonably well within its field of reference, its membership was too disparate for it to develop a coherent view on integration. While the United States had desired a maximum degree of economic unity, and while France in particular had come to see advantages in some degree of supranational organisation, Britain, backed by some of the smaller states, drew back from any extended plan, desiring only cooperation, not integration.

While cooperation may have won out over unity, the true value of OEEC lay in the foundations it established for the future, not least in the fostering of new modes of thinking. It outlived by far the three-year period of Marshall Aid, and by 1959 its original objectives had largely been reached. Almost all international trade had been liberalised to some degree; European currencies had generally become convertible, meeting one of the requirements of Bretton Woods; and in 1958 the EPU was replaced by the broader European Monetary Agreement. OEEC played a major role in driving home the realisation that European economies were mutually dependent, and that they prospered or failed together. It survived in all for twelve years. Strictly speaking, it did not die. In 1960, as a result of American worries over the split that had emerged in Western Europe as a consequence of the establishment of the European Economic Community in 1957, it was transformed, with all its institutions remaining intact, into the Organisation for Economic Cooperation and Development (OECD). The United States and Canada, only associate members of OEEC, became full members of the new body. The change of name reflected the different purpose and situation. OEEC had been constructed initially to handle the Marshall Aid programme. While it went on into new fields, it remained limited to Western Europe where, even so, it had only a limited impact upon national sovereignty. In the 1950s it was bypassed by more intense developments in economic integration which had ultimately created a dangerous economic divide within Western Europe. OECD was intended in part to counteract the danger of such a schism by concerning itself with economic coordination and long-term questions of economic development, both within Europe and the broader world economy. With the entry of Japan in 1964, the OECD finally became what in many ways had always been a latent rationale, a forum of advanced industrial democracies concerned with the effectiveness not just of the domestic economies of its members, but also of the international system. But long before then, OEEC and OECD had stopped being central to the story of European integration.

NATO: THE MILITARY ALLIANCE

Any account of the American contribution to increased West European cooperation in the years after 1945 would be incomplete without a brief consideration of the military aspects of West European security. The Truman Doctrine had been only a generalised expression of an American pledge to any individual country under threat. More importantly, the West European states themselves, though increasingly worried by their perception of a Soviet threat, had advanced little further in military cooperation than considering mutual aid treaties with one another of the traditional variety. The most important, perhaps, was the 1947 Treaty of Dunkirk between Britain and France. This agreement was expanded the following year into the collective Treaty of Brussels negotiated by Britain and France with the Low Countries. But in the light of the intensifying chill of the Cold War and the fears about Soviet intentions, the Brussels Treaty, like that of Dunkirk, was something of an anachronism, reflecting past rather than current concerns: a major objective was to thwart 'a renewal by Germany of an aggressive policy'.

Other West European states, especially in Scandinavia, were reluctant to become involved in security pacts. The Nordic states wished to retain their traditional neutrality, and for a while resisted any involvement in a military bloc that would be partisan in the Cold War. It even proved impossible for Sweden to organise a collective non–aligned security structure in Scandinavia. Any comprehensive structure in the north of Europe was finally ruled out by the peace treaty which the Soviet Union signed with Finland in 1948. The conditions imposed by the treaty upon Finland made Norway and, to a lesser extent, Denmark more nervous about the Soviet Union. Despite their desire to stay out of great power blocs, they came to accept that any collective Nordic pact, as advocated by Sweden, would be meaningless without some kind of American commitment. For its part, the United States was not prepared to furnish aid to an alliance of which it was not part. When it rejected Sweden's request to supply weapons to a Nordic alliance, the whole notion collapsed.

Given the general economic fragility of Western Europe and its military limitations *vis-à-vis* the perceived strength of the Soviet Union, what was needed was a military and defensive equivalent of the Marshall Plan and OEEC. Many European politicians had believed for some time that an American–led defensive pact was desirable and inevitable. Certainly, Britain's Foreign Minister, Ernest Bevin, had seen his country's involvement in the Dunkirk and Brussels treaties as interim measures pending the construction by the United States of a collective security system against the Soviet Union. After agreeing upon the Treaty of Brussels, he and the other signatories had immediately appealed to the United States for provision of 'what they lacked in strength'. It was early in 1949 that Western Europe eventually moved towards the formal military alliance that had been implicit in much of the thought and action of the previous two years.

In April 1949 the representatives of 12 states signed the Atlantic Pact. The United States and Canada agreed to enter into a military arrangement for the collective defence of Western Europe along with

Belgium, Britain, Denmark, France, Italy, Iceland, Luxembourg, the Netherlands, Norway and Portugal. During the early 1950s the new North Atlantic Treaty Organisation (NATO) was extended to embrace Greece, Turkey and the new state of West Germany. Anti-fascist feelings, especially in Britain, debarred Spain's entry. Sweden, Switzerland and Ireland preferred to maintain their neutrality, while Finland and, later, Austria were bound by agreement to eschew involvement in any military alliance. Those who had desired a definite American involvement in Europe had had their wishes realised.

The new Atlantic alliance was essentially a defensive agreement, seen by the United States as part of its wider strategy of containing Communism. Under the terms of the pact the member states promised to provide military forces according to their means. Certainly, a common European or Atlantic army was not the intention, and NATO never did develop a fully and effective integrated force. Each member country would provide its own battalions subject to orders from the NATO chain of command. Since the United States was the dominant partner, it was obvious that an American would be the overall military commander. This simply underlined the fact that NATO was something more than a European organisation.

The lack of integration was apparent in other ways too. In one sense NATO was basically little more than an extension of the time-hallowed tradition of bilateral treaties. Moreover, at first glance the commitment did not seem to extend to meaning a firm and automatic guarantee of action. Whereas the Brussels Treaty had guaranteed automatic military assistance to any signatory under threat, under the NATO agreement a member state need only take 'such action as it deems necessary'. The qualification had been added at the insistence of the United States, which did not want involvement without discretion: and since American involvement was the whole objective of the exercise, Western Europe, no matter what its opinion might be, had to defer. In addition, there was nothing in the agreement which specifically forbade members from decreasing their defence expenditure – in the years to come the source of constant complaints by the United States about some of its European partners – or even from using NATO-designated forces for other tasks in other parts of the world, as both Britain and France were to do in the 1950s.

The treaty was not particularly concerned with creating a net of formal institutions. However, these grew up extensively once it was realised that the alliance could only hope to operate efficiently if there was an institutional framework that permitted continuous military and political consultation. Through this framework the West European states and governments received further experience in collaboration and collective decision making. Despite the relative looseness of the structure and its limitations, the operation of the institutions was sufficiently impressive in its first years that some could suggest that NATO might serve as a base for further European integration.

But that was not the intention of NATO. And indeed, while some of its members might be willing to collaborate in a collective security structure, they were not prepared to abandon sovereignty in economic and broader political matters. Some states – Denmark and Norway, for example – had accepted NATO only reluctantly, seeing it as the least of several evils. In short, in itself the Atlantic alliance, both in terms of its institutional arrangements, practices and the varying attitudes of its members towards it, would not have provided an ideological basis for a West European political, social and economic federation. But taken together with the Marshall Plan, it helped to create a more positive environment of cooperation and a valuable learning experience. In particular, it provided a defensive shield against an external threat, giving Western Europe more space to breathe and the opportunity, if it so wished, to explore ways in which further integration might be developed.

Throughout much of this hectic period in European affairs, and as part of its own foreign policy evaluation, official American opinion had come to take a positive stand on West European union. In addition to making a contribution through the Marshall Plan and NATO, the United States also welcomed all European initiatives in that direction even when it was accepted in Washington that some, if successful, might have an adverse effect upon some American interests. But that was a price that President Truman and his administration, who became more closely involved in European affairs than any other American government before or since, seemed willing to pay.

That West European governments and politicians were able to turn in the late 1940s to debate the question of integration more intensely was due in no small measure to the healthier political, economic and military situation which the United States had helped to provide. Europe may have become an armed camp at the eye of the Cold War, but by the end of the decade whatever uncertainties there had been in the immediate postwar years had at least been replaced by a certainty: the structure of the continent had been frozen by the Cold War, with total (and probably nuclear) conflict as the only alternative. In attempting to assist Western Europe out of its payments crisis and by its commitment to the defence of the continent, the United States made an important contribution towards European integration. The moves that were to occur in that direction benefited from the more stable conditions which American action had been able to provide. But these moves were also aided by the fact that the idea of political integration had not, in fact, entirely faded with the demise of the Resistance. It still exerted a powerful appeal within the European democracies, and it is towards these European developments that we now must turn.

CHAPTER THREE
The Opening Gambits

The high hopes for a new morality in Europe espoused by the Resistance movements, and which had included European union as a top priority, seemed to be dashed by the outbreak of the Cold War and the failure of the first postwar governments to include integration on their policy agendas. Yet the idea of union did not die. To many, the postwar economic problems of the continent demanded a substantial element of very close cooperation. A myriad of associations campaigning for some form of political and economic union proliferated across all the democracies and across most political party persuasions: for example, the United Europe Movement in Britain, organised by Churchill; the Catholic Nouvelles Équipes Internationales and the Socialist Movement for the United States of Europe in France, but both with some following in Belgium and Luxembourg; and the Europa-Bund in Germany. The federalist urge remained strong, and in 1946 was consolidated internationally with the formation of the European Union of Federalists, which brought together groups in Belgium, Britain, France, Italy, Luxembourg, the Netherlands and Switzerland. As opposed to the past, many of these groups and some of their ideas found a wider audience among people with political prestige or in positions of political authority. In September 1946, for example, parliamentarians from several countries came together in an International Committee for the Study of European Questions, which published a report in favour of union. The influential European Movement, which came out of the Hague Congress of 1948, had among its patrons such politically diverse personalities as the Conservative Winston Churchill, the ex-Socialist premier of France, Léon Blum, the Christian Democrat premier of Italy, Alcide de Gasperi, and the prominent Belgian Socialist, Paul-Henri Spaak –

senior statesmen whose presence reflected the widespread appeal of the idea across political party divides. The new postwar constitutions of France and Italy (and later that of the new Federal Republic of Germany) included clauses which allowed for the possibility of the abrogation of national sovereignty in favour of supranational authorities.

TOWARDS THE HAGUE CONGRESS

Even though ferment was widespread, motivations for seeking a more integrated Europe varied from country to country, and were coloured by national perspectives. In Germany, for example, it was seen as a road by which a reconstructed German state could win rehabilitation and acceptance from its neighbours as an independent, equal and responsible partner – an attitude which, for example, was to lie behind much of the foreign policy strategy of Konrad Adenauer, the first leader of the Federal Republic of Germany, in the 1950s. In Italy integration was viewed as a counterbalance to the possible domestic instability that could arise from the presence of a large and hostile Communist Party. Many in France saw it as a route by which French prestige and French leadership within Europe could be restored.

But for most states and governments the crucial question was whether Britain would become a committed member of any European organisation. The Nordic states were reluctant to enter into any kind of commitment, but would perhaps have been willing to follow a British lead, while in France and the Low Countries British participation was regarded as an indispensable guarantee of security against both a resurgence of German militarism and the shadowy threat of the Soviet Union. While the United States, by virtue of its major input into Europe after 1941, may have been a European power, it was not and could not be a European state. During the war Britain had provided the European lead and because of its wartime role was believed to have the reasons and the opportunity to effect some kind of unity. Britain's importance was not just a matter of the political prestige gained during the war. It was also economic: for example, after 1945 British steel production was more than two-thirds of the combined total of the other European members of the future OEEC, while its coal output nearly equalled that of all the other West European states.

Both inside and outside Britain the hopes of European federalists in 1945 had been focused upon the charismatic wartime leader, Winston Churchill. It was widely believed that Churchill had been converted to the European cause during the war, and that he had kept the flame of union alight. It was he who had dramatically proposed an Anglo–French Union in 1940 just before the fall of France. Throughout the war he had returned to the theme of Europe: in a 1943 broadcast, for example, he had emphasised the need for a Council of Europe that would possess an effective network of working institutions, including a common military organisation. Consequently, federalists were shocked and disheartened by the 1945 British general election, which removed Churchill and his Conservatives from power. While Churchill might still agitate for union, it was doubtful whether the new Labour government of Clement Attlee would display any enthusiasm for it.

Churchill did continue to argue for European integration. In a major speech delivered in Zürich in 1946, he ranged widely across the whole subject of integration, arguing that it was imperative to establish a United States of Europe. This speech was his most significant review of the question since losing the premiership. It helped to spur federalists to greater efforts, and inspired the creation of new organisations devoted to the European cause.

The British Labour government watched this activity cautiously. The prime minister, Clement Attlee, and his colleagues were not anti-European, but they were opposed to any kind of integration, though the Foreign Minister, Ernest Bevin, had made it clear from the outset that he was in favour of more cooperation, especially around an Anglo–French core, and by 1947 was even indicating an interest in some kind of customs union. But the burst of enthusiasm, which had support in several European governments, was too strong to be denied entirely. Still under the aegis of Churchill, the various organisations agreed in December 1947 to establish an International Committee of the Movements for European Unity. The Committee's task was to make arrangements for a congress of all those interested in union, to impress Europe with the vitality and necessity of the cause, and to seek some institutional structures of a European organisation. Hopes were high because it seemed that Britain might be prepared to modify its position: note had been taken of a speech made by Bevin in the House of Commons on 22 January 1948 when he commented that the idea of unity was undisputable and that 'the time is ripe for a consolidation of Western Europe'. But whether Bevin wished to go beyond the kind of cooperation he was currently pursuing in the security field was a moot question.

In due course the International Committee completed its arrangements, and the Congress of Europe was held in The Hague in May 1948. With several hundred delegates from 16 states, including a group from Germany led by Konrad Adenauer, as well as observers from the United States and Canada, the Congress was an impressive display of the widespread interest in and enthusiasm for the idea of unity. Most political persuasions bar the extremes were represented, along with many influential political leaders. Most significant, perhaps, was the absence of a strong British Labour presence: indeed, the party executive had frowned upon participation, dismissing the Congress as a body composed of 'unrepresentative interests' that could not effectively advance any successful and workable form of integration.

The demands and arguments put forward at the Congress had all been heard before. Delegates wanted a European assembly, a charter of human rights, and a European court. The Congress itself was too unwieldy and too disparate to achieve any practical measure of success. It concluded its deliberations with a series of ringing statements on the desirability of a united Europe, with some common institutions, within which 'the European states must transfer and merge some portion of their sovereign rights so as to secure common political and economic action for the integration and proper development of their common resources'. Apart from the rhetoric and the generation of adrenalin, few practical measures were adopted. One, however, was the decision to establish a European Movement which would have a National Council in each country, to carry on the debate and pressure governments. This decision was welcomed by the United States, and in 1949 an American Committee on a United Europe began to give financial assistance to the European Movement. Even though Churchill was appointed as one of the presidents of the Movement, it was at this point that British leadership began to disappear from the unity movement.

THE BRITISH VIEW

Churchill himself had not been notably concerned with translating the general principle into practical realities. Moreover, his speeches had not been fundamentally concerned with 'Britain with the continent', but with 'Britain and the continent'. Rather than regarding an Anglo–French Union as a core of European unity, Churchill believed that the essential beginning was reconciliation between France and Germany. In his famous Zürich speech, for example, he had argued that these two states 'must take the lead together'. But he then went on to indicate that Britain would not necessarily be part of the new Europe when he said 'Great Britain, the British Commonwealth, mighty America, and I trust Soviet Russia . . . must be friends and sponsors of the new Europe and must champion its right to live and shine'. In short, there was not much in the end that separated Churchill from the official British position. Like many British politicians, he had accepted European unity as a valuable ideal. But Britain did not have to be part of that unity; it could only be associated with it. Indeed, the basic British attitude had been summed up admirably by Churchill himself many years earlier when he wrote, in an American periodical in 1930, 'We see nothing but good and hope in a richer, freer, more contented European commonalty. But we have our own dream and our own task. We are with Europe, but not of it. We are linked, but not compromised. We are interested and associated, but not absorbed.' For at least a further two decades that was to be the reality of an intransigent British position.

And yet the various integrationist movements, brash or hesitant, in the 1940s looked to Britain for leadership, and clung to the hope that Britain would be absorbed, not least because of concerns over security. Even Jean Monnet, the mover of much that was to occur in the future, saw Britain as the nucleus of a European Community. On the other hand, British political leaders gave priority to what Churchill had called their own dream and their own task. These had two components: the commitment to the Commonwealth, and the notion of a special Anglo–American relationship.

It was a mistake to regard the development of European integration after 1945 as the outcome of a continuing debate between Britain and the continent: all points of view could be found in all countries. Yet in a way it is a simple but effective means of analysing the subject since for much of the postwar period Britain was the leading spokesman for a particular point of view. Based upon an interpretation of the past Britain tended to give high priority to defence and security. The official policy was to establish a number of mutual aid pacts with other European democracies, a line that was shared by France until 1948. In the end the only one was the 1947 Treaty of Dunkirk with France. Its justification was primarily military – a guarantee of aid in the face of any future German aggression and, for Britain, the beginnings of an alliance against the Soviet Union – though it did provide for bilateral economic assistance and cooperation, and, indeed, a standing economic committee was established.

As we have seen, by 1948 the British government seemed to have modified its attitude, and many thought the time to be more propitious for attempting to pull Britain more firmly within the European orbit. But it soon became apparent that Britain still preferred little more than an effective interlocking system of treaties along the lines of the Treaty of Dunkirk: increasingly, if these were initiated, they would be little more than holding operations until the United States shared in the defence of Western Europe. In pursuance of his objectives, Ernest Bevin took the lead in negotiating a cooperative arrangement with France and the Low Countries. The result, the 1948 Treaty of Brussels, was a 50 year pact 'for collaboration in economic, social and cultural matters, and for collective self-defence', which Britain saw as a practical basis for cooperation, but not union. Bevin reiterated a warning against what he regarded as excessively ambitious hopes of integration. The Dutch Parliament thought otherwise, and urged its government to pursue a federal association of states with more vigour. As for the Treaty of Brussels, the general direction of its affairs would be intergovernmental in nature, the responsibility of a committee of the national foreign ministers. It seems clear that Britain at least did not envisage any institutional structures beyond this, yet some form of framework would have been necessary if all the objectives of the treaty were to be properly fulfilled.

Bevin did have a view of Europe, but it was a limited one conditioned by pragmatism and scepticism. Progress should be slow and cautious, and not be out of step with Britain's other major foreign policy concerns, the Commonwealth and the United States. He saw the Brussels agreement being extended eventually to cover the whole of Western Europe, but each step would have to be thoroughly explored, and the overall character would have to remain at the level of intergovernmental cooperation. Within a short space of time, however, there were already signs that the Brussels structure was running away from the British idea. The enthusiasm aroused in the other four members by the time of the Hague Congress was one indication that Britain was in danger of becoming rather isolated. Another was a change of heart in France. As Britain concentrated more on integrating the United States into a western defensive system, France began to see integration as a way of increasing its own influence within Europe, especially over the future of Germany. At the Congress of Europe, ideas and views had ranged from those favouring a weak form of federalism to those demanding a fully sovereign supranational authority. Even within the non-union camp, the British idea of a loose grouping of European states in close association with the United States faced opposition from those who argued for a 'third force', essentially a cooperative European security arrangement without American participation: General de Gaulle had already made it clear in 1946 that he favoured this path.

Despite British disapproval, ardent federalists hoped to utilise the Brussels Treaty as a springboard for their ambitions, encouraged by the changing attitude of the United States, now seemingly desirous of a stable and effective Western Europe. Throughout the remainder of 1948 Britain attempted to stick to its position. It again resorted to the previously tried formula of a counter-proposal that might serve as a compromise. The suggestion was that West European foreign ministers should form a semi-permanent committee that would meet at regular intervals to discuss problems of common concern. Britain wished, however, to exclude defence and economic affairs from the brief. The former would be the province of the Atlantic military alliance that Britain hoped the United States would create, while the latter were held to fall under the purview of the body established to administer the Marshall Plan. It seemed clear that anything more than a purely intergovernmental system of consultation and cooperation would be deemed undesirable by Britain.

But the force of opinion against Britain and its supporters, notably Ireland and Scandinavia, was already gaining strength throughout 1948, under the stimulus of the Congress of Europe. Churchill's proposal made at The Hague for a European Assembly had been taken up with vigour by the newly formed European Movement. In July the International Committee of the Movements for European Unity agreed to ask the national parliaments of Western Europe to lend their voices to the argument. More importantly, however, some national governments swung more firmly in favour of the idea. In July the prime minister of Belgium and a committed Europeanist, Paul-Henri Spaak, stated that he supported a European Assembly and announced that he had asked the European Movement to consider plans for such a body. At the end of the month a new government in France, with a strong pro-European cast of ministers, including Robert Schuman at the foreign ministry, contacted the other members of the Brussels Treaty, urging the establishment of a European Assembly. A proposal from Italy in the same month went further, to argue that OEEC should take the lead in the matter.

A few weeks after receiving Spaak's invitation, the European Movement responded with a memorandum on the details of the proposed assembly. In early September Belgium and France stated that they would place the memorandum on the agenda of the forthcoming meeting of the Permanent Committee of the Brussels states. In October Britain had to yield to the pressure and agree to endorse the establishment under the Brussels Treaty of a study commission on the feasibility of an assembly. The Labour government, however, still regarded the whole trend with almost unmitigated hostility, and showed its distaste by sending only a low-grade delegation to the study commission. At subsequent meetings Britain attempted to divert the discussions towards its favoured position of a permanent committee of foreign ministers. This was not at all what the supporters of union wanted, but they were willing, in order to lure and placate British opinion, to accept such an intergovernmental structure alongside an assembly. This two-tier compromise was the essence of the study commission's report issued in January 1949. Even so, the British delegation, under instructions from London, reserved its position. Eventually, after further compromises to meet British objections about the public nature of the ministerial meetings, the foreign ministers of the Brussels states issued a communiqué on 29 January 1949 in favour of a Council of Europe 'consisting of a ministerial committee meeting in private and a consultative body meeting in public'.

The British strategy had been, in Bevin's words, to ensure that the proposed structure would be 'as little embarrassing as possible'. In view of the past it is not surprising, and in view of the future it is significant, that Britain still preferred to remain aloof from Europe. These developments were not simply a confrontation between Britain and Europe. Other states shared the British unease. But whereas integrationist sympathies were widespread in many continental states, they had little purchase in Britain, especially within the ruling Labour Party.

Notwithstanding the British unhappiness, the proposals were accepted at the meeting of foreign ministers in London, where Britain had a final victory in defeating a proposal from France and Italy that the new body should be named the European Union. The Statute of the Council of Europe was signed as the Treaty of Westminster, one month after the establishment of NATO, on 5 May 1949 by representatives of 10 states, and arrangements were made for the organisation to establish permanent offices in Strasbourg. Its supporters regarded it as a happy augury that on the same day the Soviet Union finally called off its blockade of Berlin. With its aim of achieving 'a greater unity between its Members for the purpose of safeguarding and realising the ideals and principles which are their common heritage and facilitating their economic and social progress', the new body became Western Europe's first postwar political organisation, one which immediately and daringly claimed that it would work for 'an economic and political union'.

The Council of Europe has remained Western Europe's largest organisation. The original membership of 10 – Belgium, Denmark, France, Britain, Ireland, Italy, the Netherlands, Luxembourg, Norway and Sweden – had grown to 18 by 1965. Greece and Turkey joined in 1949, Iceland in 1950, the Federal Republic of Germany in 1951 (with the Saar region, disputed between France and West Germany, having associate status until its reunification with West Germany in 1956), Austria in 1956, Cyprus in 1961, Switzerland in 1963, and Malta in 1965. After the collapse of their authoritarian dictatorships in the mid-1970s, Spain and Portugal were also admitted to membership.

POLITICAL ASSOCIATION: THE COUNCIL OF EUROPE

In August 1949 the Consultative Assembly of the Council of Europe held its first session in Strasbourg. Federalists and functionalists alike regarded it as a great achievement and a decisive breakthrough in the fight for a united Europe, and immediately set out to make the new body a more effective organ of integration than was apparent in its charter. They had two primary objectives: to develop some semblance of supranational authority, and to strengthen the Assembly *vis-à-vis* the Committee of Ministers. For, despite the resounding phraseology, the creation of the Council of Europe had not in any degree diminished national sovereignty as represented by the ministers. In the last resort the aims of the Council were to be achieved by 'discussion of questions of common concern and by agreements and common action in economic, social, scientific, legal and administrative matters and in the maintenance and further realisation of human rights and fundamental freedoms'. Defence was excluded because it was controversial, given the presence as founder members of two states, Sweden and Ireland, which still professed a policy of neutrality. The Council's aims were still very generalised. In effect, while it had a wide field of reference, at the same time its ability to do things was severely limited.

Any international body could minimally agree to a framework of discussion and agreement. In many ways the Council of Europe was little more than a continuation of the traditional format of cooperation, transcribed to a bigger stage, and could not itself move forward to a supranational or federalist future. This is not to say that it would not encourage efforts at more intense integration: indeed, this was to be one of the major concerns of the Assembly.

Within the Council there were no surprises or novelties about the Committee of Ministers: with each state having one vote and a veto, it became little more than an intergovernmental conference of foreign ministers meeting twice yearly. In 1952 it adopted the practice of permitting deputies to stand in for the ministers: the deputies soon became permanent features, attending to all business except that deemed to be symbolically important. Most decisions have required unanimity, thus allowing reluctant members the right of a veto, though a loophole does allow members to pursue a policy without requiring the assent or cooperation of the others. This was not used directly until 1956, with the creation of a European Settlement Fund. The most radical innovations towards integration that were to come later were initiated outside the framework of the Council and its Committee of Ministers. In that sense the Committee has not been a true executive body; but nor was it designed to be. In relaying decisions to the member governments, it has only been able to recommend. Committee members could go their own way whenever national concerns dictated a strictly national path.

The Assembly, on the other hand, has been more adventurous and imaginative almost from the outset. At its first session in 1949 Paul-Henri Spaak became president. He presided over the first of a series of discussions on how the Council could further the cause of integration. Its members, since 1951 nominated by the national parliaments, themselves displayed a tendency in many debates to cluster around political party identity rather than nationality. But the Assembly itself was very much a talking shop; it simply did not acquire powers that matched its proclaimed functions. The basis of its existence was deliberation. It was the Committee of Ministers which had the ability to determine budgets, decide on employment in the secretariat, and rule on applications for membership. At first, the Assembly could not even decide upon its own agenda: it was only after the first session in 1949 that the Committee of Ministers agreed not to exercise its right to draw up the Assembly's agenda. It was permitted to offer only recommendations to the Committee of Ministers, without being able to bind the latter in any way: quite often, the Committee simply chose to ignore or reject Assembly recommendations. Just as the Committee was not a true executive, so the Assembly was not a true legislature.

Partly because of these restrictions on action and scope, the relationship between Assembly and Committee has often been uneasy and strained. The divergent views simply reflected their different interests. By and large, the Assembly became populated by people who went to Strasbourg because they were interested in Europe and unity, while ministers have represented national governments to which they are responsible. One frustrated delegate, the leading French politician, Paul Reynard, could assert in exasperation that 'the Council of Europe consists of two bodies, one of them for Europe, the other against it'. Despite the introduction of a liaison committee in 1950, little common ground appeared between the two sides. All of this frustrated the Assembly, whose major proposals involved the notion of greater European unity. On the other hand, there were people like Spaak and the Italian premier, Alcide de Gasperi, who were prepared to accept things for what they were, to see the Council of Europe as a first step in the right direction, not an end – and a direction which they believed to be merely inevitable.

The tensions exhibited by the Council of Europe must be attributed not only to its structure, but to the forces which determined it. The dual design had been influenced greatly by the negative British attitude, with the pro-Europeans reluctantly compromising as much as possible in order to ensure British membership. Britain's willingness to compromise had been far less marked. But the essential conflicts within the Council were not so much between the unevenly matched Assembly and the Committee of Ministers as between national perceptions of the desired shape of Europe. While France, Italy and the Low Countries were interested in developing common political institutions with a supranational flavour, Britain and its Nordic supporters wanted only the traditional form of intergovernmental collaboration. The sides were set, and national positions determined, in a debate that was to continue well into the future.

It was this seemingly irreconcilable cleavage that effectively meant that the Council of Europe was in no position to advance by and in itself the concept of European union to any great length. The failure of ambitious projects within the Council was evident by the time of its second session in 1950. Despite being buoyed by the attendance of a West German delegation mandated to support the establishment of a supranational federal authority, the federalist argument went down to decisive defeat. This had several far-reaching effects. First, any illusions that people may have had about Britain were soon dispelled: Britain still refused to accept anything above a loose intergovernmental structure. The effort to placate Britain came to an end. In the future, attempts to achieve a modicum of unity would go ahead regardless of the British position. Second, it tended to downgrade the Council of Europe, which came to be regarded by ardent Europeanists only as a symbol of unity and of better things to come. By its success in limiting the scope of the Council of Europe, Britain effectively destroyed it as a potentially powerful engine of integration, but in so doing lost whatever control of the situation it had had. In May 1950 the Assembly, almost as an act of desperation, sent a list of recommendations to the national parliaments, bypassing the Committee of Ministers. The treatment of these recommendations illustrated the gulf that was growing within Western Europe. They were positively received in the parliaments of the six states that were to take the initiative in integration in the following decade. The British parliament, by contrast, just reiterated the view that the Council should be merely a meeting place for discussion and ideas, while in Scandinavia the recommendations were not even debated.

The Council of Europe nevertheless survived and within its limited competence has reason to be proud of the work it has done since its inception. One of its major concerns has always been the securing and protection of fundamental human rights, and it sought to build further upon the UN Declaration of Human Rights of December 1948. The European Convention for the Protection of Human Rights and Fundamental Freedoms was launched in November 1950, with 12 states immediately appending their signatures. The Convention eventually came into force in September 1953, when it received the necessary 10 ratifications. Ironically, Britain was the first state to ratify the Convention, while France, for example, did not do so until 1974. In order to reinforce the obligations of the Convention, the Council fostered the establishment of a Commission in 1954 and a European Court of Justice in 1959, which was to have a deep and direct impact upon ordinary European citizens in the years to come.

Although rarely hitting the headlines, the Council continued to work to achieve integration in restricted and less controversial fields. It sponsored the European Cultural Convention of 1954 and a European Social Charter in 1961. It sought to achieve some form of policy coordination in other, more economic sectors: transport in 1953, civil aviation in 1954, and agriculture in 1955 (though the latter was essentially organised within the context of OEEC since Switzerland and Portugal, not then Council members, were also participants).

It similarly exerted itself to establish working relationships with other international organisations, so much so that the Council of Europe became a kind of central clearing house for cooperation and coordination, with the Assembly (renamed the Parliamentary Assembly in 1974) receiving and discussing annual reports from other European bodies, such as the European Community and the European Free Trade Association, from OECD, and from several UN agencies.

The first serious challenge to the Council came with the creation of the European Coal and Steel Community. However, the six states that joined in this new venture were strong supporters of the Council and saw no incompatibility between the two bodies. The Council still remains the organ with the broadest spread of democratic membership: it is the West European body which perhaps will benefit first from the revolutionary changes of 1989 in Eastern Europe precisely because of its more 'bland' nature: in 1990 Poland signified its desire to join the Council. Because of its spread of membership, it has retained value as a forum where a wide range of ideas and views can be aired for discussion. It is this which has helped to prevent it from being completely submerged by later developments. Perhaps the major significance of the Council of Europe rests in the fact that it was the first European organisation with a political flavour. As such, it was an important milestone on the road to the closer association of the European Community, a facet acknowledged by the European Union of Federalists which reported that the Council 'marked the beginning of a real and organic cooperation between the nations of Europe' and 'the end of the illusion that the aim of European unity can be achieved without political machinery on a supranational level'.

EXPERIMENTS IN ECONOMIC INTEGRATION

The honour of establishing the first postwar economic arrangement belongs to Benelux, a grouping of Belgium, the Netherlands and Luxembourg. An agreement to come together as an economic unit was reached by the exiled governments in 1944, though the scheme did not envisage any political arrangements. After the war they began to tackle problems of harmonising the three domestic economies, an essential step towards the projected customs union. The latter was to be achieved through the abolition of internal customs duties and the introduction of a joint external tariff on all imports into the three countries, and the unification of excise and other tax rates. Progress was slow, and delayed several times. The war had had a differential impact on the economies, with Belgium much less adversely affected than the Netherlands. These differences were compounded by other national interests.

Eventually, however, the common external tariff and the abolition of internal customs duties were introduced in January 1948, but this did not fulfil the initial optimism. Each state still retained a large measure of protectionism against the others, and complete free trade still remained as far away as ever. Indeed, the excise duties remained so markedly different that tax controls on the borders between the Benelux states had to be maintained. It is fair to say that by the time of the establishment of OEEC progress in Benelux had more or less ground to a halt. Its experience demonstrated the difficulties of establishing an economic union even in such a compact and relatively homogeneous area as the Low Countries, where there was also a large degree of consensus on the project. Nevertheless, Benelux did advance further than other proposals for economic union, such as that toyed at in 1945 and again in 1948 by France and Italy, and perhaps it offered valuable lessons that could be learnt by future attempts in the same direction.

The other major attempt at economic cooperation, albeit much less ambitious, took place in Northern Europe. In earlier years a great deal of lip service had been paid in Scandinavia to cooperative efforts, up to and including economic cooperation; but the several discussions had been infrequent and without any tangible results. It had been the Nordic states which had drawn back from the full implications of the Oslo and Ouchy Conventions of the 1930s. In 1946, however, they agreed to establish a Scandinavian Committee for Legislative Cooperation. Its objectives were to be quite ambitious: to vet proposed national legislation and to submit proposals for new legislation in such a way that conformity of objective and practice would be achieved, and also to ensure a coordinated joint Nordic view at international conferences. This was not meant to be any kind of supranational authority, but under the aegis of cooperation some conformity of legislation was achieved as well as some joint initiatives, one of the first being the establishment of Scandinavian Air Lines (SAS) in August 1946.

During the discussions on the Marshall Plan, Norway proposed in July 1947 that a committee ought to be established to consider possibilities of economic cooperation. The following February, Denmark, Iceland, Norway and Sweden agreed to create a Joint Nordic

Committee for Economic Cooperation. This body was to explore the possibility of the elimination of internal tariffs within Scandinavia, the construction of a common external tariff, and cooperation on labour and production developments. To some extent the work of the Committee was affected by the arguments in 1948 over a common Scandinavian military alliance. Nevertheless, it did manage to report in January 1950 in favour of the abolition of internal tariffs, the creation of a common external tariff, and a broad customs union built upon large-scale and specialised industrial production. By then, however, Norway, with the weakest and least industrialised economy of the three major states, was beginning to get cold feet and insisted upon appending a minority report saying that it could not, given its current economic situation, contemplate joining a customs union. Denmark seemed to be interested in going ahead in conjunction with Sweden, but the latter was not willing to consider this. In the face of Norwegian opposition, the Joint Committee was forced to conclude that the 'difficulties are so significant that they cannot at present be solved by the participating countries'. But even though what was being contemplated was regionally restricted, it nevertheless went far beyond what these states, following the British line, had been willing to accept at the European level.

With the failure of these discussions on economic union the Nordic states were left with the limited form of cooperation to which they had agreed in 1946, and also with Uniscan, a loose, consultative structure they had entered into, albeit reluctantly, with Britain under the latter's urging, but one which would involve little more than a multilateral attempt at coordinating economic policies. Uniscan was not complex, but simply based upon consultation at the highest bureaucratic level, with occasional ministerial meetings. While it survived, it served a useful function in obtaining agreement on some economic questions such as currency convertibility and capital transfers. Uniscan could persist throughout the 1950s without much difficulty since it in no way threatened national independence. More significant for Scandinavia was its retreat in 1950 back to limited and relatively non-controversial sectoral coordination at the regional level. For example, the states coordinated their laws on citizenship in 1950 and on communications in 1951. This pattern, on eschewing economic matters, was to culminate in the formation of the Nordic Council in 1952.

However, just as the Nordic states abandoned the idea of close economic integration, the theme was taken up in new developments elsewhere which, if they had a role model in mind, were to be based upon the more intensive ambitions of Benelux rather than the loose

41

informal formats ultimately favoured by Britain and Scandinavia. With the declaration of the Schuman Plan in May 1950, European union was to acquire a new momentum and dimension, one that would proceed on a narrower front with the involvement of only a few countries, and in policy terms with a much more specific focus than that held by those who dreamed of European political federation.

CHAPTER FOUR

The European Coal and Steel Community

During the first two years of the Marshall Plan the West European economies responded to the injection of American aid, and production rose steadily. While the administration of the Marshall Plan through OEEC was giving Western Europe a first lesson in economic cooperation, it was clear to the dedicated disciples of a united Europe that neither OEEC nor the Council of Europe could have anything more than a limited application. Given the diversity of membership within both organisations, neither was likely to metamorphose itself into a different and more integrated organisation. OEEC demonstrated how easy it was for policies of coordination to clash with national wishes and interests. Even those governments that were in the vanguard of the urging for greater union were guilty at times of dragging their heels when OEEC proposals and policies seemed likely to have an adverse effect upon the national economy. Nevertheless, throughout 1950, France, seeking to push Western Europe beyond OEEC and the Council of Europe, resisted measures agreed in OEEC for the liberalisation of trade. In the same year Italy set a new higher rate of customs duties just before a scheduled meeting of GATT was due to discuss tariff reductions. However, these irritations perhaps paled into insignificance when compared to the British position. It was Britain more than any other country which had placed a stamp on all European discussions about integration since the war. That was to change rapidly: 1950 was to be the year when efforts to build a united Europe with British participation came to an end. If unity were to be achieved, a different path had to be sought. What was needed was the necessary stimulus. That was provided by the French foreign minister, Robert Schuman, who in May 1950 cut through all the objections and hesitations within the European debate to propose a pooling of coal and steel resources.

THE SCHUMAN PLAN

Schuman's proposal was that coal and steel resources in Western Europe should be pooled and administered by both the national states and a new supranational authority acting conjointly, with the purpose of gradually eliminating all tariffs in these heavy industries. But the Schuman Plan was not just economic. Behind it lay two political motives: first, to see the Plan as the first step towards an effective political integration, and second the political conviction that stability and union within Western Europe rested ultimately upon a rapprochement between France and West Germany. And indeed this was how Schuman's declaration began: 'the French Government proposes that Franco–German coal and steel production should be placed under a common High Authority in an organisation open to the participation of the other countries of Europe'. In response to a question put to him shortly afterwards as to how many participating countries he thought would be necessary to make the proposed structure viable, Schuman simply stated, 'if necessary, we shall go ahead with only two'.

There was, in fact, nothing particularly novel about the proposal. The choice of industries and the scheme itself had been partly influenced by two recent publications, one emanating from the Assembly of the Council of Europe and the other from the UN Economic Commission for Europe. Both publications had made similar recommendations. The point was that both industries were experiencing particular problems in several countries: an acute coal shortage and an oversupply of steel. The specific plan announced by Schuman had been drafted by Jean Monnet who certainly did see it as only a first step in a chain that would ultimately lead to political integration. After a long career in public service, Monnet had been appointed as head of the French Planning Commission. His experiences there in grappling with the problems of planning the postwar development of the French economy had made him increasingly convinced that effective economic planning was beyond the capacity of any single state, but would depend upon intense cooperation between states.

There was a further reason which particularly affected France. The Cold War had effectively decided what was to be done with Germany. In 1949 two German states had emerged from the territory of the old Reich. While France was content for Germany to remain divided, it was concerned about its new neighbour, the Federal Republic of West Germany, not least about the rapid economic growth that had occurred there after a major currency reform in 1948. The Schuman Plan had been sold to a French government that was worried about the future political, military and economic potential of the new West German state in part as a means of keeping a check on that potential. For its part, West Germany was unhappy about the restrictions that had been placed upon the economic development of much of its heavy industry by the International Ruhr Authority, an organisation set up by the Allies during their military occupation of Germany: the Schuman Plan offered a way to eliminate the Authority while still satisfying West Germany's neighbours about its intentions. Monnet's original report had drawn particular attention to the fact that West Germany could easily be expected to produce steel at a cost far below what France could manage. While there was, at least for Monnet and Schuman, an altruistic motive behind the scheme, it is clear that France found the idea attractive because it offered a better way than the International Ruhr Authority of binding the new West Germany to external control while it was still relatively weak.

Schuman achieved the maximum dramatic effect by announcing his proposal at a press conference rather than as a governmental report. Even so, he had taken the precaution beforehand of secretly informing both the United States and West Germany of his plans. Neither had been expected to raise objections. The United States was still pressing for close cooperation, while the West German Chancellor, Konrad Adenauer, had on several occasions already suggested some kind of Franco–German cooperation. There were several reasons why Adenauer pursued such a line of argument: it might be a way of helping the new West German state to achieve equality in the international order; it might placate West German annoyance over the role of the International Ruhr Authority; and it might in time offer an opportunity for West Germany to regain sovereignty of the coal and steel producing Saar, which still remained in French hands.

It is noteworthy that Schuman did not contact Britain in advance of his announcement. Not surprisingly, Britain was annoyed at being excluded from any consultation. However, it is highly dubious that Britain would have adopted a stance different to that it took in response to Schuman's public declaration. For the Schuman Plan had implications beyond a simple coordination of coal and steel production. It claimed that 'The pooling of coal and steel production will immediately provide for the establishment of common bases for economic development as a first step in the federation of Europe, and will change the destinies of those regions which have long been devoted to the munitions of war, of which they have been the most constant victims'. The declaration went on to state bluntly that 'Europe must be organised on a federal basis'. This was hardly music to Britain's ears: the Labour government had vigorously resisted all such overtures since 1945.

In some ways the idea of a coal and steel community took off because people committed to some form of common future for Western Europe occupied positions of authority in several countries: Schuman, Monnet and others in France, Adenauer in West Germany, Alcide de Gasperi and Carlo Sforza in Italy, Paul-Henri Spaak in Belgium, and Joseph Beck in Luxembourg. However, even though many enthusiastically endorsed the creation of a supranational authority, there was still concern about how much power such a body might have. Consequently, there were counter-proposals that within the new organisation there still should be some kind of authoritative institution that would represent the interests of the participating states.

Britain had been content with the intergovernmental structure of OEEC. Indeed, it had even baulked over the European Payments Union for five months until it gained complete assurance that it would still be able to retain sole control over sterling as an international reserve currency. Hence it was not surprising that Britain declined the invitation to join the proposed coal and steel structure, ostensibly because it was unwilling to accept beforehand the principle of a new and binding supranational authority. Yet it was precisely to avoid the kind of obstructionism that Britain had indulged in in the past that participation in the new structure was made conditional upon prior agreement to the principle of a supranational authority. While some British officials were interested in the Schuman Plan, the Labour Party rejected it as something that would limit its ability to strive for democratic Socialism in Britain 'and to apply the economic controls necessary to achieve it'. In the House of Commons, Clement Attlee reiterated that it would be impossible for Britain 'to accept the principle that the most vital economic forces of this country should be handed over to an authority that is utterly undemocratic and is responsible to nobody'.

There might have been an economic argument for Britain to stay out, but the decision was quite clearly taken on political grounds.

Otherwise, it could have followed the Dutch example. The Netherlands had been happy to accept the supranational principle in advance, but insisted on retaining the right to withdraw from the discussions should it prove impossible in its eyes for the ideas to be turned into economic practice. In 1951, with the coal and steel discussions still going on, the British electorate returned Churchill and the Conservatives to power. But there was to be no reversal of the British attitude. The Conservative Party continued the Labour practice of remaining aloof, though never actively criticising attempts at European union as long as they did not threaten what Britain conceived to be its own vital interests. In that sense Britain was not an active opponent of the new attempts at sectoral economic unification that in the early 1950s began with coal and steel. On the other hand, however, the absence of Britain from the new developments marked the beginning of a new and decisive phase in European integration.

Britain was not entirely alone in its refusal to become involved in the Schuman plan. It was backed by its traditional allies from the debates of previous years. In the event it was only those six states in which agitation for closer political and economic integration had been strongest in the 1940s, with political support at the highest level, which entered into the discussions that led to the establishment of the European Coal and Steel Community (ECSC). The foundation of the ECSC marks the first significant step towards European union that went beyond being merely consultative and intergovernmental in character. Its architect, Jean Monnet, hailed it as 'the first expression of the Europe that is being born'. It set the tone of the renewed debate which in the coming decade was to divide Western Europe even further, at the same time as setting in motion a groundswell that eventually produced the European Community.

THE ECSC: ESTABLISHMENT AND STRUCTURE

Even though they had all agreed beforehand to the principle of a supranational institution, the six states of 'little' Europe – France, West Germany, Italy, Belgium, the Netherlands and Luxembourg – faced nine months of hard bargaining after they formally began negotiations in June 1950. In the process, the ideas that had originally been expounded by Monnet were substantially modified. The most important factor, perhaps, was the changing status of West Germany.

In the very month that the Six began their discussions, war broke out in Korea. In the process of reviewing its global commitments, the United States stressed even more the importance for the free world of a strong West German state. Insofar as this affected the ECSC negotiations, it gave West Germany a far stronger hand and enabled its negotiators to resist some of the French demands, especially those which were aimed at a deconcentration and decartelisation of West Germany's heavy industries, and to pursue more urgently its own point of view on the future of the Saar. Oddly enough, it was the United States that acted as an important intermediary in these arguments.

Finally, the ECSC Treaty of Paris, designated to last for 50 years, was signed by representatives of the six states on 18 April 1951. After lengthy debates in each national parliament, ratification took a further year to complete. The treaty was complex, with 100 articles and a considerable number of additional annexes. Despite the time that had elapsed from Schuman's original declaration to ratification, the ECSC succeeded in escaping from the drawing board relatively easily. Undoubtedly, the essentially non-problematic process was aided by the fact that the Six had been able to agree upon the basic objectives in advance – the economic objective of a common market and the political one of some kind of supranational authority – as it was also by the fact that the discussions were mainly conducted by experienced bureaucrats in closed sessions. Behind all this, however, was the fact of the strong Christian Democrat presence in all six governments throughout the crucial 1950–52 period. On the other hand, the ECSC proposals were supported by most political parties throughout the Six, though for different reasons. Only in the Netherlands and Lux-embourg can we perhaps speak of a party consensus on the reasons for support. There was some opposition in Belgium, focused mainly on worries over the fate of the country's old and inefficient coal mines. Italy accepted that there would be economic disadvantages, though in the negotiations it successfully managed to gain some important concessions for its own steel industry: but the economic worries took a clear secondary position to the political factors which were the major motives for Italy's participation.

Ironically, it was in the two countries, France and West Germany, which Schuman had seen as the hub of his scheme that the most vocal opposition was expressed. In West Germany the leader of the opposition, Kurt Schumacher, and his Social Democrat Party rejected entry on nationalist grounds, arguing that by binding the country so closely to western states which were also members of a military alliance led by the United States, Adenauer was making the possibility of German reunification even more difficult and remote. In France the concept was assailed by the powerful extremes on both the right and the left: Charles de Gaulle's contemptuous dismissal of it as a directionless 'mish-mash' was matched by the ideological opposition of the Communist Party.

The broad support that the ECSC Treaty did receive was perhaps possible because, despite its complexity, it was rather inchoate: because it was couched in rather vague and ambiguous terms, it could be interpreted in different ways. In that sense, ECSC was a child of a specific coalition of interests and a conjunction of specific events. It came into being on the groundswell of the earlier federalist enthusiasm, while still being sufficiently limited and pragmatic to be deemed feasible by senior politicians who themselves were keenly interested in fostering moves towards greater and effective cooperation. As later events were to prove, there was no guarantee that those constellations would persist over time or even continue to support moves towards integration.

The general objective of the ECSC Treaty was to foster 'economic expansion, growth of employment and a rising standard of living' in the member states through the development of a common market in coal and steel. In order to ensure a more appropriate distribution across the states of production, prices and a rational pattern of modernisation, the treaty schedule called for a five-year transitional period of two distinct stages. The ECSC would first have to dismantle tariffs and other trade restrictions. Only then could it move on to establish a free common market. Such an ambitious programme, which could have at least some negative consequences in the member states, could be achieved only under the supervision of a supranational authority with the necessary powers to determine what the policies of the member states ought to be.

The overseeing institution was to be the nine-member High Authority. Its members were to be nominees of national governments: while all the states were to be represented, not more than two members could come from any one state. In practice the three larger states were to have two nominations each, the others only one. The term of office of the commissioners was to be six years: it would be staggered, with one-third retiring every two years, so as to provide some degree of continuity and collective memory. In fact, its membership proved to be highly stable. Jean Monnet was appointed as the president of the High Authority, and his resignation from the office in June 1955 was the only occasion before the setting up of the much broader

European Economic Community in 1957 when there was a change in the membership of the High Authority.

The High Authority seemed to have a wide brief on fiscal matters such as taxes and levies, as well as upon production and restrictive practices. Its authority to work for the removal of all barriers to the free movement of coal and steel rested on a wide array of actions, ranging from non-binding recommendations to binding decisions. The latter could be reached by a majority vote among the nine: unanimity in the High Authority was not to be necessary. Its decisions could be positive, by directing investment or controlling both prices and production, or negative, through punishing those who ignored its decisions. Hence, the significance of the High Authority was its ability to influence the national coal and steel industries without being countermanded by national governments. Perhaps it was only because of the narrow range of human activities which fell within the orbit of the ECSC that the member states had been willing to cede potentially substantial powers to the body which was the fundamental supranational element of the new organisation.

Yet the High Authority was far from being a sovereign body. It was paralleled as an executive by a Special Council of Ministers which, while bound in some important respects by High Authority decisions, could nevertheless attempt to moderate the supranationalism of the latter. The Council had been insisted upon by the Benelux countries which, notwithstanding their strong commitment to the cause of integration, wanted a body whose purpose would be to watch over and defend the national interests of the smaller participants. The members of the Council were drawn from the national governments and had the task of counterbalancing the High Authority's supranationalism. On the other hand, while the High Authority required the support of the Council in, for example, any attempt to limit output because of overproduction or when seeking an equitable distribution of supplies during a shortage in output, the Council of Ministers was inhibited to some extent because the national governments did not directly finance the ECSC. Funding was received by the High Authority from a tax levied upon coal and steel production directly from the firms concerned.

A further restraint upon the High Authority, though less potent or practicable, was to be provided by a Common Assembly of 78 members (18 from each of West Germany, France and Italy; 10 each from Belgium and the Netherlands; and 4 from Luxembourg), the first international assembly in Europe with legally guaranteed powers. In terms of the ultimate political objective of integration, the Common

Assembly was designed to be the repository of ultimate control. This, however, did not materialise. The Assembly was not a true legislative body. Its significance rested upon its ability to censure the High Authority and to demand its collective resignation, a blunt sanction that was never to be applied.

Two further checks on arbitrary High Authority action were to be offered by the avenues of organised opinion and law. The treaty established a Consultative Committee whose task it was to advise the High Authority on all aspects of its work. This committee was composed of representatives of producers, employees and consumers; it too, however, could not be much of a check on High Authority action if the two bodies moved on to a collision course – something, in fact, which never occurred. Potentially more important, and significant for the further advances on European integration that were yet to come, was the decision to establish a Court of Justice. The Court, consisting of seven judges drawn from all the national judiciaries, was to have the task of ruling on the legality of any High Authority action on the basis of complaints submitted by either national governments or industrial enterprises. While this could be a check upon the High Authority, it could also be a check upon individualistic action by national governments. There would be no appeal against the Court's decisions; by rooting the whole ECSC structure in the last resort in the rule of law, the drafters of the treaty introduced a concept which was to be of tremendous importance for European integration as a whole.

THE ECSC IN OPERATION

At the outset the ECSC tended to move cautiously so as not to jeopardise expansion of the European ideal by alienating public opinion. This was reinforced by the tendency of national governments not to handle unpopular decisions if they could be transferred to the High Authority for action. While in the longer run this practice perhaps strengthened the High Authority in its relations with the member governments, the caution it induced in the High Authority, along with the ambiguity of the treaty, made for some slow progress.

The High Authority met for the first time in the autumn of 1952, and immediately set about trying to turn the principles of the Treaty of Paris into practical results. Six years later, when the launching of the European Economic Community with the same six member states had in a sense superseded the ECSC, the Authority could make a reasonably positive report. While many restrictive practices and problems remained, trade had increased within the heavy industries of the Six. The question has to be asked, however, if this was due to the activities of the ECSC or if it was merely a consequence of the sustained economic boom which affected the whole of Western Europe.

The fact of the matter is that in terms of setting up some kind of economic common market, much of the groundwork had already been done. Benelux, for instance, had already moved forward to setting up a low common external tariff with no internal tariffs. Again, in terms of the quantitative restrictions that had bedevilled trade in the past, many of these had already been swept away or modified by OEEC. The more serious difficulties, present at the outset, were political in origin. It was symbolic, perhaps, of the deep-rooted nature of national instincts that the ECSC could not agree upon a single language in which to conduct its activities. West Germany objected to French being the single language of the organisation, and the net result was that the ECSC had to operate with four official languages. Similarly, there were disputes about where the new body should be physically located. France already had the Council of Europe in Strasbourg, and it was accepted that because the Common Assembly of the ECSC would be drawn from those attending the Council of Europe, the new assembly should also be located in Strasbourg. No consensus was possible on the other ECSC institutions, and in the end it was agreed, as a provisional measure only, to place the High Authority and the Court of Justice in Luxembourg, a temporary arrangement that in effect became permanent.

The High Authority soon discovered that to use legislation to eliminate tariffs and quotas was not sufficient to generate a common market. Each of the member states had a host of other discriminatory practices that effectively distorted trade patterns. It was these which made progress relatively slow, and which on occasions even led the High Authority to bow down to views expressed in the Special Council of Ministers even where under the treaty it had undisputed authority to act. The net result was that the High Authority, and hence the ECSC, did not seem to have any grand strategy for the future in terms of planning and coordinating coal and steel output. It did launch a general economic survey in 1953, but this was at the request of the Special Council of Ministers, itself responding to national government worries about a slump in demand. But the survey led nowhere, and was never repeated.

Rather than producing a brave new economic world, the ECSC and its High Authority had constantly to wrestle with national objections and intransigence. It had, for example, to struggle with West Germany's complaints about a High Authority decision to allow French steel to be sold within West Germany with a lower level of taxation than that placed upon its own steel being sold in France. Again, by 1955 Belgian coal and Italian steel still enjoyed substantial national protection three years into the ECSC operation. At the end of the transitional phase, French government discrimination and obstruction in its subsidisation policies meant that to all intents and purposes France's coal industry still remained outside the common ECSC structure. France persisted in operating a policy of cross-subsidisation where profitable coal mines subsidised those making losses, and where in any case the profitability of the whole industry depended upon generous governmental support – both policies which directly infringed the conditions of the ECSC treaty. And it was only in 1961 that the ECSC won a victory over a French licensing system that discriminated against imports of coal into the country.

Despite such problems of national differences and policies, the ECSC experiment could claim some success, albeit only a partial one. By 1956, for instance, it had been able to overcome discriminatory practices in transportation rates and costs. Overall, it could by the end of the transitional phase claim that it had changed the basis of economic competition by removing many restrictive practices and that it had eased some of the pain of economic decline by its policies towards those aging coal and steel plants that were coming to the end of a useful life. By 1958 much trade discrimination had been eliminated, and both production and the volume of trade had greatly expanded. It could argue that while it still had to struggle with the painful problem of modernisation in much of the coal industry, its economic statistics compared favourably with those of other countries.

On the other hand, the limitations of the supranational institutions and the unwillingness of member states totally to set aside their own national interests were starkly exposed in 1959. The immediate cause was a mountain of surplus coal, generated by two mild winters and a slowing down of economic growth: coal stocks had quadrupled from 7 to 31 million tons since 1957. Initially, the High Authority took no action, believing that the problem would only be temporary. It was eventually spurred into action when the majority of the member states began to take unilateral action to control imports of coal into their own territories, so obviating the whole object of the common market since the new controls also applied to imports from other ECSC states. At the same time, Italy, which had to import some 90 per cent of its coal needs, preferred to buy cheaper, mainly American, coal on the open market rather than deal with its ECSC partners.

In March 1959 the High Authority declared that coal overproduction was such as to constitute a state of 'manifest crisis' as that term had been defined by the Treaty of Paris. Only the Special Council of Ministers, however, had the right to declare such a state of crisis. The ECSC rules required a qualified majority in the Council for such a declaration, something which proved to be impossible. The Authority's proposals had involved the imposition of import controls and production quotas. These were resisted by Italy and the Netherlands which were happy with the low level of world prices, and by West Germany which preferred to protect its own coal industry through subsidies – a route which, under the Treaty of Paris, the High Authority was forbidden to consider. At the extreme, France, which since the late 1940s had been widely regarded as the leader of European integration, even denied that the supranational bodies had the right to acquire and use emergency powers. But since the ECSC had been created, the faltering Fourth French Republic had collapsed in 1958, and France was then governed by President de Gaulle, determined to raise the status of France as a state and nation: it was a foretaste of the French attitude that was to affect integration in the next decade.

The High Authority, and through it the ECSC, suffered a loss of prestige: the supranational agencies, after all, had been established precisely to handle that kind of crisis. It was an indication of the great difficulty the European idea would have in achieving concerted action in even a single economic sector, and suggested that the recently established and broader European Economic Community of 1957 would not find it easy to secure its broad objectives of common policies and a common market. Out of the disarray into which the ECSC had fallen, the High Authority attempted to move forward to a general agreement on energy, but it was not until April 1964 that the Council of Ministers eventually agreed to a document. While the High Authority hailed it as an energy equivalent of the common agricultural policy to which the new Economic Community was committed, the document essentially confirmed the superiority of national interests. It essentially involved the coordination of existing national practices, especially on subsidies, and any element of a jointly financed common policy under the direction of the High Authority was simply absent.

The High Authority returned to the attack in 1966, seeking some kind of common agreement on levels of production. While West Germany, for example, was willing to go along with the proposal (but only if there was a joint system of ECSC subsidy financing), the net importers of coal within the Six – France, Italy and the Netherlands – were totally hostile to the notion of national contributions to a joint financing policy. Once again, the High Authority had to admit defeat, and withdrew its proposal.

The economic record of the ECSC was therefore rather mixed. It had, however, not been intended to be just an economic body. For people like Schuman and Monnet, it was to be the first unit in an interlocking sectoral integration that would ultimately fulfil the dream of political integration. The key phrase was spillover. In a functional sense, spillover was founded on the belief that contemporary economies were based upon a tangle of interrelated sectors. Once one economic sector could be integrated, the complexity of modern economies would force other sectors into similar structures and developments. More important, perhaps, was the notion of political spillover. This was based on the assumption that once supranational institutions had been set up in one economic sector, interest groups would look to that political level for the realisation of their demands, and that in time the groups would begin to appreciate the value to themselves of integration. And again, because of the nature of the modern economy, these groups would in turn lend their support to pressures for further integration.

In retrospect, the ECSC did not seem superficially to have achieved much in the political direction. The ECSC had not conditioned the European public in favour of supranationalism, nor had the key interest groups in coal and steel, whether the industries were publicly or privately owned, emerged as a vanguard of European integration. The ECSC, moreover, as the 1959 crisis had amply demonstrated, had not established an unambiguous authority over national governments and parliaments. Nevertheless, it had, on the credit side, generated a European ambience and presence. No matter how inadequately, it was a working European operation, with a physical location, to which non-members had to pay regard. Non-members like Britain, for example, found it useful and necessary to maintain permanent delegations in Luxembourg accredited to the High Authority. And by its very existence, the ECSC could add some impetus towards arguments for integration, particularly through an alliance of High Authority and Assembly. Far from restraining the former and acting as a watchdog, the

Assembly constantly urged the High Authority to make even greater supranational efforts. Within the Assembly itself, political formations were beginning tenuously to emerge along political party lines, a practice encouraged by the official recognition of, and payment of administrative expenses to, transnational party groupings. Equally important in building a framework for the future was the role played by the most anonymous of the ECSC's institutions, the Court of Justice. Almost from the beginning, it was involved in hearing complaints relating to the operation of the ECSC. Nearly all the cases that came before the Court were appeals by national governments and industries against decisions of the High Authority. What was significant was that the vast majority of these appeals were rejected, and that while the Court had no means of enforcing its opinion, its verdicts were accepted, if not immediately implemented. In that way the Court was perhaps the institution which most successfully stamped its imprint upon the ECSC, and in so doing built up a body of case law, an authority, and legitimacy that could serve as foundations for the future.

The ECSC also served to stimulate other developments. In the late 1940s integrationists had tended to desire a single federal political system, which at some point would entail a single act of abrogation of national rights to a supranational authority, whose precedence over the former national states would be constitutionally defined. The ECSC was not, and was not intended to be, that type of institution. Its method of integration was to be more gradual, retaining for long the right of national veto. What was needed, and what perhaps lay behind its inauguration, was an atmosphere of mutual confidence among its members, and especially between France and West Germany, which was to be produced through tackling together a list of specific problems by stipulated deadlines. As the barriers fell, the institutions would move on, with the consent of all participants, to a further list of commitments. While this pattern was reproduced only imperfectly in the ECSC and while a timetable of functional spillover might have taken an unconscionable time to achieve, what in the end counted for the ECSC was that it did provide an atmosphere of mutual confidence among the leaders of the member states – despite the disputes, none contemplated leaving the Community – and that this helped to pave the way for the creating of the European Economic Community in 1957. With the establishment of the latter, some immediate rationalisation affected the ECSC. A single

Common Assembly and Court would serve three distinct communities, the ECSC along with the new Economic Community and Euratom. The High Authority, however, survived as a distinct body until 1965 when it was merged with the other supranational executives.

CHAPTER FIVE
The Road to Rome

The ECSC was meant to be the first of several organisations integrating economic sectors, brought about by functional and political spillover. The six members of the ECSC, however, showed little inclination to rush matters. Despite their support for the ECSC, the member states seemed wary about losing sovereignty and their own political control over an important industrial sector, and were loath to allow the High Authority to exercise its full constitutional competence. These reasons partly explain the imperfect development of the ECSC during the 1950s. However, the Treaty of Paris had confirmed and inflamed the enthusiasm of those whose dream was a united Europe; several ideas about similar schemes were advanced almost before the ink had dried on the Treaty of Paris.

However, while these ideas were based upon the projected outcome of the ECSC, they did not originate within that organisation nor from any kind of collaboration among its constituent members. They were to be sponsored by the Council of Europe and, to some extent, by OEEC. In November 1950 the Council endorsed the idea of 'specialised authorities', something which the OEEC also favoured. In the discussions which had led to the creation of the ECSC, other economic sectors such as transport and agriculture had been highlighted as being ripe for similar developments. It was transport which became the first post-ECSC target. But transport networks spread far beyond the Six, and any meaningful cooperation would have to include all or most of Western Europe. This was the thinking which lay behind the Bonnefous Plan, named after Edward Bonnefous, who was the main architect in the Council of Europe for a European Transport Authority linked to the Council. Given the wide diversity of views within the Council about the nature of economic cooperation, let alone its political implications, it was not surprising that if anything positive was to come from the idea, it would be little more than a minimalist option. That indeed was the case, with the appearance of another loose intergovernmental structure, a Conference of European Ministers of Transport, which could only suggest and advise – though it did have some success in persuading ten states to sign a convention on cooperation and coordination of their rail networks in 1953.

Agriculture was also a popular theme for discussion in the Council of Europe. Perhaps the first significant initiative came from France, although the Dutch politician, Sicco Mansholt, had already drafted a plan for agricultural free trade that would benefit Western Europe as a whole, but especially the cost-effective Netherlands agricultural industry. Late in 1950 the French Minister of Agriculture, Pierre Pflimlin, announced at the Council of Europe – and proposed later in March 1951 to the non-member states of Austria, Portugal and Switzerland – something which amounted to a second Schuman Plan, in that it contained similar ultimate objectives: a common market directed by supranational institutions. Again, it fell foul of the divergent views within the Council of Europe on integration. By the time the member states were ready to discuss it in March 1952, the document under consideration had been so diluted from the original scheme as to present no dangers at all to national authority control over agriculture. Even so, the proposal failed to progress any further.

The Council of Europe, backed by the OEEC, ran into similar problems in the first half of the 1950s over proposals on the health, postal services and communications sectors. While some cooperation and coordination in a specific sector might be possible, as long as the hope was to embrace the whole of Western Europe in its ambit, any scheme could only be minimalist. If the sectoral approach and spillover were to achieve any great potential, they could only do so on a more limited front – that is, by the six states which had already agreed to the supranational principle by forming the ECSC. Yet the Six themselves did not seem prepared to launch any further sectoral integration, at least in the short run. Indeed, the initial experiences of the ECSC had led some to argue that rather than pursue a sector by sector strategy, it would be far easier and more logical to plan for the integration of whole economies. In that sense, the sectoral approach was already being rejected: ECSC might well have been its end rather than its beginning. That the sectoral approach was to receive a new lease of life was due to events beyond the control of the Six, or even Western Europe. And the focus of the new interest was not to be on those sectors originally envisaged as targets, but on the unlikely and controversial issue of defence.

FAILED COMMUNITIES

During the initial negotiations over ECSC, the international climate changed for the worse as conflict broke out in Korea in June 1950. It was inevitable that the war in Asia would affect politics in Western Europe, most obviously in the military sphere. Korea had not just intensified the Cold War with, for example, analogies being drawn between the partitioned Korean peninsula and the divided nature of Germany; it also placed an extra burden on American resources. The United States, faced with an allocation problem, began a review of its defensive commitments that led it to the conclusion that in the event of a military confrontation with the Soviet Union in Europe, the resources it could commit to the fledgling NATO alliance would be insufficient. Seeing no need why it alone should be expected to make up the deficit, it requested its allies to increase their defence expenditure. The European response was negative. The United States then argued that if the European members of NATO were unwilling or unable to strengthen the alliance, then this would have to be achieved by permitting West Germany to rearm.

On 12 September 1950 the United States formally proposed West German rearmament within NATO. With increasing persistence it continued to argue that West Germany should be brought into the western defensive system with its own military forces. The West German government was not averse to the idea of rearmament. Konrad Adenauer had already suggested that West Germany should be allowed the means to defend itself, and that the surest way of winning the population over to a massive commitment to democracy was to give it a stake in the responsibility of defending Western Europe. Otherwise, he argued, many Germans might be seduced by the lure of a neutral, but unified Germany which would inevitably be susceptible to Soviet influence.

Although it was hardly disputable that a West German contribution to NATO would be invaluable, especially as the other European members did not wish to, or could not, meet the new levels of requirement set by the United States, the American demand caused consternation and an agonising evaluation of its consequences in the capitals of Europe, and nowhere more so than in Paris. After 1945

France's primary objective had been the prostration of Germany. It had continued to seek to absorb the Saar even after the formation of the West German state, and relations between the two countries, collaboration in ECSC notwithstanding, were not entirely cordial. In many ways France was content with a divided Germany. A rearmed West Germany merely served to revive all the old French fears about security.

But to all West Germany's neighbours, the idea of a German military force only a few years after the defeat of Hitler's armies was still repugnant. On the other hand, it seemed obvious that the United States would not back down – and Western Europe was still heavily dependent upon the United States. The European problem was not to oppose the American proposal adamantly, but to find some compromise that would both satisfy the United States and assuage European fears of a revitalised German militarism. The shackling of a West German military contribution to NATO would have to be achieved by placing it under non-German control. Moreover, whatever the course adopted, it would have to receive the blessing of Germany's traditional enemy, France, for it to have any chance of success.

An alternative was already available: the idea of a European army. This had first been mooted by Konrad Adenauer in 1949. In August 1950, shortly after the outbreak of the Korean War, France had advocated the idea of a European army in the second session of the Council of Europe Assembly. The idea was strongly opposed by Britain, and quickly vetoed by the Council of Ministers. Nevertheless, this was the route that France chose to follow as an answer to American pressure, since one of the underlying assumptions was that it would preclude a distinct German army under a separate German command. It became known as the Pleven Plan, named after the French premier, René Pleven, who took an outline drafted by his earlier mentor, Jean Monnet, and laid it before the French Parliament on 24 October 1950.

The Pleven Plan, like other suggestions that had recently come out of the Council of Europe, followed the outline and objectives of the Schuman Plan very closely. The proposal was accepted in principle by the French National Assembly, and in calling for a 'common European army' with a European 'minister of defence', it was to be the basis of discussion about the establishment of a European Defence Community (EDC). Given Adenauer's earlier views, it was to be expected that an EDC would be supported by West Germany, though there was considerable opposition within the country, especially by the opposition Social Democrat Party, to the whole notion of rearmament. By contrast, the initial American attitude was cool. But the American High Commissioner in West Germany and the American commander-elect of NATO lent their voices to the idea, and the United States quickly became an important supporter of the project. However, West Germany would levy a price for its involvement: the agreement of the Western Allies formally to end their occupation and to give full sovereignty, including control over foreign policy, to the West German state.

The other important state to win round was Britain. Pleven hoped that Britain would join the project: indeed, much of the French support for the EDC was predicated upon the necessity of British participation. When Churchill, who had supported the earlier Council of Europe proposal, returned as premier in October 1951, many hoped that that participation would now be forthcoming. Only one month later, however, the new Foreign Secretary, Anthony Eden, firmly announced that Britain would not become a member of the EDC. The Conservative government preferred to follow the Labour route of seeking to expand the 1948 Treaty of Brussels to incorporate Italy and West Germany. The British rejection weakened the force of the proposal and was probably a factor in its slow progress. Britain's traditional supporters fell into line, and Pleven's blueprint was taken up only by the six states of the ECSC. Even so, it was not until 27 May 1952 that sufficient of the detail had been thrashed out for the representatives of the six countries, meeting in Paris, to be able to sign the treaty establishing the EDC.

The EDC was to be a military organisation, but for many it was also to be a further step along the road to European integration. In addition to a common army, there was to be a common budget and common institutions. Indeed, in some ways the EDC treaty went beyond the ECSC in that Article 38, which had been included at the insistence of Italy, required the Common Assembly to study ways of establishing federal institutions along with a popularly elected legislature. At first glance it seemed that the vision of Monnet and Schuman of gradual sectoral integration binding the participants even closer together was one important step nearer realisation.

However, the EDC may superficially have followed the sectoral pattern of the ECSC, but its fundamental implications were different. First, its supranational executive, a Board of Commissioners, would have considerably less leverage than the ECSC High Authority against the national representatives in the Council of Ministers. Unlike the ECSC, the whole concept had been modelled as a body in which

Britain might participate: this may partly account for the diluted supranational element. Second, unlike the ECSC, it was not to be a partnership of equals. The EDC had been suggested and was designed as a means of preventing West German military parity. West Germany was to be the poor relation, with all its military units being placed under the integrated command structure. The other EDC members would allocate only a proportion of their armed forces to the European army. Additional protocols reinforced the French desire for guarantees against West Germany. The mutual defence link with NATO was stressed again. France also persuaded the United States and Britain to join it in a joint declaration that a threat to the EDC would be treated as a challenge to their own security, and that this would be symbolised by the two Anglo-Saxon countries agreeing to station troops on the continent. A final protocol sought an agreement between the EDC and Britain, whereby the latter would agree to provide military aid to any one of the EDC states should it come under attack. In many ways, these additional protocols reinforced the impression that for France the EDC was designed as a guarantee for itself against possible German aggression as much as it was to be an anti-Soviet organisation. Even if it had survived, it is a moot point how long this bias would have been tolerated by West Germany.

Notwithstanding these problems, there was reason to believe in late 1952 that the push towards integration had passed a critical threshold, and so could only go forward at a much faster pace. The ECSC and EDC, it was believed, would finally consign the shibboleths of nationalism to a tardy grave. Having accepted that previous attempts to build a comprehensive Western Europe had failed through the efforts to incorporate Britain into the design, there was now a widespread conviction that a multi-purpose unit could be fashioned by the little Europe of the Six.

A principle source of the new enthusiasm was a problem raised directly by the EDC concept itself, a dilemma summed up by Konrad Adenauer on his first visit to the United States in April 1953, when he said in New York that a European army without a correspondingly unified European foreign policy would be rather illogical. This was welcome news to those who sought a federal Europe, for the federalist implications of the dilemma were very clear: a European army would need European political control of a type that could not be provided by the EDC institutions. It was evident that in neither the ECSC nor EDC could the supranational agencies have powers commensurate with their responsibilities: the ECSC was already giving indications of the resilience of national governments. This was the reasoning which led to discussions on the possibility of a European Political Community.

Article 38 of the EDC treaty, with its federalist implications, offered a way forward with its statement on the role to be played by the projected Common Assembly. Paul-Henri Spaak, back as premier of Belgium, suggested that since the EDC Assembly did not yet exist, the Assembly of the ECSC could turn itself into an ad hoc EDC body specifically to consider a more wide-ranging political cooperation. This procedure was accepted by the foreign ministers of the other five states, serving in their capacity as the Council of Ministers of the ECSC. Accordingly, the ECSC Assembly, enlarged to give it the number of representatives the projected EDC Assembly would have, was invited on 10 September 1952 to consider and report within six months on the feasibility and structures of a European Political Community. This it duly did, accepting, though not without some strong opposition, the draft of a working party on 10 March 1953. The opponents of the draft within the ad hoc assembly were primarily on the left. The West German Social Democrats were hostile to the whole concept, as they were to the EDC and West German rearmament, while some French Socialists were unhappy about the proposals on how the new structure would relate to Britain. But this did not prevent assembly acceptance of the plan.

The European Political Community was not to be just a third community, but nothing less than the beginning of a comprehensive federation to which the ECSC and EDC would be subordinated. The draft treaty of the Political Community, with 117 articles, was presented in Strasbourg on 10 March 1953. Its institutional structure was to be complex and far-reaching, with a European Executive Council, a Council of National Ministers, a Court of Justice and a popularly elected Parliament. The rapid progress towards integration which seemed to be occurring also, in December 1952, led the Dutch foreign minister to write to his counterparts that the extent of political and military integration currently under consideration should be accompanied by an equally extensive economic integration – in short, by a common market. His suggestion was welcomed, and two months later the six foreign ministers passed it on to experts for their consideration.

The European Political Community was not, however, in its outline to be the kind of federation that federalists had wanted. The supranational principle was diluted by the retention of an executive body representing national interests, and the extent of responsible government would be limited. It was perhaps more of a confederal scheme than a federal one. Even so, it was a problematic proposal, and the publication of the draft treaty proved to be the high watermark of European union in the early 1950s. The pace and enthusiasm flagged considerably when attention had to switch from abstract or grand designs to the nitty-gritty of practical details. In the upheaval that was to come during the next 12 months, only the ECSC seemed to have avoided the scrapheap. A withdrawal from the frontier of full integration was noticeable in the further discussions of the six countries in the latter half of 1953, when the topic was debated only in very general terms.

That, however, was due not just to the complexity of turning the Political Community treaty into reality, but to the problems that the Six were facing in getting the EDC off the ground. Despite its implications, the great argument was not over the Political Community, but over the EDC, for the former stood or fell with the ratification of the latter. The EDC treaty had not been ratified by any state when the proposed Political Community treaty was published. There were still arguments over the additional protocols insisted upon by France. Without them there was little hope of French approval; if they were retained, there were serious doubts about their acceptability to the other signatories. Eventually, West Germany and the Benelux states ratified the treaty early in 1954, though in the former this was only after a prolonged political battle in which the Social Democrat Party took its opposition to the EDC all the way to the country's supreme court. In Italy an ailing Alcide de Gasperi also faced formidable opposition, but fortunately was never obliged to put the EDC to the test, preferring instead to postpone the potential confrontation until after France made its decision. Thus the fate of the new Europe hinged upon France, the original sponsor of the EDC.

France had never at heart been enthusiastic about the EDC, regarding it at a minimum as perhaps a lesser evil: fundamentally, it did not want West German rearmament. Schuman had not wished to introduce the measure in the French Parliament after the treaty was signed in 1952 because he feared that he could not guarantee its success. In the following two years French governments repeatedly reaffirmed their support for the EDC, but did not submit the treaty for ratification. In addition to their fears that ratification would fail and perhaps also their own doubts about the enterprise, French governments argued that ratification must await agreement by their proposed partners on suggested modifications to the treaty, as well as upon a clarification of the British attitude. All were merely delaying tactics designed to conceal the basic French distaste for West German rearmament and the weakness of French governments. The British attitude had long been clear: the 1951 Conservative government had continued to follow the line laid down by the previous Labour foreign minister, Ernest Bevin, who said in the House of Commons in November 1950 that Britain preferred an expansion of the Treaty of Brussels to serve as the basis of military cooperation within NATO, but would not object to the EDC were it to be established. The other interested party, the United States, was totally unsympathetic towards the domestic French ramifications of the treaty, and ultimately showed its impatience with the threat of an 'agonising reappraisal' of policy should France delay the rearmament of West Germany and the strengthening of NATO much longer.

But the problem was not an easy one for France. Since 1950 the pro-European parties had declined in strength in the legislature, and even without the EDC dilemma, governmental survival at the best of times was problematic. In addition, France was increasingly concerned about the deterioration of its economic position, particularly with regard to that of West Germany. Since 1951 the West German economy had greatly expanded, while in France a deficit had persisted. The French economy was so weak that in 1953 it had to renege on an OEEC agreement of two years earlier. One of the problems of the economy was the level of its resources that were being sucked into the long-running colonial war in French Indo-China, a war which France could not win and one which was effectively concluded by the humiliating surrender in May 1954 of the cream of the French army at Dien Bien Phu. The inexorable course of this colonial war meant that many people in France, especially within the army, were not prepared to entertain anything that entailed France giving up military sovereignty.

But something still had to be done about the EDC and its ratification. From its inception until 1954 the EDC treaty hung like a sword of Damocles over French politics, albeit only one of many problems that afflicted government. The political parties of the narrow and fragmented centre of the political spectrum, from which all governments had to be drawn, were agreed only on the fundamental issue of preserving the Fourth Republic: they had, as it were, reserved their right to disagree on everything else. The consequence was inertia; no controversial issue could ever hope to be resolved satisfactorily, so governments, preoccupied with survival, merely tended to forget about them or postpone them to some indeterminate future date.

It was Dien Bien Phu which offered a way out of the dilemma. It helped bring to the premiership Pierre Mendès-France, a member of the influential Radical Party and a man of energy who commanded considerable personal loyalty. In order to inaugurate his declared policy of economic renewal, Mendès-France had first to remove from the agenda the two pressing crises which had crippled French political life: Indo-China and the EDC. On the EDC Mendès-France at first followed the route of his predecessors, seeking to persuade Britain to reconsider its refusal to join the EDC, and arguing with his partners for a dilution of the supranational element in the proposed structure, especially where it could affect the French military contribution. Like his predecessors he failed to make any headway. The United States continued to be irritated, while Britain's response was that even if France sabotaged the EDC, it would not prevent West German rearmament. Two of his prime ministerial colleagues, Adenauer and Spaak, reflected the view of the other five when they insisted that any further French delay over the EDC could not be tolerated. Accordingly, on 30 August 1954, Mendès-France submitted the EDC treaty to the National Assembly. The submission, however, was not accompanied by any governmental endorsement or comment, bar the statement that Mendès-France did not regard it necessary to resign if the motion was defeated. In other words, the treaty was simply introduced as a hindrance that had to be disposed of before other business could be tackled: the vote, negative as expected, was in fact not on the treaty itself, but on whether it ought to be discussed.

This procedural tactic was the burial ceremony of the EDC, and a setback for both the plans for a more effective Western defence system and the hopes and ambitions for a more united Europe. The rejection of EDC also meant the fall of the even more ambitious European Political Community, which had as yet not advanced beyond the stage of a draft treaty. The EDC concept was perhaps too idealistic to have had great hopes of concrete achievement, and in its implications for European integration perhaps something of a paradox. The sensitive area of defence should more realistically have been one of the last spheres for the renunciation of national sovereignty, with a solid background of integrative experience and mutual trust behind it. But in any case the concept of supranational defence integration had not been as carefully considered and researched, and its potential participants fully persuaded of its value, in advance as had been the case with the ECSC. Indeed, the efforts of people like Monnet were still focused more strongly upon the negotiations over, and the consolidation of, the ECSC. The EDC was treated almost as an afterthought.

WESTERN EUROPEAN UNION

The damage done to the cause of integration was severe. Only the ECSC survived, but even it did not entirely escape the shockwaves. Jean Monnet announced his decision not to seek re-election as President of the High Authority. He planned to pursue integrative schemes as a private citizen and it was thought doubtful whether he could achieve the same effect in that capacity. Almost simultaneously de Gasperi died; his successors were not able to stamp the same authority on Italian foreign policy. At the same time, Schuman ceased to be central to French foreign policy. The forces of federation and supranationalism were in disarray, and at the time it seemed natural to conclude that the whole momentum of European integration was lurching to a halt, in particular because the EDC debacle had opened up a rift between France and West Germany.

The two states had, despite the EDC, succeeded in signing a bilateral cultural treaty in 1954. But in February 1955 France complained bitterly that the agreement had been infringed by the West German decision to make English the main foreign language to be taught in all schools. In its turn West Germany criticised France's economic stance, particularly what it regarded as protectionism and obstruction to freer trade between the two states. Above all, however, the major bone of contention was the fate of the Saar, something which might have been settled if the EDC and the Political Community had succeeded. The small region, with its coal and steel resources, had not been treated by France as part of its zone of occupation after 1945. Instead, in 1947 it was organised as a politically autonomous territory in an economic union with France, and treated almost as a colony. West Germany's support in 1952 and 1953 for the Political Community had in part been predicated on the idea that it could resolve the Saar issue: the territory was due to become a separate 'European' area. It is, however, likely that the Europeanisation of the Saar could, for West Germany, only be a temporary measure. The region was overwhelmingly German in character, and in a sense its problem would have to be resolved before Franco–German relations could return to a more normal footing. As a result of a referendum in the Saar in October 1955, when 96 per cent of the electorate voted against Europeanisation in any shape or form and for incorporation with West Germany, France bowed to the inevitable. One year later the Saar was handed over to West Germany. Resolution of the Saar question was to be an important factor aiding European developments in the late 1950s.

Despite the blow that the failure of the EDC and the Political Community struck against integration, the first pressing need to salvage something out of the debris was in defence. The United States had accepted the EDC as part of its strategy: the rejection of the EDC did not mean any amendment to the American insistence upon a West German defence contribution or greater inputs from the other states. An alternative to the EDC had to be found. The search was very brief. All else failing, Western Europe fell back, with British encouragement, upon the 1948 Treaty of Brussels. In 1955 the new British Conservative premier, Anthony Eden, took the lead in salvaging something from the wreck of EDC. He took the opportunity to bring forward again the British view that West German rearmament could easily be achieved, and with the necessary level of supervision to quell the worries of France and others, within NATO itself. And Britain was quite happy for the Brussels Treaty, suitably rephrased, to be expanded to include West Germany and Italy, since it would involve nothing beyond intergovernmental collaboration. Konrad Adenauer, who saw rearmament as an indispensable part of his own Western-oriented policy of strength, quickly fell into line behind Eden, and the others followed shortly thereafter. To remove the anti-German emphasis in the original treaty, a protocol was added to the preamble, deleting the statement that one of the objectives was 'to take such steps as may be necessary in the event of renewal by Germany of a policy of aggression'. In its place there was a declaration of the intention 'to promote the unity and to encourage the progressive integration of Europe'. Having got the kind of structure it had always insisted upon, it seems clear that Britain had no qualms about such a statement being used to promote some version of supranationalism. On the other side, to mollify France, it was agreed that British participation in the revamped body would involve the stationing of British troops in West Germany unless a majority of its partners consented to their withdrawal; however, Britain reserved the right to do so if an emergency situation elsewhere demanded a redeployment of its military forces.

The new body was to be called Western European Union (WEU). An independent structure for the organisation was out of the question. It was too weak to support one, and in any case Britain would almost certainly refuse to commit itself to anything that smacked of supranationalism. All that was added to the loose intergovernmental structure of Brussels was a Consultative Assembly, whose function would be performed by the relevant national delegates to the Common Assembly of the Council of Europe. WEU also took over the social and cultural responsibilities outlined in the Brussels Treaty, but since most of the original military functions had become redundant with the creation of NATO, it was decided that WEU could perform best by being directly incorporated within the broader defence alliance. Ironically, therefore, the French rejection of EDC resulted in what France, in originally introducing the Pleven Plan, had most desired to avoid: the creation of a separate West German army.

Apart from advancing West German claims for equality, and thereby effectively removing one of the striking drawbacks which the EDC would sooner or later have had to face, the WEU structure achieved no significant results. It was not, and could not be, a vehicle for European integration. In the 1950s it was only occasionally activated, with nominal headquarters in London; and indeed any proposals on defence that emanated from its Consultative Assembly were invariably ignored by the member governments. If WEU had a role, it was to ensure the closest possible cooperation within NATO, and although it did play a limited role in the Saar settlement, it remained essentially a paper organisation. With the handing over to the Council of Europe in 1960 of the social and cultural responsibilities it had inherited from the Treaty of Brussels, it seemed that to all intents and purposes WEU had become moribund.

It was saved from total extinction by two developments. The first was the division of Western Europe after 1957 into the European Economic Community of the Six and the rest. In the 1960s once Britain's decision to apply for membership of the Community was blocked by President de Gaulle, WEU did serve as a conduit, no matter how limited, between Britain and the Six. The second development was the French decision in the 1960s to leave the NATO command structure. Once the prickly and nationalistic de Gaulle had retired from French politics, France suggested in the early 1970s that WEU might provide a link between it and NATO. France returned to the theme in 1981, proposing reactivation of WEU as a liaison body. But it was not until after 1984 and the growing rapprochement and détente between the superpowers that WEU began to re-emerge as a body that could have real value. It was an excellent vehicle for an emerging West European voice on defence issues as distinct from a NATO position in order (with France still outside NATO) to establish some kind of common ground at a time when it seemed possible that the two superpowers might actually manage to reach an agreement on levels of nuclear armaments that might not take Western European interests into account.

By 1987 the new spirit of collaboration on defence had developed to the extent where the Netherlands could suggest that WEU was an appropriate body that could, for the first time, seek a common European position on a non-European issue, the long-running war between Iran and Iraq and the deepening Persian Gulf crisis. In the end, West Germany, constitutionally prevented from deploying its forces outside Europe, agreed to provide additional naval cover in the West European arena as a replacement for the British and French ships sent to patrol in the Persian Gulf. If WEU has a role to play in integration, that kind of defence collaboration is what it is peculiarly able to do. It can offer something different from both NATO and the European Communities, in the case of the former because it can concentrate on a European rather than a trans-Atlantic perspective, and in the second because since 1973 neutral Ireland has been a member of the Communities. This may have been what WEU was originally intended to do, but nevertheless its belated reincarnation in the 1980s could not disguise the fact that its role in the process of European integration has been rather marginal.

NEW DEPARTURES

Despite the mood of despondency that seemed to shroud the whole idea of European unity in the mid-1950s, there was nevertheless a wide array of cooperative bodies in which the European democracies were involved to a greater or lesser extent. The Council of Europe, the OEEC and NATO had been joined in the 1950s by WEU. Alongside these were the working examples of a more intense economic integration of Benelux and the ECSC. Further afield there was a new Scandinavian venture in closer collaboration, the Nordic Council, launched in 1952. Western Europe had come a long way since 1945. The crucial question was less whether the integrative urge had dissipated entirely, but more whether an appropriate context could be found for channelling its energies.

World events following the fall of the EDC conspired to make Europeans more aware of Europe as an entity. The failure of the 1953 and 1956 uprisings in East Germany and Hungary respectively, as well as the abortive Anglo–French Suez expedition of 1956, were further reminders of the contraction of Europe's world role. A similar lesson was being provided by the surge of nationalism in Asia and Africa, which precipitated the end of the colonial era and which geographically entailed a retreat back to Europe. Furthermore, with the death of the Soviet dictator, Stalin, and the arrival of thermonuclear stalemate between the United States and the Soviet Union, the new superpower interest in peaceful coexistence, for a while at least, seemed to permit an air of greater relaxation after the tensions of the Cold War. Taken together, all these factors allowed a greater breathing space for a consideration of Europe, especially as the democracies had entered a period of unprecedented economic prosperity, something which tended to demote the urgency of protection for specific national interests.

One general problem was that the very number of international organisations had divided the democracies and had created several different Western Europes. All attempts to link the countries more closely together through the Council of Europe, the most appropriate body because of the wide spread of its membership, did not get very far. On the other hand, it was quite often the same people who represented their countries in the various bodies: when the ministerial organs of the OEEC, Council of Europe, NATO or WEU were examined, the overlapping nature of their memberships was very apparent. But two other factors were more important than the simple diversity of organisations. The first was the division that had existed since at least 1948 on the extent to which coordination and integration should entail a formal abrogation by states of some of their national sovereignty. The most elaborate response for broad-ranging rationalisation had come from Britain in 1952 with the Eden Plan, but this had been a response to Britain's anxiety about what the little Europe of the Six might achieve. It was aimed at enabling Britain to remain a decisive player in Western Europe without committing itself in any way to supranationalism. The other factor was the assessment by committed federalists and functionalists of exactly what had been achieved. Despite all efforts, Benelux had still not acquired its economic union. In 1955 the three states did accept an agricultural common market, though in the event a further seven years elapsed before it was established. Scandinavia had had even less success in the numerous discussions on a customs union, and the topic had been given no priority in the plans of the Nordic Council. Even the ECSC was experiencing problems in sectoral integration, while the other agencies were all merely intergovernmental in character.

While there were, therefore, good grounds for pessimism about future progress, the question of whether integration could proceed beyond a limited sectoral level was answered three years later by the Treaty of Rome. Protagonists of unity may have been despondent about the loss of the EDC and the European Political Community, but were not routed. On the other hand, the experiences of the early 1950s had made some of the proponents of unity more cautious, especially in France and West Germany. However, almost before the dust had settled on the Political Community, voices were raised in favour of further efforts. Jean Monnet continued to urge further sectoral integration in the fields of transport and energy. The Benelux states, however, wanted a more decisive effort, and suggested that instead of further sectoral integration to supplement the ECSC, the target should be nothing less than a comprehensive economic community. Not surprisingly, the indefatigable Paul-Henri Spaak was in the forefront of these arguments for new departures. Through his active involvement in European institutions – serving, for example, as president of both the Assembly of the Council of Europe and the OEEC – he had been given the accolade of being 'Mr Europe'. The ECSC Common Assembly threw its weight behind the establishment of a committee that would explore means of founding a common market. Jean Monnet also continued his efforts through the Action Committee for the United States of Europe which he had founded in 1955. On 18 January 1956 the Committee's Joint Declaration rejected the notion that integration should be confined to only six countries. Yet it was in those six countries that it enjoyed the greatest influence and where it was able to generate the most support. Monnet himself seemed to be rather more cautious about going too fast too quickly, and seemed to hanker still for sectoral integration in the first instance, especially in the developing field of nuclear energy, as a strategy which stood a better chance of succeeding in the short term.

The integration cause and its stress upon a broad economic approach were also aided by the current pattern of international trade and by the limitations of the OEEC, which could not sponsor any forward movement without the consent of all its members. There was, therefore, a legitimate argument that could be used to spawn a common market, membership of which would be open to any willing OEEC signatory. The lines of division over political unity and economic integration versus association and cooperation had already been clarified and hardened in the previous debates over the future of Europe. Thus it was not surprising that the initiative to take up again the idea of a common market, first raised back in 1952 by the Netherlands at a ministerial meeting of the ECSC as a way of combatting the limited effectiveness of both the OEEC and the sectoral approach, as well as Monnet's arguments for cooperation in nuclear energy, were grasped only by the six countries of little Europe.

In mid-1955 the foreign ministers of the Six met at Messina in Italy to launch 'a fresh advance towards the building of Europe' and to create a market 'free from all customs duties and all quantitative restrictions'. Despite the phraseology, the Messina declaration did not seem to have much impact at the time; it was not seen as a dramatic move towards supranationalism. But the six ministers did draft a joint proposal for the pooling of information and work on the uses of nuclear energy, and for the establishment of a customs union that would lead to a common market. The agreement at Messina was attributable in no small degree to the groundwork and preparation of the three Benelux states, especially by the Dutch Foreign Minister, J.W. Beyen. He, along with Spaak and the long-serving Luxembourg premier, Joseph Beck (who chaired the meeting), were the driving force at Messina: they were, in fact, the three men who in exile had drawn up the plans for Benelux. At Messina they succeeded in winning the support of Italy for a move towards broad economic integration, triumphing over both a more limited conception advocated by West Germany that fell somewhere between supranationalism and the old sectoral route, and the doubts of France over the whole concept of a common market.

In the end, Messina reproduced much of the original Benelux position on matters other than the broad principle of the common market. The final document referred also to transport, the harmonisation of social regulations, hours of work and overtime, and the creation of an investment fund. Paradoxically perhaps, the linking of a common market with nuclear energy helped the cause of each. West Germany, for example, liked the idea of a common market, but had doubts about the utility of a nuclear energy agency, while France held the reverse position. The Six agreed to hold an intergovernmental committee, to be headed by the tireless Paul-Henri Spaak, which would consider, flesh out and report back on the various proposals. Before they disbanded, the ministers had one concrete task to fulfil: to appoint a new President of the ECSC High Authority. Monnet had resigned in February 1955 in the wake of the EDC failure, but was still in position since the Six had not been able to find a successor. This they eventually did at Messina – another positive augury for the future, perhaps – appointing to the post René Mayer who was, in fact, an associate of Monnet.

The Spaak Committee met near Brussels between July 1955 and March 1956. Despite the difficulties that emerged during the discussions, usually over the nature of the common market and its timetable (with France being the main objector), Spaak managed to retain a decisive influence over the direction taken by the committee. When it issued its first interim report in the autumn of 1955, it was clear that it had narrowed its focus to the two core projects raised before Messina, the Netherlands proposal for a common market and Monnet's ideas for a nuclear energy community. It is striking, in fact, how much the latter idea seemed at the time to dominate as a first priority. This, however, may have been nothing more than the fact that nuclear energy constituted a clearly defined and nascent policy sector, and one which, since unlike other policy areas such as coal or agriculture there were hardly any national interests or groups to consider, could quite easily be separated from the rest of national policy making. In addition, it was widely believed in the 1950s that nuclear fission would be a cheap and increasingly important source of energy in the future. By setting up a nuclear energy community at the outset, it was believed that it could provide an important impetus towards closer integration.

The Spaak Report was unveiled for public debate in March 1956 in a special session of the ECSC Common Assembly, where only one vote was registered against its proposals (though it should be noted that the extremes of the political spectrum were not represented in Strasbourg). The Report was also approved by the foreign ministers of the Six meeting in Venice on 29 May 1956. The Spaak Committee was turned into a conference charged with drafting the appropriate treaties. This conference worked in Brussels throughout the remainder of the year. Finally, in February 1957 a series of meetings of experts and foreign ministers was held in Paris, culminating with agreement of the six premiers on the last points at dispute. The following month two treaties, one establishing a European Economic Community (EEC) and the other a European Atomic Energy Community (Euratom) were duly signed by the Six in Rome and referred to the national parliaments for ratification. The Six took pains to make it clear that their intention was not to form an exclusive club: Christian Pineau, the French prime minister, was particularly insistent that they hoped other countries, especially Britain, would feel able to join in the initiative. The most striking feature about the Treaty of Rome, however, was the speed with which it had been reached. Only three years after the collapse of the projected EDC and Political Community structures, European integration was poised to take a great leap forward.

CHAPTER SIX
The European Economic Community

As Paul-Henri Spaak was later to remind the Consultative Assembly of the Council of Europe in 1964, 'Those who drew up the Rome Treaty . . . did not think of it as essentially economic; they thought of it as a stage on the way to political union'. Walter Hallstein, the West German representative at Messina and the first President of the EEC Commission, had earlier stressed the same point: 'We are not integrating economies, we are integrating politics. We are not just sharing our furniture, we are jointly building a new and bigger house.' In other words, the objectives of those who had contributed to the developments that culminated in Rome were ambitious and overtly political. The Six had reverted to Schuman's view that political union could be achieved in the long run through a sustained effort at economic integration across a broad front. The sector by sector approach of the ECSC had proved too problematic. In the end the ECSC was still trying to integrate only one part of complex industrial economies, and could not possibly pursue its aims in isolation from other economic segments.

Euratom would probably have run into similar difficulties even if the EEC had not been in place. In fact, Euratom was to be the poor relation of the Rome Treaty, slow to begin its work and very soon unable to prevent national interests exerting themselves. France had been the major supporter of Euratom; as the only one of the Six already possessing a nuclear programme, it obviously hoped to benefit most from the joint funding of the Community and to establish a domination of the nascent industry. Almost inevitably, perhaps, as the industry developed, national interests asserted themselves. As early as 1959 West Germany and Italy had begun to build their own industries to prevent France gaining too much dominance in the sector. Euratom failed completely to control and direct developments, or indeed to resist governments that wanted to weaken the supranational element in this policy area. By the early 1960s Euratom had sunk further into decline, suffering an increasing shortage of funding as the member states preferred to give priority to their own national programmes. When both France and West Germany decided to launch their own fast breeder reactor programmes, Euratom was finally doomed as an effective agent of integration. After 1967, when it was no longer a separate organisation, it had to be content with only a provisional annual budget.

To some extent, the problems of Euratom were those of a sector which had, especially in France, high political salience. Because of that prominence, it proved difficult to develop that element of compromise and bargaining which would have been essential for integrative success. But it also reaffirmed the difficulties of a purely sectoral approach to integration. The same was not true of the broader European Economic Community, which despite its wider brief demonstrated that it had both strength and flexibility. In addition, the Six had learnt some lessons from the past, and hoped that the adoption of a long-term perspective would also avoid a clash of economic interest with the OEEC. Tariffs and trade restrictions were to be reduced only gradually, so allowing the EEC to concur with the world organisation, GATT, to which the OEEC states belonged. Signatories of GATT could institute tariff changes which might discriminate against third parties only if done over a long period of time, so giving those third parties the opportunities of adjusting to the change without suffering severe economic disruption.

In the shorter term the drive towards integration was aided by a conjunction of political and economic factors both inside and outside the Six. The EEC, while ambitious, was on the surface less revolutionary than the European Political Community. It placed an economic dressing over the political goals in the hope that it could accommodate as many interests and groups as possible. The most favourable circumstance was the existence of governments in the Six which were broadly consensual in their view on integration. In France it was the pro-European government of Edouard Fauré that endorsed the new structures. The other five were well aware of the fragility of the Fourth Republic, especially after the 1956 French election, and fearing that the EEC might not happen with a different government in power in Paris, were keen to get things moving as quickly as possible. On the other hand, this enabled France to gain concessions in the negotiations which, in the words of a National Assembly resolution in January 1957, would enable France to 'guarantee [its] essential . . . economic interests'. Many French demands, it is true, were modified or rejected, but it is striking how far the other five were prepared to go to accommodate France. They agreed to assist and aid financially the socioeconomic development of French overseas territories, to align social legislation on holidays and equal pay with that of France (something which would raise production costs in all five countries), to allow France to retain its system of export subsidies and import taxes until it could acquire financial equilibrium. By contrast, France did have some strong incentives to work with the other five. The Saar settlement had given a strong boost to Franco–German relations, while those with Britain had deteriorated because of the failure of the Suez venture. And in particular, the last governments of the Fourth Republic did not want a repetition of the EDC episode.

The other key actor was West Germany where Adenauer's European policy was now supported by the Social Democrats. The main opposition, in fact, came from some of his ministerial colleagues, especially his eventual successor as Chancellor, Ludwig Erhard, who preferred a broader and looser arrangement. Most West German interests, however, stood behind Adenauer. The EEC offered West Germany and its booming economy a huge outlet for its industrial goods, in the same way as it offered France some export benefits for its large agricultural sector. Within the Community both would have some protection from outside competition. While some might see in all this nothing more than economic fulfilment, the ultimate political goal, with which the other four signatories were more in sympathy, was already implicit in the Rome Treaty's preamble with its desire 'to establish the foundations of an even closer union among the European peoples'.

THE TREATY OF ROME: OBJECTIVES AND STRUCTURES

After the fiasco of the EDC, the French National Assembly was generally regarded as being the place where the Treaty of Rome would stand or fall, particularly as the Fourth Republic was entering its final prolonged crisis, with ever weaker governments struggling to survive. In the event, the treaties easily overcame this potential baptism of fire; in fact, the French Parliament was the first to approve ratification. Finally, with ratification by the Netherlands in December 1957, the EEC and Euratom were ready to operate.

The EEC began its existence with an Assembly meeting in Strasbourg in March 1958. Meeting in the home of the Council of Europe, it brought back memories of that body's inaugural session a decade earlier; the same tangible mood of excitement and sense of history was present. It called itself the European Parliamentary Assembly and symbolically arranged the seating of delegates by political affiliation rather than by nationality. The buoyancy of the moment led also to the rejection of the nominee of the six foreign ministers for the presidency of the Assembly. Instead, the delegates honoured one of the pioneers of integration by electing Robert Schuman to the post.

The immediate general objectives of the EEC, as laid out in the Treaty of Rome, were 'by establishing a Common Market and progressively approximating the economic policies of Member States, to promote throughout the Community a harmonious development of economic activities, a continuous and balanced expansion, an increase in stability, an accelerated raising of the standard of living, and closer relations between the States belonging to it'. The new organisation was enjoined to end restrictions such as price fixing, limiting production, dumping, and all elements of protective government aid (for example, subsidies) to ensure free and fair competition. It was also expected to work for the coordination of economic and monetary policies and the harmonisation of fiscal and social policies, and of law. Though these objectives were expressed in economic terms, it was clear that a political purpose lay behind them. This was equally true of the specific objectives listed: a customs union and a common agricultural policy. Inevitably, because the new organisation was to range over an extremely wide area of activity, the provisions of the Treaty of Rome were necessarily complex, running to 248 articles supplemented by 4 annexes, 13 protocols, 4 conventions and 9 declarations. In aiming to be more than a mere common market, the Treaty emphasised the principle that the problems of one member state would be the problems of all. And it did not mention a fixed life-span, with provision for renewal or renegotiation: the Treaty was to remain in force for 'an unlimited period'. This meant that it could not be revoked, a view with which, for instance, West German courts have agreed.

Broadly speaking, transformation into a common market was to be spread over a period of between 12 and 15 years, with a stepwise progression through stages of four years each. The common external tariff would be based on an average of the existing duties levied by the member states at their national borders, though with some downward adjustment. There had been disagreements over the timetable: France thought the transitional period was too short, while others wanted even faster movement. The latter were mollified to some extent by the exclusion from the Treaty of anything that would bar some members from forming a smaller customs union ahead of the EEC schedule. This provision was directed towards the Benelux states, and was permissible 'to the extent that the objectives of these regional unions are not attained by application of this Treaty'. In fact, immediately upon accepting the Treaty of Rome, the Benelux states agreed in substance in February 1959 to a new treaty of economic union, beginning in January 1960 and to last for 50 years, several years ahead of the Rome programme.

As has been indicated, some provisions implied more than a customs union: membership of the EEC meant a commitment to the free movement of both capital and labour, a common investment policy, and the coordination and rationalisation of social welfare goals. To assist the EEC in these objectives, three funds were to be set up: a European Social Fund to develop 'employment opportunities for workers' and to raise their standard of living; a European Investment Bank to further economic expansion through the use of loans and guarantees; and a European Development Fund targetted upon the associated French overseas territories. On the other hand, there were several escape clauses within the Treaty which permitted divergence in national policy should a state decide that this was necessary on grounds of national security.

Furthermore, while the main thrust of the treaty had a very clear specification of the timetable and the procedures to be followed, it was rather vague on several other points which were announced only in terms of general principles. This was true of the declared intention to establish not just a common commercial policy once the transitional period had been concluded, but also of objectives which were to be sought during the transitional phase: a common transport policy, free movement of workers, and a common agricultural policy. In view of future events it is important to note the absence of detail on agriculture, even though this had been designated a special economic activity which would be handled completely at the supranational level. The treaty gave no indication of what a common agricultural policy would be other than something that would increase agricultural productivity, ensure a fair standard of living for the agricultural population, guarantee regular supplies of produce on the market, and ensure reasonable food prices for the consumer. Even within these admirable phrases one can detect the difficulties of achieving a common policy: what those principles could produce, if put into practice, would not be free trade, but only a limited liberalisation that would seek a balance between EEC principles and the protection of national agricultural interests.

The treaty would be administered through an institutional framework. Its institutions were drawn, perhaps not surprisingly, from their ECSC predecessors. The supranational and bonding element was to be provided by the quasi-executive Commission of nine members appointed for renewable four-year terms by the national governments. West Germany, France and Italy were each entitled to two commissioners, the other states to one each. The Commission's primary task would be to recommend policies and to administer the Treaty of Rome. The Commission was seen as the guardian and embodiment of the European ideal. Though appointed by the member governments, the commissioners were not to be representatives of national interests. Upon appointment each commissioner was to take an oath of loyalty to the EEC including 'neither to seek nor to take instructions from any Government or body'. The Commission was to have not just the right to initiate and recommend policy to its executive partner, the Council of Ministers, but also the task of ensuring that the provisions of the treaty and policies emanating from the Council of Ministers were carried out by the other institutions and the member states. It was to be based in Brussels.

Though in 1965 the Commission eventually absorbed the parallel executive bodies in the ECSC and Euratom, it was, despite the high-sounding phrases, to have rather less scope for individual initiative in decision making than the ECSC High Authority. The reason was that the latter had been given, once and for all, a large grant of power in a defined sector. The conception of Rome was different: it was a framework treaty covering a wide area, where agreement by the drafting partners (the member states) on everything would not have been possible and probably not advisable. Nevertheless, although possessing a less extensive grant of power, the Commission was widely expected to be the dynamic element in further moves towards integration.

Paralleling the Commission was the Council of Ministers, the organ of the national governments, which was to carry the main burden of coordinating policies. Despite the euphoria which surrounded the creation of the Commission, the Treaty of Rome ultimately rested the future of the EEC in the member governments. Nowhere was this more apparent than in the complicated pattern of voting that was drawn up for the Council, varying according to the nature and source of the issue under discussion and ranging from simply majorities through qualified majorities to unanimity. Although the Council was to have only six members, it was to receive 17 votes. The pattern was one of weighted voting by which states received votes commensurate with their size. West Germany, France and Italy were each to have four votes, the Netherlands and Belgium two votes each, and Luxembourg only one vote. On a simple majority requirement therefore, victory could be achieved by any two of the big three if they gained the support of one of the smaller members, or by an alliance of the three large states. In practice, however, simple majorities were to be applicable only in six very minor and procedural areas. Most issues were to be decided unanimously, where any one state clearly had a veto, or by a qualified majority of 12 votes from at least four states: this was designed to protect the interests of all states, not just the smaller members. The complexity was intended to last only for a transitional period. The treaty anticipated that by 1966 the Council would move to a situation where a simple majority would suffice, as an important step towards a stronger supranational and political EEC.

While it was clear that as long as unanimity or qualified majorities were required, it was possible, as several of the member states were to do, for states to drag their heels and delay a programme. It was the ECSC experience which had occasioned the acceptance for an interim period of a change in the relationship between the supranational element and the member governments. It had been learnt that progress could not be made if a member state objected strenuously to a particular part of a programme. This had especially been true of the larger members. The EEC structure was designed therefore to bring about a closer collaboration between the Commission and Council. As in the ECSC, the two executives were to be supported and supplemented by a consultative committee representing the several national interest groups. This Economic and Social Committee would only be an advisory body, even though it would have to be consulted by the Commission and the Council of Ministers on a wide range of topics and issues. Its membership, appointed for renewable four-year terms, has grown over the years and has proved, as it was intended to be, a useful sounding board, especially as it quickly subdivided itself into specialist groups of experts on specific topics – in which, in fact, most of the work of the Committee was to be done.

The third major institution of the EEC was the Parliamentary Assembly, which replaced the ECSC advisory body, though with the membership increased from 78 to 142. Under the Treaty of Rome its powers were defined as the supervision of both the Commission and the Council of Ministers, including the right to put questions to the Commission and to discuss the latter's annual report, to discharge the annual budget, and to censure the Commission. The latter was a heavy weapon which has never been used, since it would involve the removal of the whole Commission if an Assembly vote of no confidence gained a two-thirds majority. Its legislative powers were far more limited, although on paper at least its budgetary powers, with it jointly forming the budgetary authority with the Council of Ministers, appeared rather more substantial. None of this, however, made the Assembly a legislative authority. It was not a directly elected body, though it was given the right under the Treaty to draw up proposals for direct elections. However, such proposals would need ratification by the two executives. There were, in fact, large areas of responsibility where the Assembly had to be consulted by the Council of Ministers, but its suggestions and amendments could safely be ignored with impunity by the Council. In short, a European parliament still had to come into existence.

The final major institution was to be the Court of Justice, not to be confused with the European Court of Human Rights set up under the 1950 Convention and based in Strasbourg along with the Council of Europe. The EEC states were prepared to accept the jurisdiction of the latter court in cases of human rights. The EEC Court of Justice, however, was set up to interpret the Treaty of Rome and ensure that both the EEC institutions and the member states were fulfilling their obligations under the treaty. The Court of Justice was to be composed of seven judges, one from each member state plus one other, appointed by the Council of Ministers for renewable six-year terms on the nomination by member governments. The Court was given the responsibility of handling cases arising from all three Community treaties or from disputes between members. Its decisions were to be by majority vote, and its verdicts would be final. However, in the last resort the interpretation of its decisions would depend upon the national governments and the national court systems. Even so, it was not long before the Court would find against every government and against the Commission. As the Community shifted away in the 1960s from whatever supranational bias it possessed, this binding role of the Court as, as it were, the 'guardian' of the Communities became much more important, both before and after the enlargements of the organisation in the 1970s and 1980s.

In short, the Treaty of Rome created a body, the Commission, that would have the responsibility of initiating policies and of implementing those already agreed upon. It was paralleled by a Council of Ministers whose main function would be to take action and legislate on the basis of the Commission's proposals. The Parliamentary Assembly and the Economic and Social Committee were primarily or wholly advisory in nature, with very little checking power, while the Court of Justice could interpret the provisions of the treaty and the decisions of the EEC.

THE EEC IN OPERATION

Inevitably, decision making in an organisation like the EEC would be complicated, especially as the treaty provided for several different kinds of decision. The Commission and/or the Council of Ministers could formally issue regulations, directives, decisions, recommendations and opinions. As the term is usually understood, legislation refers to regulations and directives. These are initiated by the Commission and adopted by the Council of Ministers. The difference between the two is that whereas a regulation is universally binding on all member states, a directive is specifically aimed at a named member state, informing it that something must be done, but leaving the way in which it is to be achieved to the discretion of the national government. Decisions are issued by either the Commission or the Council of Ministers: they derive directly from the authority given to them by the Treaty of Rome or from previously issued directives or regulations, and they too are binding upon the governments to which they are addressed. By contrast, recommendations and opinions are not binding.

One problem raised by the creation of the EEC was the proliferation of institutions within the Europe of the Six. A first rationalisation was achieved by making only one assembly and one court serve the ECSC, EEC and Euratom. It was not until 1965, however, that the treaties were revised to provide for a single Commission and Council of Ministers. The 1965 changes were the first significant constitutional development since 1957, in that they provided for a review of the purposes and activities of the Community, incorporating also a schedule for a single European Community by 1970. But that is moving ahead of the story.

The first test of the Treaty of Rome came in January 1959, when the preliminary stage of tariff reductions was due to go into operation, with customs duties being reduced by 10 per cent and import quotas increased by 20 per cent. There was some apprehension, not only because of the newness of the organisation and the awareness that hitches could easily occur, but also because of possible French recalcitrance. The tired and weak Fourth Republic had finally collapsed in 1958, to be replaced by a Fifth Republic headed by Charles de Gaulle, whose nationalist prejudices were already well-known. In the event, President de Gaulle and France, still preoccupied by the war in Algeria which had toppled the Fourth Republic, did not obstruct the deadline, choosing not to invoke the escape clauses which France had insisted be incorporated into the Rome Treaty. Indeed, this first step proceeded so smoothly that the EEC decided to speed up the timetable of tariff reductions.

During these first years of operation, progress towards some of the economic goals continued to be satisfactory. By 1961 internal tariff barriers had been substantially reduced and quota restrictions on industrial products had been largely eliminated. Trade within the EEC had expanded at a rate double that of trade with non-members, and the EEC had also become the world's largest trading power. Of some of the other developments outlined in the Treaty of Rome, a European Investment Bank, based in Luxembourg, had been set up immediately to provide capital for the future balanced development of the Community. By the end of 1961 the Bank had provided substantial loans for development, mainly to Italy, the poorest member of the Community. A joint system of security for migrant workers had been introduced in 1958. In May 1960 the EEC began to look at ways of liberalising the movement of capital, and the following year issued the first regulations governing the existence of cartels. Again in 1960, the EEC had begun to look at the problem of discrimination in transport, and in 1961 a Monetary Committee was established, as well as one charged with examining trade cycle policy. The one area where nothing seemed to have occurred was in setting up a Social Fund, since the Six had even begun to grasp the nettle of a common agricultural policy, agreeing in January 1962 to introduce common target prices for the most important farm products and a levy on agricultural imports into the EEC.

The seemingly positive advances on the economic front re-emphasised the fact that the Treaty of Rome had skirted around the question of political cooperation. Economic progress helped spur new thinking on the political direction of the EEC, especially as the Commission, under the forceful presidency of Walter Hallstein, had exceeded the expectations of many in terms of the activist role it had pursued. It was, perhaps rather surprisingly, the Fifth French Republic which agitated most strongly for an acceleration of political momentum. In June 1959 President de Gaulle had contacted West Germany and Italy to suggest regular meetings of the leaders of the EEC governments. The Benelux states were hostile to the suggestion, because they hoped that a geographical expansion of EEC membership, including British participation, would occur before concrete political plans were discussed. The Six eventually reached a compromise in November 1959, agreeing that the foreign ministers should meet regularly on a biennial basis. De Gaulle returned to the attack with an even more ambitious scheme for regular three-monthly meetings of the heads of government, supported by a permanent secretariat. This again met with a cool reception from the other five, first because it might foreclose the question of EEC enlargement, and second because it seemed to seek to push the EEC more in an intergovernmental direction.

On the whole, however, the Six seemed to be satisfied with the initial operation of the EEC. Certainly it would not have been a viable proposition if it had run into serious trouble within a year or so of its launch. A measure of its success and an indication of the magnitude of its task could be gleaned from Benelux. The EEC was attempting to do within its transition stage of fifteen years what Benelux did in three: and yet it was only at the end of its transitional period that Benelux had had to face up to serious difficulties in seeking to achieve its ambitions. The wider scope of the EEC and its larger membership might well impose strains long before the end of the interim period. Yet paradoxically, this very scope itself demanded rapid resolution of such stresses, particularly since as time went on it would become more apparent that a much greater momentum and will than that supplied by the Treaty of Rome would be required to push the Six firmly into economic union and political unity.

This is not to denigrate what the Six did achieve economically and politically during the first few years of the organisation. On the other hand, it is clear, as has already been indicated, that the establishment of the EEC and its initial development was assisted by a conjunction of favourable political and economic circumstances. The late 1950s and early 1960s were the heyday of the economic boom that Western Europe had entered in the early 1950s. Continued economic expansion and the widespread belief that Keynesian economic techniques provided governments with an effective tool for managing the economy had engendered the belief that the future would be like the present, but better, that economic growth would simply continue into the indefinite future, bringing more and greater benefits to all segments of society. In such an optimistic climate it was easier for national governments and interest groups to go along with the economic ambitions of the EEC; it was not seen as a great threat to their own concerns.

The political climate was also favourable. Economic prosperity and satisfaction led many, perhaps, to look rather benignly upon Hallstein's activist Commission and not to be unduly worried by the possibility of it developing into some kind of European government. The importance of the international climate must also be reiterated. In the late 1950s Western Europe was still basking in the afterglow of the 1955 Geneva summit, the first since the war between the United States and the Soviet Union. Détente was the catchphrase in which Western Europe wanted to believe – although, despite the wish to be master of its own destiny, Western Europe was nevertheless still not prepared to relax its concern about security as expressed through NATO. Finally, beginning with the resolution of the Saar issue, there had been an increasing rapprochement between France and West Germany. This grew with the coming to power of de Gaulle and the personal understanding he was able to reach with Adenauer. The process, which had been one of the original aims of Schuman and Monnet, was to culminate in a formal treaty of friendship in 1963.

In short, progress in the first years after 1957 was sufficiently gratifying to all who had backed the formation of the EEC, and sufficient to oblige other states to take more account of it. In effect, it seemed that notice had been served that the EEC was a successful operation. In 1959 Greece and Turkey had already drawn this conclusion, and had applied for some form of association with it. And in 1961 Britain publicly changed its attitude towards the principle of the EEC and formally applied for membership. The British decision confirmed what had become increasingly apparent since 1958, that the EEC was central not just to European integration, but to Western Europe as a whole, and that after 1957 the history of West European cooperation would centre upon the EEC, upon both its activities and the response to it by the other European states.

CHAPTER SEVEN

The Europe of the Seven

The countries of the Six geographically formed the core of Western Europe. They had been in the forefront of developments since the late 1940s, progressing far beyond what other states, for varying reasons, were prepared to accept. In fact, outside the Europe of the Six very little had been achieved and very little interest had been displayed in integration and cooperation beyond the all-European organisations that had been set up at the end of the previous decade. The most significant developments occurred in Scandinavia where there was a long tradition of limited cooperation, or at least of a belief in a common cultural area which made such cooperation valuable, if not almost inevitable. The major organisation had been the venerable Nordic Inter-Parliamentary Union, founded in 1907. During the interwar years there had been several proposals for something that would go beyond this to involve governments, and in 1938 the idea of a Nordic Council had been proposed by Denmark. The issue was raised again by Denmark after the war, first in 1948 and then successfully by the premier, Hans Hedtoft, at a meeting of the Nordic Inter-Parliamentary Union in 1951. Denmark found strong support in Sweden. Norway was more cautious, with several influential politicians fearing that even a limited form of cooperation might erode national sovereignty. Finland, bound by its treaty of friendship with the Soviet Union, effectively ruled itself out of any participation for the time being.

Norway's suspicions were soon set aside, and the country joined with its two neighbours in setting up a Nordic Council in 1952. None of the three states desired anything that would even smack of supranationalism, and their creation of the Nordic Council emerged as a faint mini-version of the Council of Europe. The Nordic Council was deliberately limited to being an intergovernmental consultative body, with a brief to seek Nordic cooperation across a broad front, but on a voluntary basis. Its limited nature was underlined by the absence of any statutes and of any permanent headquarters or secretariat, or an ability to force governments to act upon its recommendations. It met as a kind of annual conference. The voting members were elected by the national parliaments; ministers who attended did not vote. Even during its first few years, however, the Nordic Council began to achieve a considerable degree of coordination in the legislation of the three states, though these related to practical matters that did not seem to threaten national independence. If it was thought that a consensus could not be reached, then the Nordic solution was very simple: the matter was not raised. Hence defence was not an issue because it was not discussed, since Sweden's neutrality clashed with the NATO membership of Denmark and Norway. This consensus by unanimity was reinforced in 1955 when Finland joined the Council.

The most striking absence of progress was in economic policy. For example, Denmark, with its efficient agriculture, could not seriously propose a common agricultural policy because of the importance that Norway and Sweden attached to their own less economic agriculture. On the other hand, economics could not be excluded entirely from Council sessions. In 1954 the Nordic Council agreed to work for as comprehensive a Nordic common market as possible, and a committee was set up to study the question. This committee was still to report when the Council in 1958 felt it necessary to reiterate its interest in a common market. But by then any Nordic creation would have been a reaction to the EEC. It is perhaps doubtful whether the Nordic states were really prepared to go the whole way to a common market. Finland's participation would clearly have been dependent upon the consent of the Soviet Union. While a common market would most clearly benefit Sweden, which had the largest economy, the question would have to be raised whether participation would compromise its political neutrality. And for Norway and Denmark it would raise awkward questions about reorientating their trade, since for both states Britain was the most important trading partner.

What is clear is that for different reasons the Nordic states were disinclined to pursue closer economic integration wholeheartedly, or were at least following their customary practice of slow and cautious deliberation to try to pinpoint and resolve in advance any possible difficulties. But events elsewhere were passing them by, and by 1958 customary caution and reluctance had led the Nordic states to the point where any move would be a reaction to external developments, a point wryly made later by Per Haekkerup, the premier of Denmark: 'No stone was left unturned, no question unanswered. . . . But while we were discussing and elaborating these problems from every conceivable angle, developments in Europe passed us by.' Not only would the Nordic states have to reconsider what their relationships would be to the EEC, they, and especially Denmark and Norway, would be particularly interested in Britain's relationship with and attitude towards the new organisation.

BRITAIN IN THE WINGS

The advance towards the EEC had, of course, taken place without British participation, since Britain could not accept the fundamental supranational principle. In fact, in many ways Britain disapproved of the whole venture, though continuing to lend vocal encouragement to the idea of unity. The drive towards integration upset British conceptions about its relationship with Europe. For most countries outside the Six, Britain was the natural leader, not just because of historical relationships, but because it would have by far and away the largest European economy outside the EEC. Several states might have been willing to follow the Six in their ventures if Britain had been willing to join.

Though not prepared to join the ECSC, Britain had accepted a treaty of association with it in December 1954, although it was a further 11 months before the treaty was ratified. Britain had been equally emphatic about the EDC, believing that there were simpler ways of achieving West German rearmament. Again, however, once it seemed that the EDC had the support of the Six, Britain was willing to accept it and work with it. After the defeat of the EDC the British approach to Europe during the remainder of the 1950s consisted of three phases: WEU, the so-called 'Grand Design', and the European Free Trade Association.

The WEU, which began life in May 1955, was in many ways an irritant to Britain, placing upon it a burden as great as membership of the EDC might have done, with the pledge to maintain British forces in West Germany. In 1957, for example, when Britain decided to switch the basis of its defensive system from conventional to nuclear arms, it had to negotiate through WEU to secure a reduction in the level of its troop commitment on the continent. WEU was an anomaly: a defence organisation designed to permit West German rearmament. Yet West Germany was soon an independent member of NATO, a *de facto* situation that could not be reversed against the will of the Federal Republic without disrupting the whole alliance.

Once the original rearmament furore had subsided, WEU largely became a useless appendage, existing passively within NATO. While it did establish an institutional structure, its meetings were sporadic and its commitments overlapped with those of NATO, the Council of Europe and OEEC. It might have served as a link between Britain and the Six, but it was not until after its first application to join the EEC had been rejected in 1963 that Britain began seriously to consider this as a possibility. Until then Britain, which had taken the initiative in founding WEU out of the wreckage of the EDC, tended to place little credence in it. Politically, Britain was not prepared to allow WEU to intrude upon Anglo–American relationships, and placed it a poor second to NATO.

Quite simply the gulf which separated Britain from the Six, apparent long before the WEU was created, was far too wide to be bridged by such a tenuous organisation. But for Britain, WEU was perhaps satisfactory: it allowed for the possibility of British association with the leaders of integration, if necessary, and may have permitted some form of British influence upon the latter. This state of affairs changed abruptly with the Treaty of Rome and its implications. If Britain wished to retain some semblance of leadership in Europe or even to maintain what it regarded as its special position there *vis-à-vis* the United States, some new arrangement would have to be found. In fact, some members of the Six had been more positive than Britain about the potential of WEU. In 1955 and 1956 West Germany and Italy in particular thought it could be an effective bridge between Britain and the Six. Paul-Henri Spaak even wrote a personal letter to the British prime minister, Anthony Eden, which, in appealing for discussions within WEU, pointed in the same direction.

It was the speed of developments after the 1955 Messina meeting which forced a British reappraisal. Britain, in fact, had been explicitly invited to attend the foreign ministers' meeting in Messina. This was probably a consequence of British membership of WEU, but Britain's recent agreement to a treaty of association with the ECSC may have led the Six again to think optimistically of a British change of heart. Attendance, indeed, would not have cost Britain anything or compromised it in any way, since unlike the meeting called to consider the ECSC, participants at Messina were not required to accept the principle of supranationalism in advance. The extent of Britain's interest can be gauged by its response to the invitation: it sent only a civil servant to the preliminary discussions on a common market, and he eventually withdrew completely in November 1955. Britain simultaneously wrote to West Germany, stressing its opposition to a common market of only six countries, and asking for West German support for a much broader free trade area based upon the OEEC states. Britain reiterated its view that membership in a European common market was not compatible with its membership in the Commonwealth, and that in fact a common market of the Six would not fit with the aims and membership of OEEC. It is perhaps also true to say that, underneath, Britain, in regarding the Messina plan as too ambitious, was also quietly confident – particularly after the collapse of the EDC and the Political Community – that the scheme would come to nought. At an OEEC Council meeting, Harold Macmillan, then Chancellor of the Exchequer, is reputed to have said that he had become aware of some archaeological excavations at Messina about which he expected to hear no more.

An expanded free trade area that would incorporate the proposed EEC was a view which Britain began to expound in OEEC meetings after June 1955. The arguments were fleshed out by the Foreign Minister, Selwyn Lloyd, at a NATO Council meeting in December, where he introduced proposals for what became known as the Grand Design. These were further elaborated at the Consultative Assembly of the Council of Europe the following year. The essence of the British suggestion was that the time had come to rationalise the proliferation of European institutions that had sprung up over the past decade, most specifically by introducing a single European assembly which, unrelated to any one organisation, would serve them all. The second part of the British design was a comprehensive free trade area covering the whole of Western Europe. Britain had its supporters outside the Six, notably the Nordic states with which it held regular meetings within Uniscan to discuss and coordinate views on European developments and their possible implications. It was the British proposals which, as much as anything, stalled Scandinavian discussions on a Nordic common market, for if Britain was to be fortunate in its attempt to forge something beyond the Europe of the Six, the Nordic states would have little choice other than to follow the British lead. As the government of Norway was to state during the free trade discussions of 1958, 'whatever the United Kingdom does we must do as well'.

While the implications of Messina worried all the OEEC states outside the Six, the British proposals, by contrast, immediately aroused the suspicions of the Six. It seemed typical of previous British offers: so vague as to be almost meaningless or free to be interpreted in innumerable ways. At the extreme it was seen as a plot to sabotage the projected EEC. Suspicions were easily aroused, for it was also at this time that Britain announced its desire to reduce the number of its troops stationed in West Germany under the WEU agreement, as part of its switch to a nuclear-based defence. Nevertheless, the British proposals were discussed and, since the talks ranged widely over defence, economics and politics, involved the whole of Western Europe.

By 1956 Britain had become concerned about the impact the EEC would have on its own economy and political role. The British economy suffered more than most from low productivity as well as from an adverse balance of payments. Ironically, part of the British problem was due to the success of the OEEC and EPU: under their efforts sterling had become convertible in most circumstances into other countries' currencies, leading to the end of Britain's restrictions on sterling which in the past had enabled it to protect its markets in the sterling area. Politically, Britain feared that if the Six were to go ahead and form the EEC, it would generate a unit that would be dominated by West Germany. While Spaak and his Committee wished to give priority to their own plans and timetable, the British argument struck a chord with some. Spaak himself feared that the post-Messina negotiations might fail; to avoid this he urged Britain to join in the negotiations currently being conducted by the Six.

The signals coming from Spaak and others may in the end have led Britain to underestimate the determination of the Six and to overevaluate its own ability to pull the OEEC states, including the Six, round to its own viewpoint. But in fact it was too late, if indeed it had ever been possible after 1950, for Britain to assert its will on the Six, especially upon France. By the time that the OEEC Council agreed in October 1957 to set up the so-called Maudling Committee, named after Reginald Maudling who was appointed by the British premier, Harold Macmillan, in July 1957 to conduct the negotiations on Britain's proposals for a wider free trade area, the Six had in a sense already passed the point of no return. Discussions on the Treaty of Rome had entered their final stages, with ratification outstanding only from France and West Germany.

It was not surprising, therefore, that while the Six were willing to discuss the Grand Design within the OEEC context, they saw it as an addition to, not a replacement for, their own plans. Britain's strategy was not just to block the Six, but to have something in place should they succeed in getting their common market off the ground. To counteract the possibility of discrimination by the EEC should it be able to establish a common external tariff, the other OEEC states would need to accept a lowering of or even an end to their tariffs, providing the Six would waive their common external tariff on goods coming from the rest of the OEEC. In short, the British strategy was for a free trade area in industrial goods, but with no external tariff surrounding the free trade area. Instead, members would negotiate separate tariffs with non-members. By contrast, Britain did not find much support across the OEEC for its proposal to exclude agriculture from the free trade area. To the cynical and not so cynical, it seemed clear that Britain was seeking to secure the best of two worlds: to take advantage of the market opportunities for its own industrial goods that a free trade area would provide, while still retaining its special economic arrangements with the Commonwealth, especially its cheap food policy.

Britain was willing to make some further concessions on the political front, with some kind of executive body administering the free trade area. This would be a Council of Ministers with majority voting being permissible on a 'limited field of discussion', but this would still be something that would lack the reality of supranationalism. If Britain had suggested something like this several years earlier, it might have found some support within the Six, but by 1957 they had already passed far beyond that point. It says something, perhaps, about the persisting British inability to realise the depth of commitment to something totally new that existed among the Six. On this political front, the British line was assailed by federalists for seeking to wipe out all the advances made since 1950 and to freeze Western Europe in the more primitive mould of the Council of Europe. From the other side, the British scheme ran into objections from the neutral states which wanted to avoid both the close integration of the Six and military entanglements within NATO. In the end, the main argument took place over an amendment from Italy that would limit the single assembly to the EEC, WEU and the Council of Europe.

The key concern of these debates, however, was the economic component of the British proposal. The idea of a broad free trade area was, on the whole, acceptable to the Six, but only if it was supplementary to, and not a replacement for, the EEC. Within the Six, the strongest support came from the West German Finance Minister, Ludwig Erhard, who had long favoured a broader European grouping than that being developed by the Six. But Erhard did not have the ability or the power to divert his premier, Adenauer, from a strong commitment to the EEC. Indeed, given the level of activity within the Six at this time and the patent way in which Britain's Grand Design seemed to go against everything they were working for, it is surprising that the Six were willing to discuss the scheme in the first place.

The opposition within the Six came from several sources. There was the clear economic argument which believed that countries outside the EEC, particularly Britain with its preferential Commonwealth arrangements, would be in too advantageous a position. Further opposition came from those who, no matter how much they might desire British association with their ambitions, saw a free trade area as a retrograde step, and feared its adverse effect upon the ultimate goal of political unity. And within the Six there was an almost unanimous rejection of the British arguments that an institutional framework above that provided by the OEEC was not necessary, and that what the Six wanted to achieve could equally easily be reached by strengthening the OEEC. In particular, men like Paul-Henri Spaak, who had worked so hard for the EEC, were conscious of the fact that many economic interests within the Six supported the foundation of the EEC primarily because of the advantages they believed would be accruable to themselves. If the free trade discussions were pushed too hard, Spaak and others feared that they might prove more attractive than the EEC to many interests. If benefits could be obtained without the closely-knit EEC structure, then the whole drive towards integration might well falter or collapse.

The key lay with France and, to a lesser extent, West Germany. If these two states had agreed to the Grand Design, it may well have succeeded. It was an open secret that the scheme had its supporters in West Germany. Ultimately, however, the German decision lay with Adenauer who was strongly committed to the Europe of the Six. In addition, because of the course of world events, he was turning to look more closely to France for political support. France itself had an almost proprietorial interest in the EEC: after all, the Europe of the Six was very largely a French creation. Certainly, it regarded itself as the leader of the Six: the British proposal would weaken that position. French governments in 1957 had become progressively weaker and more short-lived, paralysed by internal conflict and the war in Algeria. With the establishment of the Fifth Republic in 1958, the new president, de Gaulle, was able to offer a more decisive French lead.

In December 1958 the free trade area negotiations were abruptly terminated by France. De Gaulle had accepted France's commitment to the EEC. Although it was not entirely to his liking, politically it was preferable to a free trade area where Britain would play a leading role. He looked to West Germany for support, holding two meetings with Konrad Adenauer during the second half of 1958. At the second meeting, in November, they agreed to call a halt to the free trade area negotiations. Adenauer went along with de Gaulle's views because of the renewed pressure upon Berlin by the Soviet Union during the same month and his fears of a wavering United States commitment: strong French backing would be highly welcome. De Gaulle had already made up his mind, having already instructed the French representatives on the Maudling Committee to convey the view that France did not believe it was possible to create the free trade area for which Britain was pressing. De Gaulle's price for lending strong support to West Germany was reciprocity with his views on the Grand Design. The other EEC members had to follow the French lead or risk the unravelling of the EEC. The latest effort to prevent too wide a wedge being driven through the concept of Europe had failed.

The net result of the abortive free trade area negotiations was a sharp deterioration in intra-European relations. They had done nothing to diminish Britain's isolationist attitude, and simultaneously had confirmed the widespread belief that any British proposal was a wolf in sheep's clothing. Above all, Britain had failed to convince the new French president that it could be nothing but a rival to France for European leadership. De Gaulle's known views – fashioned by his interpretation of the collapse of France in 1940 and his resentment over the refusal of Britain and the United States to treat him as an equal in prosecuting the war effort, on the failings of the Fourth Republic, on reforming NATO, on the need for France to acquire greater international prestige, along with his ambition to affect a lasting reconciliation between France and West Germany (ideally on French terms) – all influenced his decision to terminate the Maudling Committee negotiations, and all were still influential in his rejection a few years later of the British application to enter the EEC.

THE EUROPEAN FREE TRADE ASSOCIATION

With the collapse of the Maudling negotiations, Britain's next act was to go ahead with the formation of a European Free Trade Association (EFTA), along with Austria, Denmark, Norway, Portugal, Sweden and Switzerland. Finland also participated in the discussions that produced EFTA, but did not become a member. It hoped that the involvement of neutral states like Austria, Sweden and Switzerland – all of whom obviously did not see membership as compromising their neutrality – would persuade the Soviet Union that the new association was sufficiently politically innocuous for Finland to be able to join it in the not too distant future.

Sweden tried to take the first initiative only two days after the ending of the Maudling negotiations, inviting other states to send representatives to Stockholm to discuss how their trade policies might be better coordinated. Although the invitation was surprisingly withdrawn the following day, Sweden had ensured that some free trade momentum would be maintained. Indeed, paralleling the work of the Maudling Committee, Britain and the Nordic states had discussed the idea of a loose inter-governmental consultative mechanism known as Uniscan during 1958. At the same time, Switzerland had strongly affirmed its interest in the notion.

It was the fact that the seven states which formed EFTA were already in broad agreement as to what they wanted, particularly within the Uniscan core, that enabled the further discussions and an agreement to be reached extremely quickly. With Britain playing a prominent role, government officials met in Geneva at the beginning of December 1958 to discuss, without being bound in any way by their own governments, the possibility of rescuing a smaller free trade area from the wreck of Maudling. A second meeting was held in Oslo three months later. The ground was sufficiently well prepared for formal negotiations to begin in Sweden in June 1959. Within two weeks the participants were able to agree upon a draft plan. By the end of the year the Stockholm Convention had been signed, with the launch of the European Free Trade Association being set for May 1960.

By contrast with the Treaty of Rome, the Stockholm Convention was quite modest, in both length and ambition. It consisted of only 44 articles and seven appendices. Its immediate economic aim was to work for the reduction and eventual elimination of tariffs on most industrial goods among its members. The Convention set a transitional period of 10 years, with an industrial free trade area coming into being by 1970. Special provisions were to be made for agriculture and fisheries. But there the EFTA's work would be at an end. It was not designed to continue to seek closer economic unification. Indeed, in terms of the Convention, EFTA looked like a temporary or transitional arrangement. Unlike the Treaty of Rome, where acceptance was totally contractual, membership of EFTA could be renounced upon giving only one year's notice of withdrawal. Not surprisingly, given the well-known stance of the Seven on political unity, EFTA was not intended to have any political implications, and so it was not deemed necessary for it to have an elaborate institutional structure. Its institutions would be confined to a Council of Ministers, meeting only two or three times a year. The Council would be supported by a group of permanent national representatives, serviced by a small secretariat, which would meet weekly in Geneva.

Some doubts were raised over Britain's real motives for encouraging the foundation of, and entering, EFTA: economically, the smaller members were likely to benefit far more, which indeed did prove to be the case in the 1960s. Quite possibly the ulterior motive was to convince the EEC states of the virtues of EFTA's low tariffs, with the end objective of persuading them to return to the conference table to negotiate a multilateral trading agreement that would hold the two parts of Western Europe together. This was a prevalent interpretation within the EEC, and one which was reinforced by the tone of the debate in the British House of Commons upon the Stockholm Convention, in which most speakers concentrated more upon the relationship with the EEC than upon the organisation and aims of EFTA. One of the few salutory notes in the debate was provided by the Labour Party spokesman, Roy Jenkins (who was to become President of the EEC Commission in the late 1970s), who said,

> In negotiating the EFTA we have been too much concerned with showing the Six that what they rejected is a perfectly workable arrangement. I think that the EFTA will be perfectly workable, but I do not believe that in the last resort the Six rejected the Free Trade Area because they thought it would not work. They rejected it because, whether it worked or not, it was not what they wanted.

That is precisely the point. EFTA was to be just a free trade area; as such, there was no agreement on barriers being set against third parties. That barrier, a common external tariff, was integral to the Treaty of Rome, which wanted to go beyond a free trade area to a customs union, which the Six believed was a far more effective way of developing the potential of their internal market, the logic of which would ultimately oblige them to adopt common policies and harmonise their regulations. That in turn would hopefully provide an impetus for closer political union.

The EFTA states were agreed on only one thing: they rejected the sequence of events beyond a free trade area postulated by the Treaty of Rome, accepting EFTA as the only possible alternative that would offer some benefits to its members should the EEC prove effective. They were otherwise a very disparate group of seven. Four were members of NATO; the other three were neutral. Portugal was ruled by an authoritarian dictatorship, and so was at odds with the principles of liberal democracy that were deeply embedded in the life of the other six. They were also disparate in economic terms, and not just because of the dominant size of Britain. Three – Britain, Sweden and Switzerland – traditionally were low tariff countries with an industrial economy that relied upon the import of most of the necessary raw materials. Denmark and Norway were rather similar, but with high non-tariff barriers against certain manufactured goods. By contrast, Austria maintained high tariff barriers, while Portugal had an extremely limited industrial base. Given this diversity, it is not surprising that EFTA, with its limited infrastructure, looked a rather makeshift organisation. It was hard to avoid the conclusion that while pique may have played a part in its foundation, it had come into being not so much to benefit its members in terms of strengthening trade within the seven, but on the basis of a belief that in unity there was strength: in other words, as a group of seven they would be in a less disadvantageous position vis-à-vis the Six than if each separately attempted to negotiate some accommodation with the Six.

In short, as the 1950s came to a close, Western Europe was truly and literally at sixes and sevens. It had taken 10 years for the states definitely to decide where they stood on the question of integration or association. On the other hand, the numerous developments and debates of the decade had not persuaded a single country to shift from the position it had originally adopted on the European question in the 1940s. In 1960 the pattern which had emerged seemed likely to remain in force for some time to come, with the EEC countries preferring a maximum of integration and the remainder opting for a minimal level of intergovernmental association. This arrangement might well have been satisfactory, with some accommodation between the two sides being not too difficult to achieve, but for the rancour that had been aroused in recent years. The EEC and EFTA seemed determined to go their separate ways, and to regard each other as a rival, not a partner.

Since most of the states were members of its western alliance and important for its own economy, this rift was a matter of grave concern to the United States, which saw the abrupt ending of the Maudling negotiations as effectively signifying the ending of the OEEC's role as the leading West European economic organisation. American policy disliked EFTA as an unnecessary complication, not for what it was, but because the EEC seemed to fit better with its own strategic, if not economic, interests. The United States therefore stepped into the European argument, seeking to preserve some semblance of economic consensus. While wider economic considerations were relevant, the European rift between Six and Seven was a major factor in the American initiative for a reconstruction of the OEEC so as to allow non-European membership. The OEEC was transformed into the OECD (the Organisation for Economic Cooperation and Development), charged with concentrating upon international problems of economic strategy and development. The establishment of the OECD, however, also reinforced the lessons of the late 1950s that Britain was not something special. The EEC would inevitably have a powerful voice in the corridors of the OECD, with direct links to Washington. Britain, to which the other West European states had looked after 1945 for a lead, was, if any further evidence had been required, clearly in the wings.

CHAPTER EIGHT

De Gaulle and the EEC

As the 1960s opened the future for European integration continued to look bright. Western Europe and the world were continuing to enjoy growing economic prosperity, though there were signs, as yet unheeded, that the rate of growth was slowing down. Politically, too, despite tensions over Berlin and the building of the Berlin Wall in 1961, the furore over the U2 incident when an American reconnaissance plane was shot down over the Soviet Union, and the shock of the Soviet lead in space exploration and technology, tensions between the two superpowers had not returned to the glacial levels of a decade earlier. Indeed, the growing rift between the Soviet Union and China, which became public and final in 1963, heralded the end of world bipolarity, something which it was hoped would give Western Europe more room to consider its own development.

On the surface, the major problem within Western Europe seemed to be the division between the EEC and EFTA. In 1960 EFTA still hoped for a multilateral solution, within the ambit of the OECD, to the economic differences between the two organisations. But to the EEC this looked too much like the British proposals of the late 1950s, and it declined the overtures from EFTA for the same reasons as in the past. However, even though the two bodies seemed to be in competition, the edge was held by the EEC. It was the more coherent organisation and perhaps the one with a clearer and more positive economic future. EFTA simply had to try to keep pace with its rival: when the EEC, for example, accelerated its timetable for tariff cuts in May 1960, EFTA had to follow suit with its own revised programme the following February, simply to keep in step with the EEC.

Even so, the tensions between the EEC and EFTA abated somewhat in the early 1960s. By 1962, in fact, it seemed not just that accommodation was possible, but that EFTA might well become a footnote in history. The crucial factor was the reversal of the British stance towards Europe. Britain, along with Denmark and Norway, as well as Ireland (which was not a member of EFTA), had lodged applications to join the EEC, and their initial negotiations with the Six seemed to be progressing satisfactorily. Indeed, the EEC, in anticipation of its enlargement, had also begun to consider how it might accommodate the remaining EFTA states, all of whom for varying reasons could not consider joining the EEC, or were precluded from doing so. The issue of enlargement, however, proved to be contentious. It, and particularly the British application, jarred with President de Gaulle's conception of Europe and the EEC. The issue is sufficiently important to justify separate treatment in the following chapter. Here we shall concentrate upon developments within the Six.

Economic progress within the EEC had been satisfactory. The goals of the first transition phase, the first series of internal tariff reductions and measures designed to reduce the differences in the external tariffs of the Six, had been achieved without too much hardship or dispute, and the Commission was looking forward with confidence to shortening the planned duration of the second transition phase. Negotiations on the establishment of a customs union were ahead of schedule, and the Commission was forecasting that the union could come into effect by 1967, three years earlier than originally planned. In addition, under strong pressure from France, the EEC had also taken the basic decisions on a common agricultural policy, to which it was committed by the Treaty of Rome. So great had been the pace of development that the Commission was also recommending that attention should be turned to the much more complicated task of establishing a genuine economic union. Again, the political and economic circumstances seemed favourable. Some member states, for example, were beginning to register large trade deficits while West Germany's trade surplus continued to grow to embarrassingly large proportions: these discrepancies had made the national governments more interested in the idea of an economic union with coordinated monetary and budgetary policies.

The success story of the EEC was obvious on the economic front, something which was probably not just due to the favourable world conditions, important as these were. The political story gave indications of following along parallel lines. The most important indicator was the role of the Commission which under the guidance of Walter Hallstein had played the active role hoped for by ardent Europeanists, overcoming the diminution of the supranational element in the EEC as compared to the ECSC. The Commission had taken seriously its constitutional role of initiating proposals, and seemed poised to take over some of the work load allotted by the treaty to the Council of Ministers. Hallstein himself in 1964 dismissed national sovereignty as a doctrine of 'yesteryear', arguing that it was no longer true that 'the national unit, relying on itself, its own strength and skills, should be the final and only yardstick of the historical process'. As to what should take, or was taking, its place in Western Europe, Hallstein seemed to be in no doubt: it was the EEC and its Commission. The following year he could comment to journalists that he, as President of the Commission, could be regarded as a kind of European prime minister.

To some extent, the Commission could be so active because the national governments, through the Council of Ministers, had been content to allow it to be so. Even President de Gaulle had on the whole been quite circumspect about the Commission. On the surface, de Gaulle even seemed to favour the idea of the EEC as a political unit. In 1961 he suggested that the EEC consider more seriously the issue of political union, though, as we shall see, his conception of political Europe was very different from that of the supporters of supranationalism. Equally significant for the political equilibrium was the rapport which de Gaulle and Adenauer had with each other. The growing rapprochement between France and West Germany peaked in January 1963 with a formal Treaty of Friendship between the two states. This included provisions for institutional cooperation between Bonn and Paris across a wide range of policy areas, something which was quite compatible with the political objectives of the EEC.

Yet within the space of only a few years, all this optimism, not for the first time, was in tatters – against a world backdrop that was also changing: the waning of American economic strength; the rise of Japan; the rapid expansion of decolonialisation; new superpower hostility with the Cuban missile crisis; the slowing down of economic growth and indications of problems to come. Within the EEC the commitment to the Community seemed to be less; or at least it was rather different. In part, this shift of emphasis was due to political changes within the member states. To a considerable extent the Europe of the Six had been a Christian Democrat creation. By 1963 while the Christian Democratic Union still governed West Germany, the elderly Adenauer had been forced out of the chancellorship. He had been replaced by Ludwig Erhard, who did not have the same degree of commitment to a Franco–German core within the EEC.

In Italy the Christian Democrats had accepted the 'opening to the left', cooperation and alliance with the Socialist Party, as the only practical option for stable governmental coalitions: inevitably, they would have to pay some heed to their new partner. A renewed politicisation of linguistic divisions in Belgium was beginning to create problems for the Belgian Christian Social Party, while rapid secularisation in the Netherlands would push the several religious parties to the brink of what would be a dramatic decline in support. Above all, a conservative revolution had placed Charles de Gaulle in a dominant position in France, with the Christian Democrats not just in opposition, but heading precipitately towards extinction.

De Gaulle had already had arguments with the other five over his 1961 blueprint for political union. His veto on British membership in 1963 effectively blocked any geographical enlargement of the EEC. At the same time, disputes between France and the rest over institutional, political and economic plans grew to the extent where they called into question not just the desirability and possibility of the ultimate goal of political union, but also the current shape and even the viability of the Community. Throughout all the arguments and disputes of the 1960s the shadow of de Gaulle loomed large. The interlocking crises of the decade, with de Gaulle as the leading player, are the theme of this chapter, except for the issue of enlargement which is reviewed in the next chapter.

THE FOUCHET PLAN

The tendency in the 1950s to regard the essence of the European debate being simply between Britain and the Six blurred several divergences of opinion within the latter about the nature of integration and the way it should develop. While these differences had not been allowed to stand in the way of the launch of the EEC and its immediate economic schedule, as the organisation moved on to more of its objectives it was always probable that these differences would gain greater expression. They were not caused by the coming of de Gaulle: that merely served to crystallise them. In effective control of France and the situation in Algeria by 1960, de Gaulle was able to turn more of his attention to European affairs. While there were 'Gaullists' in every member of the Six, the debate within the EEC in the 1960s was essentially between de Gaulle and the other five. The first clash came over de Gaulle's ideas on political union.

De Gaulle and his disciples had had a view on Europe since the 1940s. It was a view which in essence called for a confederal or intergovernmental mould, rather closer perhaps to the British stand than to the vision of Monnet or Spaak. Indeed, in 1949 Michel Debré, a leading Gaullist and the first prime minister of the Fifth Republic, had called for a 'union of European states' that would improve upon the limitations of the Council of Europe. He returned to the same theme in 1953, but this time to counteract the ambitious European Political Community. French cooperation in the EEC in the years immediately after 1958 could perhaps best be described as the lull before the storm. It would only be a matter of time before the strong-willed de Gaulle would seek to reshape the EEC according to his own conceptions.

His first move came in Rome in 1959 when he proposed regular meetings of the six foreign ministers, backed up by a permanent secretariat. A sensible idea, it received particularly strong support from Italy and West Germany. In November the Six agreed that their foreign ministers would meet every three months. Three such meetings were held during the course of 1960. De Gaulle's conception of Europe, however, went beyond the Six. At the same time he was pursuing his preference for bilateral meetings: these culminated during the first two months of 1961 with his meeting first with the British premier, Harold Macmillan, and then with Konrad Adenauer.

Within the EEC de Gaulle's efforts led to the first summit meetings of the Six since the Community began, in Paris in February and in Bonn in July. It was in Bonn that the heads of government agreed to explore further de Gaulle's proposal, which he had been propounding regularly since the previous year, that the Six should consider ways of reaching greater political cooperation. They endorsed a committee, to be led by Christian Fouchet, the French ambassador to Denmark, to consider the matter. Fouchet and his committee produced a draft treaty for a 'union of states' by November 1961. The French proposals had four key institutional ingredients: a council of government heads or foreign ministers that would meet regularly, but where decisions would be taken only by unanimous agreement; a permanent secretariat based in Paris which would also be intergovernmental since it would be composed of 'senior officials of the Foreign Affairs Department of each Member State'; four permanent intergovernmental committees to take care of the policy fields of foreign affairs, defence, commerce and cultural affairs; and a European assembly whose members would be appointed by the national legislatures. Originally, France had argued for these plans to be confirmed by popular referendum (de Gaulle's favoured electoral ploy), but this was strongly opposed by West Germany on constitutional grounds.

The original Fouchet recommendations, a revised version submitted by France, and counter-proposals from the other five were all polished and discussed by the committee and later by the foreign ministers. Simultaneously, de Gaulle was pushing his ideas in a parallel series of bilateral meetings, arguing the case with Adenauer in February 1961 and then with the Italian premier in early April. All the French efforts, however, came to nought. They ran into strong opposition from the smaller states, especially the Netherlands; nor were Italy and West Germany totally convinced. Later in April discussions on the Fouchet Plan were abandoned, never to be resumed.

There were several reasons for the collapse of the Fouchet Plan. It was essentially a scheme which would have entailed the coordination of foreign and defence policies outside the Treaty of Rome. The other five, West Germany and Italy in particular, feared that this might weaken both NATO and the EEC. In addition, because of its essentially intergovernmental nature, there seemed little doubt that it would have reduced the role and significance of the EEC Commission and its bureaucracy in Brussels. Moreover, by 1961 the EEC was about to engage in serious discussions with Britain and the other applicant states about membership. Benelux in particular objected to the vigour with which de Gaulle and France were pushing the Fouchet Plan, and argued that fundamental decisions such as those raised by the plan should be deferred until at least the question of British membership of the EEC had been resolved. In essence, they were worried about Gaullist ambitions for French domination in Europe, particularly in view of the close relationship de Gaulle was establishing with Adenauer. They desired Britain as an EEC member as an essential counterbalance. In some ways de Gaulle and France were trying to turn the clock back. The Six, in the Treaty of Rome, had gone beyond what the new France wanted. While all the objections to the Fouchet Plan were interrelated, the main factor influencing its rejection was ultimately the fear that it would weaken the Rome treaty and whatever political objectives it implied, to the advantage of the national capitals, especially Paris.

Nothing much of the original French strategy survived, including much that was useful. For example, no further summit meetings were arranged for quite some time, and the notion of regular summits had to wait until 1974. The failure of the Fouchet Plan did have one negative impact. The memory of it and the attitude of the other states rankled with de Gaulle, and undoubtedly strengthened his already considerable doubts about the wisdom of allowing Britain into an organisation which he wished France to dominate. The one positive consequence was the survival of a severely truncated Fouchet Plan in the Treaty of Friendship signed by France and West Germany on 22 January 1963, a kind of bilateral version of the original scheme with its provisions for institutional cooperation in the four policy areas of defence, foreign affairs, education and cultural affairs. The Treaty was to provide in the future a solid core of cooperation between the two states and which, on the whole, probably benefited the EEC. At the time, however, it was widely criticised as a threat to European collaboration and integration. The Socialist parties of the Six attacked it for putting at risk the trust that had developed within the Community and for seeking to return to the 'outworn concept of the absolute sovereignty of states'. The Christian Democrat prime minister of Italy, Amintore Fanfani, was more forthright in his condemnation, arguing that the treaty was 'harmful to the Common Market, harmful to the progress of European unity, and harmful to the internal equilibrium of NATO'.

THE 1965 CRISIS

The crisis within the Community which began with the abortive Fouchet Plan deepened with de Gaulle's veto of British membership in 1963. It was not just the veto which caused a crisis of confidence: every member had the right to blackball an applicant. Rather, it was the manner and forum – a press conference in Paris – in which de Gaulle had announced his verdict, without formally discussing it with the other Community members. Walter Hallstein and the Netherlands were particularly critical of France, and the tension between the latter and the other five increased significantly. Further unhappiness and a similar rift were generated over opinion and strategy in defence, where de Gaulle was striking out on a path different from that of the other Western allies, a path that culminated in the withdrawal of France from the NATO military command structure in 1966, necessitating the removal of NATO headquarters from Paris to Brussels. Just as the Fouchet Plan was a French attempt to prevent the EEC Commission acquiring too much influence over the national governments, so the attitude on defence was a reaction to de Gaulle's dislike and distrust of the United States, which he felt wielded undue influence in Europe. This attitude also led him to express his distaste for the American-sponsored discussions on world trade, known as the Kennedy Round, that were currently being conducted within GATT: again, he suspected that they would produce a heightened American influence in Europe, something that would not be in Western Europe's or France's interests.

The crisis hardened two years later in 1965 in clashes over, among other things, the question of a common agricultural policy. The dispute led to a French boycott of meetings of the Council of Ministers, effectively preventing the EEC from launching any new developments. It was in many ways a logical consequence of de Gaulle's seeking to impose upon his partners and neighbours, and to put into practice, his vision of the future Europe, a vision which contrasted sharply with that of the pioneers of the Six. It is perhaps ironical that while the decision by Britain to apply for EEC membership implied a tacit acceptance of the supranational principle inherent in the Treaty of Rome, the Gaullist design for Europe, which de Gaulle called the 'Europe des Patries', was very similar to the kind of traditional scheme so popular in the past with British politicians – an alliance sustained primarily by frequent conversations between national governments, in which national sovereignty would not be compromised. Such a blueprint could not help but postpone indefinitely important questions facing the integrative bodies already in existence. Indeed, for it to succeed, the progress and plans of the EEC would have to be reversed. In some ways, therefore, France had to find a way of forcing the other five members into line behind his conception of an intergovernmental association of European states that would ultimately expand far beyond the Six, to what de Gaulle described as a Europe extending from the Atlantic to the Urals. His earlier effort, via the Fouchet Plan, had been blocked. In addition, the regular meetings with West Germany under the 1963 Treaty of Friendship were yielding little in the way of positive results. Adenauer had gone, and the new West German government under Ludwig Erhard would probably, if pushed to the limit, prefer to maintain an alignment with the United States rather than with France.

It was in any case only to be expected that a serious move by the Community to advance further through a reduction of national sovereignty and freedom to act independently would generate a nationalist opposition. As for de Gaulle, his views were already well-known, and it could only be a matter of time before he attacked Hallstein and his Commission. The skirmishes of the past became in 1965 a full battle over the Council of Ministers and its powers to take decisions. Despite the disputes that had occurred, and even though 1963 gave a strong indication that de Gaulle's interpretation of the treaty might be very different, the Six had still in many ways continued to work in reasonable harmony on the Rome timetable. However, by the mid-1960s the question had to be asked whether decision making would be more in the hands of the states, operating through bargaining and trade-offs, or rest with the Commission. Early in 1965 Hallstein attempted to push the Community more firmly back on the supranational path.

The crisis that hit the Community in 1965 was a complex nexus of proposed policies affecting Commission and national governments alike. To begin with, three separate issues were involved. First, the European Parliament, supported by the Netherlands, wished to acquire more substantial powers for itself, especially over the EEC budget, and so begin to look more like a genuine legislature. Second, the Commission was urging that the EEC, by which it meant itself, should have an independent source of revenue out of which it could finance its own activities: the EEC was still dependent upon direct contributions from national treasuries. The Commission was seeking control of the revenue raised from the tariffs imposed upon imports from third countries. There was a link between the two proposals. If the EEC were to acquire its own resources, then the organisation would lose the element of control over its spending that came with the existing system of national contributions: Hallstein could then argue that giving the European Parliament more authority would provide the necessary democratic control over the Commission. If adopted, both proposals would increase the supranational characteristics of the EEC. It was for that reason that France was hostile to both proposals: de Gaulle had already expressed his belief that the Commission already had too much power.

The third proposal before the EEC involved the finalisation of the financial regulations concerning the adjustment of the several national agricultures, on which the Six had agreed in principle in 1962. This, it was hoped, would mark the end of a long-running saga. A common agricultural policy had been on the agenda of Europe ever since Sicco Mansholt had put forward an early version to the Council of Europe in 1950, though its roots lay further back in time in a series of discussions sponsored by the European Movement. France, with its large agricultural production, was a strenuous protagonist of a common agricultural policy, believing that it would be a major beneficiary of such a programme. Farmers elsewhere were not so enamoured of the idea. Despite their efficiency and high productivity, farming organisations in the Netherlands had declared a preference for free trade. Those in West Germany were utterly opposed, partly because the policy proposals, they had developed, also contained the long-term aim of reducing in a painless manner the number of small, less efficient farm units; small farms predominated in many parts of West Germany.

While it is an oversimplification to view the first decade of operation as some kind of golden age, it is fair to say that until this point the EEC had worked fairly smoothly. All, or most, major socioeconomic groups and the six governments had believed that its benefits for their own interests outweighed its disadvantages. Despite the earlier declaration of principle, agriculture perhaps was an area where there always would have been a high probability of a clash of interests between supranationalism and national concerns. Agriculture was still a major economic activity in the first postwar decades, and the ability to control the food supply was widely regarded as central to national sovereignty. In 1965 the clash was more marked because for the first time the EEC was seriously attempting to inaugurate a common policy. The French enthusiasm was counteracted by a reluctant West Germany, worried that the policy would adversely affect its own agriculture; and the governing Christian Democrats did not in 1965 wish to risk alienating one of its most important electoral clienteles, the farmers, just before the impending general election later in the year.

The Commission took the lead in seeking a way through the conflicting demands, attempting to bring all three proposals into one package deal. This was in line with a practice already utilised quite extensively by the Commission. Since the early 1960s it had increasingly opted for linking very different issues in a single package, hoping that because the latter offered something to each of the Six the whole would prove acceptable to all. And indeed, linking these three proposals did have a certain logic. If the EEC did wish to go beyond the 1962 agreement on agriculture, the arrangements of which were in any case due to expire in 1965, if financing was permitted to come from the EEC's own resources, and if the latter were to be levied on imports, then it was sensible for the EEC budget to come under the control of the European Parliament.

What the package meant for France, therefore, was that if it wanted an agriculture settlement, it would have to accept an increase in the supranational characteristics of the EEC. This the French government was not prepared to accept. It adopted a new approach, arguing for a continuation of EEC funding from national contributions until 1970 when, under the Treaty of Rome, the single market stage was due to be introduced. This counter-proposal, however, was not acceptable to the other states, which were not happy with the way in which the scale of national contributions to the EEC, adopted in 1962, had operated in practice. The major critics were Italy and, to a lesser extent, West Germany.

In June 1965 France increased the pressure on the other five to agree to its proposed financial arrangements. Its partners had probably accepted that they would have to acquiesce to some kind of compromise within the package deal. What they perhaps did not realise at the time was that France was not prepared to compromise. De Gaulle wanted the agricultural settlement but was not prepared to accept it at the price of giving in to the other five and the Commission on the issues of resourcing and budgetary control. When it became clear by the end of the month that the EEC would not be able to concur on the financial arrangements for the common agricultural policy, the French Foreign Minister, Maurice Couve de Murville, whose turn it was that month to chair the Council of Ministers, abruptly terminated the session despite the objections of the other ministers. France simply refused thereafter to attend any further meetings of the Council of Ministers, provoking what came to be known as the 'empty chair' crisis.

The point was that France was protesting not so much about its inability to get its way on agricultural policy nor about the latter's incorporation into a package, but more about the political or supranational elements of the package. This was not surprising in view of the known Gaullist attitude that the Commission was already too powerful. The French view was reiterated by de Gaulle at a press conference in September when he attacked the Commission for acting unconstitutionally in attempting to take power away from the national governments, concluding with the statement that France would not participate in the Council of Ministers until the Commission retracted. The essence of the Gaullist critique is brought out well in his highly publicised comment that

> we know – and heaven knows how well we know it – that there is a different conception of European federation in which, according to the dreams of those who have conceived it, the member countries would lose their national identities, and which . . . would be ruled by some sort of technocratic body of elders, stateless and irresponsible.

Hence de Gaulle was striking at the heart of the Community structure itself. He had not given up hope of reshaping it along the lines he had already supported in the abortive Fouchet Plan. What he wanted in its place was put more colourfully, but very succinctly, when he said, also in 1965, 'However, big the glass which is proffered from outside, we prefer to drink from our own glass, while at the same time clinking glasses with those around us'.

The French objective was spelled out more clearly in November by Couve de Murville who argued for a complete overhaul of the Community institutions, in effect implying a revision of the heart of Rome. The time was additionally ripe for this Gaullist critique, for behind the French attitude towards the Commission package was a more fundamental worry, the fourth and perhaps the most important element of the crisis. The Treaty of Rome outlined a change in voting practices from unanimity to majority voting, with most cases to be decided by majority voting after January 1966. As we have seen, most situations had previously required the unanimous agreement of the member states, with most of the remainder requiring qualified majorities under the weighted voting system. The change required by the Treaty of Rome would have a tremendous impact upon the EEC, and it was an impact that was antithetical to de Gaulle. Finding himself in a minority of one in 1965 over the Commission's package of proposals, De Gaulle either had to cede the day to the Community and hence accept the principle of majority voting, or block the effective working of the Community. France was simply not willing to resume participation until these fundamental features of the Treaty of Rome were modified or dropped. De Gaulle wanted first for the Commission to end the pretence that it was a potential European government, and also its efforts to impose itself on national governments; and second that if the Treaty of Rome requirements about majority voting were to apply, they should not be permitted to do so in situations where a member state deemed its vital interests to be at risk. And for de Gaulle each state should have the sole right to decide what its vital interests might be. The dispute brought out into the open the argument about the kind of Europe the Community ought to be building, an argument which had simmered beneath the surface for some time, but which until now, partly deliberately and partly unconsciously, had been successfully avoided.

For a while the other five members dug in their heels and also refused to alter their stance. The French boycott of the Council of Ministers lasted for seven months. Only junior representatives were sent to sessions of the Council in order for routine business to be carried out. But France pointedly refused to participate in meetings where substantive decisions affecting the nature of the EEC were scheduled to be taken. While the EEC did not disintegrate under the conflicting pressures, by the end of 1965 the stalemate could not have been permitted to persist for much longer lest the Community itself be endangered. New decisions and directives were needed. Either the five had to be willing to take these alone, or they had to yield somewhat to encourage France to return. Similarly, France had to accept some relaxation in its position or risk seeing the five go ahead by themselves: the latter option would undoubtedly see a reduction in French influence as well as the likelihood of the five soliciting British membership. The five had always perhaps accepted the necessity of compromise. France was pushed to the same position in part because of the above considerations, and in part as a consequence of the French presidential election of 1965 in which de Gaulle, because he failed to win an absolute majority and was forced into a second run-off election against his nearest contender, suffered a not inconsiderable loss of prestige. In addition, the angry reaction of French farmers to de Gaulle's policy demonstrated how much France, and the government, would lose in agricultural terms. De Gaulle had not set out to destroy the EEC, but to remould it in a more appropriate form, where the 'ambiguities' and 'mistakes' which he believed to be contained within the Treaty of Rome would be eliminated. In the end he had to accept some compromise, or risk severely mutilating the EEC.

THE LUXEMBOURG COMPROMISE

The crisis of 1965 was a continuation of the argument that had begun in 1961 with the Fouchet Plan and that had resurfaced over the application by Britain to join the EEC. All these disputes were about the same theme: the nature of the Europe that the Six wished to construct and the proper relationship between the Community and the member states. Throughout all these episodes France had believed that its basic national interests were being threatened – in 1961 and 1965 by developments within the EEC itself, and in 1963 by Britain (and, by implication, the United States). What de Gaulle wanted was not just a 'Europe of states', but one that would both be free from what he believed to be an intrusive and unacceptable American influence, and acknowledge some substantial element of French leadership. Ever since his return to power in 1958, his foreign policy had been pointed in that direction: his development of an independent French nuclear deterrent and his growing estrangement from NATO are part of that

113

general background against which his treatment of the EEC in 1965 must be understood.

The effects of the dispute on the EEC were significant. French leadership of the European movement, which it had held since at least the early 1950s, was severely shaken and no longer undisputed, even though its influence would remain strong. On the other hand, there was no heir apparent ready to occupy the throne: West Germany, the only possible contender, understandably showed a marked reluctance to do so. In that sense the Community moved to a more communal, balanced leadership. By contrast, while de Gaulle failed to bring the other five completely to heel, he did succeed in achieving some of his objectives: the supranational element within the Community was reduced, and a more widespread use of majority voting was prevented. Thus, while the five may have remained united, and the EEC survived intact, the 'victory' went largely to France. In addition, in the short run at least, the door to membership remained closed to Britain. More important, perhaps, the crisis was resolved by negotiations and discussions between national governments.

In January 1966 the Six agreed in Luxembourg to the retention, in practice if not in theory, of unanimity in the Council of Ministers, as well as informally accepting that Commission activism should be limited. Hallstein's Commission was widely blamed for provoking the 1965 crisis by pushing too hard for more powers for itself and the Parliament. France in particular had resented the fact that Hallstein had first raised the question of greater budgetary powers for the Parliament in the assembly itself rather than in the Council of Ministers. The key sentence in the Luxembourg Compromise of 1966 was the statement that

'Where, in the case of decisions which may be taken by a majority vote on a proposal from the Commission, very important interests of one or more partners are at stake, the Members of the Council will endeavour, within a reasonable time, to reach solutions which can be adopted by all the Members of the Council while respecting their mutual interests and those of the Community'.

In addition, the Six noted 'that there is a divergence of views on what should be done in the event of a failure to reach complete agreement', but that 'this divergence does not prevent the Community's work being resumed in accordance with the normal procedure'.

The Six therefore simply accepted to resume collaboration even though they had failed to reach a resolution acceptable to all governments: in essence, they agreed to disagree. In particular, the

Luxembourg Compromise permitted a state to plead special circumstances in the Council of Ministers; in other words it would be able to exercise a veto on matters which it believed and claimed might adversely affect its own vital national interests. At heart, this was probably almost as welcome to the other five as it was to France. A further important consequence was an increase in the importance of the national governments relative to the authority of the Commission. The latter was in practice obliged to pledge that it would consult and inform governments at all stages of any initiative, that it would cooperate more closely with the Council of Ministers, and that it would not seek in the future to behave like a government. In short, the crisis resolved some of the ambiguity in the Treaty of Rome between supranationalism and intergovernmentalism. The effect of the crisis and its resolution through the Luxembourg Compromise was that the future development of the EEC would be much more as an intergovernmental union of independent states.

CHAPTER NINE
The Question of Enlargement

The founders of the EEC had made it clear from the outset that what they were creating was not a closed shop. In particular, they hoped that one day Britain would abandon its aloofness and accept that it was in its best interests to seek membership. Apart, however, from allowing for the possibility of expansion under the terms of the Treaty of Rome, and of coming to an agreement with France over its overseas territories, the Six had not immediately concerned themselves with formulating a policy that would govern the external relationships of the Community, though the Treaty of Rome did permit the EEC to make agreements with other countries on the basis of reciprocity of rights and obligations.

The EEC was very quickly obliged to consider accommodation with third parties which did not themselves wish, or on criteria adopted by the EEC were not eligible, for membership. The first approach to the EEC was made, in fact, by Israel in October 1958, the first of several unsuccessful attempts by that country. In June of the following year Greece applied for association with the EEC, with the possibility of a move to full membership when the Greek economy was sufficiently developed and robust to permit it. The Greek request was quickly accepted in principle by the EEC. Two months later a similar request was lodged by Turkey. Although the EEC was delighted by these applications, since in a way they were recognition of the potential future importance of the Community, the subsequent negotiations did not seem to be treated in an urgent manner by the Six; for many it was not perhaps the first external step that the EEC should make.

The EEC eventually concluded an accord with Greece in July 1961, establishing associate status for the country, and providing for a sequence of transitional adjustments of Greek tariffs to bring them into line with EEC developments, with the promise of full membership within 22 years. Negotiations with Turkey proved more difficult. Its first application was shelved in May 1960 by a new Turkish government, only to be taken up again in 1961 and 1962 with a further change of government in Ankara. The unstable nature of Turkish politics and doubts about the strength of its democratic credentials were further factors delaying agreement until September 1963, with a similar transitional phase of 22 years beginning in December 1964. But long before then the question of associate status for such 'peripheral' countries had been overshadowed by the prospects of an immediate enlargement of the Community and the consequences this would have for relationships between the EEC and EFTA. The catalyst was Britain's reversal of its attitude towards European integration. It would create a furore which, along with the 1965 crisis, would colour EEC politics throughout the 1960s.

THE REVERSAL OF BRITISH POLICY

In July 1961 the Conservative government under Harold Macmillan destroyed traditional British policy in a stroke with the announcement of its intention to apply for admission into the EEC. What was at least as surprising as the fact of this reversal of policy is that it occurred only two years after Britain's own brainchild, EFTA, had begun to operate. EFTA had been established, in British eyes, as a counterweight to the EEC. That Britain was ready to abandon so quickly a creation for which it had largely been responsible said something perhaps about the relative effectiveness and prospects of the two West European organisations.

Several factors had contributed towards the revision of Conservative party thinking on Europe, though Macmillan himself as well as some of his colleagues had been sympathetic towards closer European involvement for some time. The first reason was that while EFTA may have been living up to its limited expectations, it had done little to counter the growing importance of the EEC. This was true not just of the developments which had occurred within the EEC and the prospects of further progress in the near future, but also of relationships between the EEC and individual EFTA states. Some members of EFTA – Austria and Switzerland as well as Britain itself – were still trading more with the EEC countries than with their EFTA associates. As the EEC seemed likely to move ever more rapidly towards a full customs union, Britain felt it imperative to safeguard its important trade with the Community. If this were lost by remaining outside the external tariff wall that the EEC might construct, it could not be compensated for through EFTA. The problem with EFTA was that it still had the appearance of a temporary organisation. Geographically disparate, it lacked any strong rationale for Britain other than being a marriage of convenience, and this was reflected in Britain's general lack of interest in it: certainly, its market was far too small for a major country like Britain.

The basic value of EFTA, in fact, lay further north in the boost it gave, with the membership of Denmark, Norway and Sweden, to greater Nordic economic cooperation and interchange. This was something the three states had conspicuously failed to achieve by themselves over the previous decade. Nordic cooperation was further enhanced by the emergence of Finland from its Soviet-inspired isolation to become an associate member of EFTA in 1961. While several EFTA states were prepared to seek no more than a limited agreement with the EEC, Denmark was keen to come to terms with, and even join, the Community. Only the importance of the British market for its export-oriented agricultural economy held it back. In a sense, therefore, the survival of EFTA seemed to hinge on Britain. Britain's problem was that it seemed to give EFTA a low priority. One of the most striking examples of the weakness and looseness of EFTA occurred, in fact, a few years later in 1964 when the newly-elected Labour government in Britain unilaterally imposed a 15 per cent surcharge on imports from EFTA states. What this meant was that the EFTA states enjoyed hardly any preferential treatment in the British market: in fact in several ways they were worse off, for example in terms of prior notice, than the United States.

The second factor was the continuing assessment by the British government of its diminished role and waning influence in world politics, in particular with regard to the United States and Commonwealth. As the Commonwealth expanded in numbers with decolonisation, it had become clearer that Britain, while still dominating trade with most of its ex-colonies, could not retain the same exclusive trading advantages as before. The Commonwealth states wished to develop economically themselves and to diversify their own trading patterns. Projections of the future suggested that trade with the Commonwealth would steadily decline as a percentage of Britain's total trade.

On the political front, it had become more painfully obvious since the damaging Suez episode of 1956 that Britain's influence outside Europe had been markedly reduced, and in particular that the United States either interpreted the 'special relationship' very differently or chose to ignore it. The reorganisation of the OEEC into the OECD in 1960 emphasised this point since the American objective was to limit the damage done by the division of Western Europe into the Six and Seven, and to give general support to the idea of European integration. The problem was heightened by the election of John Kennedy to the American presidency in 1960. Kennedy's vision of the relationship between the United States and Western Europe envisaged interdependency, expressed as a political, economic and military partnership. The basis of European participation in this partnership, however, was contingent upon Western Europe putting its house in order, upon both the success of the EEC and its enlargement. Britain would have no special favours if it persisted in remaining outside the Community by choice. This American policy stance was laid before Macmillan during his visit to Washington in April 1961.

A further motive which pushed the Conservatives towards considering EEC membership was worry about Britain's economic performance. In the 1950s the West European economies had experienced a sustained period of economic growth, with none of the boom–slump cycle that had typified earlier economic periods. There were, however, significant national variations in economic growth. West Germany was the market leader throughout the 1950s and early 1960s, giving rise to the mystique of the German 'economic miracle'; the growth rate of several other countries, however, was equally impressive. By contrast, Britain was at the foot of the growth league table. Though the British economy did grow in the 1950s, with a performance superior to that of the interwar years, it persistently lagged behind that of its major competitors. Britain may never have had it so good, as the Conservatives had proclaimed in the 1959 election slogan, but the prosperity was only relative: the sluggish economy would also diminish Britain's world and European influence. To turn the British economy around in the right direction, however, would be difficult. Macmillan feared that the appropriate medicine would be politically unpopular. While he was concerned about the level of British industrial productivity, he did not want the changes necessary for raising that productivity to disrupt the prevailing political consensus: a government programme to tackle the problem would inevitably become a party political issue. Entry into the EEC was seen as a way of possibly changing the economic agenda without destroying that consensus. It would be industrial competition from within the EEC which would administer the cold shower of reducing problems such as overmanning and low productivity.

The final factor was the development of the EEC itself. Quite simply, the EEC worked. As we have seen, in 1960 the Six had declared an intention to speed up the programme of movement towards a common market. A few months later, de Gaulle had urged the Six to consider ways of introducing political union, and in 1961 the EEC had set up the committee under Christian Fouchet to study the question. These developments served notice not only that the EEC was proceeding towards becoming a viable economic unit, but also that it was serious and confident about its long-term ambitions. While the latter were precisely what Britain had objected to ever since the end of the war, if the EEC's plans were successful, Britain's political influence and perhaps also its economic fortunes would be reduced if it stayed outside the EEC. The later that Britain took the plunge in reaching a decision about wishing to join, the more difficult it would be to obtain satisfactory terms, and the harder the problems of adjustment to membership. At a meeting of Commonwealth heads of government in Accra in September 1961, Macmillan not only put the economic case as to why Britain should join the EEC, he also stressed that while it did not mean abandoning the Commonwealth in favour of Europe, the move was nevertheless necessary 'to preserve the power and strength of Britain in the world'.

THE FIRST APPLICATIONS

The British application to join the EEC was lodged in Brussels on 10 August 1961. It said, however, that Britain still would have 'to take account of the special Commonwealth relationship, as well as of the essential interests of British agriculture and of the other members of EFTA'. Negotiations on the application opened in Brussels three months later. As has been noted, the reason why Britain had decided to seek EEC membership seemed to be that no other option was reasonably available: in other words, there was perhaps little sense of positive commitment. This kind of negative tone characterised the announcement of Britain's intention by Macmillan in the House of Commons, where it seemed to be put as merely necessary rather than valuable. Again, Macmillan stressed the economic reasons for seeking membership, though the political motive was equally important.

Nevertheless, the British application broke the West European deadlock between the Six and the Seven, and set in motion a snowball of approaches to the EEC. Almost simultaneously, Denmark and Ireland also lodged an application for membership. Denmark was pleased by the British decision; of all the EFTA states it had come to be the most positively oriented towards the EEC. In depositing its application in Brussels on the same day as Britain, it nevertheless stressed the need for some accommodation with the remaining EFTA states as well as asking the EEC to take account of Denmark's general relationship with the other Nordic states. Ireland's application was perhaps something of a surprise. It had studiously avoided most European entanglements: most particularly, it was not a member of NATO, and possible EEC cooperation on defence could possibly jeopardise Irish neutrality. In economics, Ireland had avoided involvement in European multilateral trading agreements, contenting itself with special arrangements with Britain. Irish trade, however, was so bound up with Britain that it had little choice other than to follow Britain. Norway also felt obliged to follow the British lead, again for economic reasons: however, because its constitution had to be amended to permit the transfer of at least some sovereign authority to a supranational body like the EEC, the Norwegian application was not submitted until April 1962. It drew attention to the 'special problems' which Norway faced, arising from the country's 'geographical location and economic structure', which would need to be resolved by the negotiations.

With the probable defection of three of its members, EFTA would be even more of a rump organisation and no longer able, if indeed it ever had been, to present itself as a rival to the EEC. The remaining EFTA states, most feeling unable to consider EEC membership for political reasons, had nevertheless to reconsider their position. Sweden, faced with the decision by Britain and its Scandinavian neighbours, felt obliged to request a special associate arrangement with the EEC in 1961. Austria made a similar request at the same time, and Switzerland followed suit a few days later. A submission from Portugal did not come until June 1962: unlike the other EFTA survivors, Portugal was not neutral, but since it was governed by an authoritarian dictatorship, it had little hope of being allowed to join the EEC. Outside the EFTA states, Greece had already reached an association agreement, discussions towards the same end were continuing with Turkey, and in early 1962 further requests for association were made by Spain and Malta. It appeared as if the dream of a comprehensive European community had received its greatest impetus since the Six had first decided to go their own way.

The several applications received a generally warm welcome from within the EEC, though some doubts were expressed over Ireland's application, first because the country was a member neither of EFTA nor NATO, and second because its economy, still heavily rooted in agriculture, was much weaker than that of either the current members or the other applicants. The smaller EEC states in particular welcomed the British application, seeing British participation as a valuable counterbalance to the emerging Franco–German axis within the Community. On the other hand, there were still lingering suspicions that British policy on the desirability of European integration had not changed: the concern about whether Britain's intentions arose merely from expediency were not entirely allayed by the tone of the British application.

Inevitably, because of Britain's economic and political importance, it was its application which lay, either directly or latently, at the centre of all discussions and debates. In addition, the EEC felt it did not have the capacity to handle so many bilateral negotiations simultaneously. Since many of the applications had been influenced by the British move and since the British negotiations would be at least among the most complex, the EEC decided to concentrate its energy in the first instance upon the British application. The EEC also decided that the negotiations could not be the sole responsibility of a Community institution, that is the Commission, but would be conducted by representatives of the six national governments. One complicating factor was that the Six also had their own schedule to meet. They were under pressure to agree to a common agricultural policy and to renegotiate the original agreement covering relationships with the overseas territories which was due to expire at the end of 1962. In addition, they were in the throes of discussing the Fouchet Plan.

Because of these factors, serious negotiations with Britain did not begin until the spring of 1962, Britain concentrated heavily upon relations with and safeguards for the Commonwealth during the first phase of the negotiations. It also, perhaps ill-advisedly, argued forcefully for concessions on agriculture; it had in 1961 hoped that the EEC would defer taking any action on agricultural policy until after British entry had been achieved. Britain also had to stress the EFTA commitment: it was bound by the so-called London Agreement of June 1961, whereby EFTA states applying for EEC membership pledged themselves not to accept membership unless satisfactory safeguards were guaranteed for all EFTA states. Whether it was discussing agriculture, the Commonwealth or EFTA, Britain pushed for a whole range of detailed concessions. Overall, its stance perhaps reinforced the scepticism of the doubters within the EEC, at times giving the impression of being a potential benefactor rather than a supplicant. To some extent it would be fair to say that the original outlines presented by Britain's chief negotiator, Edward Heath, if they had been accepted, would have involved a rather radical shift in the operation of the EEC – even at times to the degree of hinting its possible submergence in some greater, but vague Atlantic–cum–Commonwealth system. On the other hand, the relatively hard line pursued by Heath and the other negotiators was to a considerable extent designed for domestic consumption. There were still considerable doubts within Britain on the virtue of joining the EEC, except perhaps on the very best of terms. The EEC had become a political issue, with the opposition Labour Party arguing that 'history would not forgive us' for accepting membership on unsatisfactory terms.

While the negotiations between Britain and the Six proved to be slow, they did progress, with the main theme being a gradual but steady retreat by Britain from its original position. By the end of 1962 it seemed as if a final agreement was in sight. It was at this point that hopes for the future were dashed. It was widely recognised that the main objections to British membership would come from France; de Gaulle, indeed, is reputed to have expressed considerable reservations over the whole exercise to Macmillan during a visit the latter made to Paris in December 1962. These doubts were crystallised and the negotiations brought to an abrupt end as the result of a press conference given by de Gaulle on 14 January 1963. In response to a question asking him to define the French position towards Britain's application and future developments in Europe, de Gaulle announced what amounted to a veto on British entry, emphasising that in his view Britain was not prepared to join the EEC on terms which France would find acceptable. De Gaulle's statement summed up almost 20 years of difference between Britain and the Six, and is worth quoting at some length:

> The Treaty of Rome was concluded between six continental states – states which are, economically speaking, of the same nature . . . . Moreover, they are adjacent, they inter-penetrate, they are an extension of each other . . . . It so happens, too, that there is between them no kind of political grievance, no frontier question, no rivalry in domination and power . . . . Great Britain posed her candidature . . . after having earlier refused to participate in the Communities which we are building, as well as after creating a sort of Free Trade Area with six other states, and finally – I may as well say it as the negotiations held at such length on the subject

will be recalled – after having put some pressure on the Six to prevent a real beginning being made in the application of the Common Market. England [then] asked in turn to enter, but on her own conditions. This poses without doubt . . . problems of a very great dimension. England in effect is insular, maritime, linked through her trade, markets and supply lines to very diverse and often very distant countries . . . . The nature, structure and economic context of England differ profoundly from those of the other states of the Continent. . . . The question is to know whether Great Britain can now place itself, with the Continent and like it, within a tariff which is genuinely common, give up all preference with regard to the Commonwealth, cease to claim that her agriculture be privileged, and even more, consider as null and void the commitments she has made with the countries that are part of the Free Trade Area. That question is the one at issue. It cannot be said that it has now been resolved. Will it be so one day? Obviously only England can answer that.

The French argument was based upon its interpretation of the Treaty of Rome and on doubts about the sincerity of Britain's intentions. There was, as we have seen, some justification for the latter view: Britain's arguments in the negotiations for Commonwealth preference and on behalf of its own agriculture had irritated France. In addition, the Labour Party had come out strongly against EEC membership. Other factors, however, were probably more important in influencing de Gaulle's views. One was the fear that British participation might mean a challenge to the strength of French influence inside the EEC and to de Gaulle's own bid for European leadership, which he saw as resting primarily upon a Franco–German axis. He was also concerned that the negotiations with Britain, despite the problems, would soon be successfully concluded: indeed, his depiction of the British position in his press statement more accurately reflected Britain's starting point in the negotiations rather than the current state of play.

An equally important factor was de Gaulle's interpretation and dislike of the American role in Europe. The Cuban missile crisis of October 1962 had reinforced his belief that in the last resort the United States would take its own decisions irrespective of Western Europe's position and views. Western Europe, for de Gaulle, ought to be in a similar position of strength if threatened. Hence he was strongly opposed to the concept of Atlantic partnership outlined by President Kennedy. In July 1962 Kennedy had also warmly welcomed the potential British entry into the EEC as strengthening Atlantic interdependence. De Gaulle's resentment of what he saw as the exclusiveness of the two English-speaking countries had been smouldering since their curt dismissal of his 'troika' proposal of 1958 for tripartite summit meetings. The agreement reached between

Kennedy and Macmillan at Nassau, only one month before he gave his historic press conference, under which the United States would provide Britain with a quasi-independent nuclear deterrent in the shape of the Polaris missile, served him as both pretext for, and further confirmation of the correctness of, his course of action.

Of course, at the same time de Gaulle believed that the initiatives he had advocated within the Six, particularly his arguments for a political union and his support for the Fouchet Plan, were more important than Britain's entry as a first priority. However, he saw the other members, especially the Netherlands and Belgium, becoming more and more reluctant to accept any progress in the directions he desired until the matter of Britain's application had been resolved. And if Britain did enter, de Gaulle was convinced that his blueprints would never see the light of day, and that only the 'perfidious' United States would benefit. De Gaulle was not at all enamoured with the political future that the drafters of the Rome treaty had held: the previous year he had declared that 'There can be no Europe other than the "Europe of the States" – except, of course, for myths, fictions and pageants'. But he was at least equally opposed to a Europe of states dominated by the United States. To accept Britain would, he believed, be to accept an American Trojan horse. In the same 1963 press conference he went on to state:

> It must be agreed that the entry first of Great Britain, and then of [other] states, will completely change the series of adjustments, agreements, compensations and regulations already established between the Six . . . . We would then have to envisage the construction of another Common Market which . . . . would without any doubt no longer resemble the one the Six have built. Moreover, the Community, growing in that way, would be confronted with all the problems of the economic relations with a crowd of other States, and first of all with the United States. It can be foreseen that the cohesion of its members who would be very numerous and diverse, would not hold for long and that in the end there would appear a colossal Atlantic community under American domination and leadership which would soon swallow up the European Community. This is an assumption that can be perfectly justified in the eyes of some, but it is not at all what France wanted to do and what France is doing, which is a strictly European construction.

France had a perfect right under the Treaty of Rome to exercise a veto on any prospective member: entry into the Community had to be by the common consent of all its members. The reactions of the other five were a mix of sadness and anger. But despite the assertion of their conviction that negotiations would continue to a satisfactory outcome and their annoyance over both de Gaulle's verdict and the format in which he had chosen to deliver it, the veto had to hold. While the EEC might suffer without British participation, it could not exist without French membership. Three days after the notorious press conference, the French Foreign Minister, Couve de Murville, officially demanded that the negotiations in Brussels between Britain and the Six be suspended.

It seemed therefore that for several years at least a united Western Europe would be restricted to the Six. Although the veto did not necessarily apply to the other three applicants – as de Gaulle made clear to Jens Otto Krug, the premier of Denmark – these were not prepared to pursue the matter without Britain. The most disappointed state was Denmark since it had always been more interested in the EEC. The most relieved was Norway where, although due to the lateness of its application substantive negotiations had barely begun, some opposition to the application had been voiced. A similar reaction occurred, with the exception of Austria, among those EFTA states which had been interested in reaching a special arrangement with the EEC. Austria never formally withdrew its request, mainly because West Germany was by far and away its most important trading partner. Discussions between Austria and the Six continued, in a rather desultory fashion, throughout the remainder of the 1960s. However, the persistent opposition of the Soviet Union to any agreement, on the grounds that it would violate Austria's commitment to neutrality, and after 1967 the dispute between Austria and Italy over the South Tyrol and autonomy for the German speakers of the province were two factors which prevented the negotiations reaching any resolution.

THE SECOND APPLICATIONS

The general gloom which descended on Western Europe in the wake of de Gaulle's press conference seemed to be confirmed by the election of a Labour government in Britain in 1964, since the party had been strongly opposed to Macmillan's decision to seek membership. On the other hand, the EEC displayed a marked resilience after the failure of the British application: even though the veto helped to plunge the Six into a crisis which lasted for several years, the EEC was not torn apart. Despite the discontent generated, the degree of commitment to the Community demonstrated how much the bonds between the Six had grown since the first steps in 1950.

With British entry into the EEC blocked, EFTA experienced something of a renaissance. In Lisbon in 1963 its members agreed upon a new speeded-up schedule for further tariff reductions in order to allow their industries to plan ahead more effectively. In 1965, Ireland, the 'outsider' in the first round of applications to the EEC, became linked to EFTA through the Anglo-Irish Free Trade Area, an agreement which abolished quotas and the surviving duties on imports between Britain and Ireland. By the end of 1966 EFTA had its industrial free trade area, three years earlier than the original schedule. However, there was no intention to synchronise their external tariffs, merely to reduce the barriers between the member states. While this was beneficial for trade, it did little to tackle the problem of the EEC and its much greater market. As the EEC proceeded with its own programme, the economic division within Western Europe remained as broad as ever. The consequences and problems for the non-EEC states remained the same as in the early 1960s. Almost inevitably, perhaps, Britain returned to Europe in 1967, this second application being lodged by a hitherto hostile Labour government. Once again, Norway, Ireland and Denmark announced that they too would wish to consider EEC membership. And again there was an expression of interest among the remaining EFTA states in some kind of association with the EEC. However, there was in this second round no mention of the 1961 London Agreement under which the applicants would bear in mind the situation of their EFTA partners.

While a majority of the party's rank and file still evinced strong antipathy towards European involvement, the British Labour leaders seem to have been converted, like the Conservatives before them, by the actualities and problems of government. The new prime minister, Harold Wilson, had begun by trying to forge a closer link with the United States and to strengthen the political ability of the Commonwealth. It was now even clearer that the economic bonds between Britain and the Commonwealth were still in decline. The political limitations and Britain's military weakness had also been underlined by the unilateral declaration of independence in 1965 by the white minority regime in Rhodesia; despite the application of sanctions, a rather hesitant British government failed to bring the regime to an end. The American attempt in the mid-1960s to strengthen cooperation throughout Western Europe by an initiative in the military sector – its idea for a Multilateral Force (MLF) built up of nuclear units mixing servicemen from various NATO members – further emphasised Britain's reduced status. Equally important, the domestic economy, plagued by continued slow rates of growth, a large balance of payments deficit and a large borrowing requirement, contrasted sharply with the healthier economies of the Six, especially that of West Germany.

Between 1965 and 1967 pronouncements by Labour spokesmen on the need to come to some kind of arrangement with the EEC were strongly reminiscent of those issued by the Conservatives between the failure of their free trade area proposals at the end of 1958 and the 1961 decision to seek entry into the EEC. The need to maintain Britain's political influence and to secure its economic prosperity drove the government to apply for EEC membership. Wilson, continuing the technological theme of his 1964 and 1966 election campaigns, pointed to American predominance in high technology fields such as space research and computers, and backed the application by arguing for the broadest possible West European cooperation in technological development, and that British membership would enhance the EEC in these fields.

Superficially, the prospects looked bright. Since July 1963 Britain had maintained some contacts with the EEC through a partial reactivation of the WEU, with an agreement for the seven members to meet every three months; among other things, they would exchange 'views on the European economic situation', with the EEC Commission being represented in such discussions. The possibility of a second British application had been discussed in WEU in 1966, where French spokesmen seemed to indicate that France was not 'doctrinally' opposed to British membership.

However, despite radical changes in the conception and political operation of the EEC since the first round of applications that had been occasioned by the 1965 crisis, nothing had occurred that would persuade the French president to change his mind. At a press conference in May 1967 de Gaulle, stating that he would limit himself to reviewing the implications of British entry without prejudging the outcome of the forthcoming negotiations, nevertheless repeated almost verbatim his remarks of January 1963. Six months later, on 27 November, with the negotiations barely having got off the ground, de Gaulle delivered a second veto, again in his favourite forum of a press conference. Likening the British application to the 'fifth act of a play during which England has taken up very different and apparently inconsistent attitudes' towards the EEC, he explicitly confirmed 'the impossibility of bringing the Great Britain of today into the Common Market as it stands'. Once again, there was anger and disappointment in the other five EEC states, with the Dutch Foreign Minister, Joseph Luns, caustically commenting that 'press conferences do not constitute a method of negotiating'. As before, the other three states which had expressed a desire for membership chose not to pursue the matter further without Britain.

The second veto confirmed that as long as de Gaulle remained at the helm of French politics, British entry was impossible. De Gaulle recognised that he was perhaps the sole barrier: commenting upon criticisms of his first veto in 1963, he said that 'Britain will enter the Common Market one day [but] no doubt I shall no longer be here'. The consequences were not so glacial as in 1963. Britain worked hard to keep open channels of communication, and in December 1967 it was made clear that 'there is no question of withdrawing Britain's application' which remained deposited, so to speak, on the doorstep of the Six. Through WEU and the European group within NATO, Britain, with a certain degree of success, also took the lead in urging a more effective level of cooperation and harmonisation within NATO. EFTA too began to press for some kind of interim arrangement with the EEC to help overcome the gap between the two, though this met with little positive response from the EEC. Within the Six, advocates of British entry in both government circles and private associations such as Jean Monnet's Action Committee also worked hard to maintain contacts between the two sides. But that was all that could be hoped for as long as de Gaulle remained as president of France.

CHAPTER TEN

Movement on all Fronts

In structural terms the Treaty of Rome had been a political mix of intergovernmental and federal characteristics. It indicated, perhaps, the uncertainty or rather the difference of opinion within the Six as to what structure the EEC should possess. The resolution of the 1965 crisis effectively swung the balance towards intergovernmentalism. What 1965 meant was that for the foreseeable future at least, the EEC would advance as a unit of independent states, or it would not advance at all. The new kind of Community would be reinforced by the developments of the 1970s. On the other hand, there remained within the Community a widespread acceptance of its aims: important national groups and associations increasingly tended to define their interests and values and to plot their actions with reference to the EEC, and public opinion was consistently in favour of unification. The economies were becoming more interlocked, with intra-EEC trade having grown since 1958 at almost triple the rate of that with third countries. And despite the climacterics of the mid-1960s, the governments of the Six still professed a basic acceptance of the value of the EEC. In the face of French obstructionism the other five had had to accept that the alternative of risking the destruction of the Community over the issue of British membership was unthinkable. On the other side, France had to accept the need to pursue at least some elements of the EEC timetable in order to preserve its own influence. Despite its boycott and the worries of its associates, France did cut internal tariffs at the end of 1965 according to schedule. There was, in other words, a realisation among all of the fundamental importance of the Community. Integration had become, at the governmental level, a positive political concept like democracy; but like democracy the problem was that it was prone to many different interpretations.

The 1960s had also seen a steady increase in the world influence of the EEC. The Six had begun to act as a bloc in trade negotiations with external bodies, despite the considerable internal obstacles to reaching a common position. The size of their combined economies and the more persistent singularity of their voice was giving them considerable leverage and bargaining power, as for instance in the GATT discussions on the Kennedy Round of tariff cuts in 1967, when the Six agreed that the Commission should be their sole negotiator. The EEC had also spread its trade tentacles to most of the Six's ex-colonies. The 1963 Yaoundé Convention between the EEC and 18 African states was a first step towards the aim of offering preferential treatment to all developing countries on most imported industrial goods. Under Yaoundé the African countries were designated as Associated States having reciprocal preferences except where products conflicted with the Community's agricultural policy; on the reverse side, the Yaoundé states had to give preference to EEC exports. The associates were also offered the opportunity of receiving investment grants through the European Development Fund set up for that very purpose, and loans through the European Investment Bank. To ensure a continuing dialogue between the two sides, joint institutions were established along familiar EEC lines: a Council of Associates which had powers of initiation and decision making (though most business was handled by a committee of ambassadors), a parliamentary conference, and an Arbitration Court. A second Yaoundé Convention in 1969 re-emphasised the importance of development funds and lowered the EEC common external tariff on tropical products.

Yaoundé and the Kennedy Round were examples of the EEC appearing to behave as a single entity on the international stage. It is true that states sent ambassadors to Brussels as they would to any foreign country (76 diplomatic relations had been established by 1969), but the Commission was prevented by the Council of Ministers from sending its own ambassadors abroad. All this cooperation, however, could be easily offset by others emphasising the supremacy within the EEC of national interests: for example, in UN votes the six states behaved independently almost as often as they adopted a common position. Hence, despite some appearances to the contrary, foreign policy and external relations were the province of the Council of Ministers and through them of six independent governments.

Internal progress within the Community was perhaps not so dramatic. The new start in integration began to run into problems, with slow movement towards economic integration and hardly any at all on political union. Benelux too found progress slow on its plans to end inter-state barriers completely, implement fully the agreement on excise duties made as long ago as 1950, and create a true economic union. In 1965 the Council of Ministers eventually accepted the 1962 Commission proposal on fiscal harmonisation, and set 1970 as the date by which all members would have introduced a value-added tax (VAT): in the event only four did so (France in 1967, West Germany in 1968, the Netherlands in 1969, and Luxembourg in 1970); VAT appeared in Belgium in 1971, but in Italy not until 1973. An industrial customs union was declared fully operational in 1968, 18 months ahead of schedule, with a single external customs duty and the abolition of all internal tariffs. On the other hand, the union concealed a multitude of sins, the survival of a host of equally important non-tariff obstacles such as national variations on safety regulations, taxation policy, or production standards and requirements. Also in 1968 the principle of the free movement of labour was introduced, though with little immediate effect – and in any case it did not cover the professions or state employees; a parallel free movement of capital, however, still had to be broached. Yet too negative an assessment might be to underrate the slow accretion of solid foundations that were being built for, and that would affect, the future. Nowhere was this more true than in the major innovation of the late 1960s, the establishment of a common agricultural policy.

SETTING UP THE COMMON AGRICULTURAL POLICY

Agriculture had been an important economic activity in the Western Europe of the 1950s, still employing some 15 million people, or one fifth of the work force, at the end of the decade. After the war all governments had encouraged a massive growth in agricultural output: each state was determined, through subsidies and discrimination, to protect its own agrarian economy and reduce dependence on external food supplies. While such a policy contributed towards inflationary pressures, despite its higher yields, it tended to be costed politically rather than economically. The economic costs were considerable. Only the Netherlands within the Six had successfully developed an export-oriented agriculture. In the other five states agriculture was, in general, heavily labour intensive, fragmented into small farm units, and lacking a satisfactory level of mechanisation, with farm incomes falling behind the rest of society during the prolonged postwar boom.

The size of the agricultural sector meant that it was essential to any economic union. A common agricultural policy had been advocated several years earlier. Its major supporter was the Dutch politician, Sicco Mansholt. Since Mansholt became a founder member of the Commission and the one responsible for agriculture, the economic sector was certain to be high on the EEC agenda. It had in any case been singled out in the Treaty of Rome for immediate action. It was an appropriate area in which to seek a common policy, since that would imply uniform prices for agricultural produce throughout the EEC, which in turn would require a centralised mechanism for determining both price and production levels.

Discussions headed by Mansholt resulted in 1960 in the enunciation of three principles that were meant to be the guiding light of a common agricultural policy: the farming population must be guaranteed a reasonable standard of living; markets must be stabilised; and consumers must be guaranteed fair food prices. Between 1962 and 1967 a start was made in establishing common prices for important farm products. Agreement on a common policy, however, was one of the victims of the 1965 crisis. The quest was resurrected again in 1968 as a revised Mansholt Plan. The new plan argued for both aid and reform. EEC prices were to be fixed at a relatively high level, with the total abolition of all existing intra-EEC duties, quotas and subsidies. The common price would be protected against external pressures by a levy on all food imported into the EEC to bring its price into line with that of domestic produce. In addition, where there was domestic overproduction, the common price would be supported by EEC intervention, buying up and storing surpluses for a possible resale at a later date within the Community or (if necessary at a loss) to external countries. The plan also called for a rationalisation of agriculture: a reduction in the total acreage, a smaller farming population, and larger and more efficient farm units. The costs of the programme were to be met from the European Agricultural Guidance and Guarantee Fund (EAGGF), established in 1962. The guarantee element of the Fund would deal with price mechanisms, the guidance section with structural reform.

The Mansholt Plan, if adopted in its entirety, would in the longer term have reduced the likelihood of escalating expenditure on price support, though the short-term costs, especially on structural reform, would have been considerable. Given future developments, it is surprising to find that farmers more or less everywhere rejected the plan vigorously. Governments had more mixed feelings. While at least partially committed to it ideologically, especially France which saw the EEC market as an outlet for its own large production, there was some concern about the costs involved and the possible political repercussions of restructuring. In the event the outline of the Common Agricultural Policy (CAP) that was accepted in July 1968 was a watered down version of the Mansholt Plan. The important variation was the rapid disappearance from the CAP of the structural reform elements as the incompatibility within the scheme between producer and consumer interests asserted itself. The strength of national farm lobbies, once they had been persuaded of the virtues of the system, and perceptions by politicians of their political strength, would keep the CAP in the tradition of protectionism. The CAP was to provide a single market for agricultural products with common prices throughout the EEC, supplemented by a common external tariff barrier and common financial responsibility. It endorsed a system of guaranteed prices to farmers through intervention buying by the EEC of surplus produce either when supply exceeded demand or if prices dropped below a previously defined threshold. One important factor in the acceptance of the CAP was the support for it from France and West Germany as part of a quid pro quo. Through it France would gain access to West Germany which was only some two-thirds self-sufficient in food: in return, West German industries would gain a better entry to France's heavily protected industrial market.

Initially the CAP did encourage production and productivity, and there was a limited decline in the number of people on the land, but to a much lesser extent than if Mansholt's original scheme had been accepted in its entirety. Very little attention would be paid to reducing acreage and the number of farmers or to boosting efficiency through larger farm units. The CAP's credibility suffered a further blow as world food prices fell shortly after its initiation, leaving EEC prices stranded at a level some two to four times higher than those on the world market. The CAP rapidly became what it has remained ever since: ironically in an organisation committed to the liberalisation of trade and the ending of national protection, it became essentially an instrument of sectoral and European protectionism. Once EEC support prices went far above world levels, so the consumer had to pay more for food, not just through higher prices, but also through the higher levels of taxation that were required to finance the Community budget for farm support. Abroad, it raised an outcry from the United States and other countries over its alleged protectionism – with some justification, since the EEC figured largely on the world stage.

Though its import needs were less than 10 per cent of its total food requirement, it was one of the world's largest food importers, consuming just under one quarter of the world's agricultural exports. And, of course, once the price guarantee system was in force, farmers would be totally opposed to any question of reconstruction. Very little money, in fact, would be available for agrarian structural reform: it all would be needed for price maintenance. The CAP was to be constantly criticised for ignoring the consumer, failing to stabilise production, and encouraging inflationary prices, all at a high cost to the taxpayer. Under strain virtually from its birth and assailed from every quarter – including farming organisations – it had, by the early 1970s, become something of a Community sacred cow, not least perhaps because it was almost the only common policy to which the EEC could point. Its viability and rationality were to be continually questioned in the expanded Community after 1973, especially by Britain.

TOWARDS NEW POLITICAL DIRECTIONS

The architects of the Treaty of Rome had created a dual executive, with the Commission being weaker constitutionally than the Council of Ministers. The first years of the EEC, however, had seen a dynamic, rather aggressive Commission under the presidency of Hallstein that proposed and pushed hard for initiatives to such an extent that it was widely regarded as the motor force of the Community. From another perspective, however it could be said that the Commission, though energetic, was ultimately only carrying out the timetable set down in Rome to which the Six had committed themselves. Whatever the truth of the picture, there was a new reality after 1965. First, de Gaulle obtained his final revenge against Hallstein when France opposed his reappointment as president of the Commission; rather than fight, Hallstein chose to resign. When the newly merged executives of the three original communities began to work as the Commission of the re-named European Communities (EC) in July 1967, it was headed by Jean Rey of Belgium. Second, the true implication of the Luxembourg Compromise was a significant increase in the importance and influence of the Council of Ministers. Since the Council met infrequently, in effect this meant an increase in the influence of COREPER, the Council's Committee of Permanent Representatives. Members of COREPER enjoyed ambassadorial status in representing their countries in Brussels. Their task is not only to prepare briefs for their respective ministers on the Council, but to decide among themselves on those less controversial issues that do not require a political decision. COREPER, because it met weekly with the Commission, became a crucial and influential hinge between the two executives of the Community.

The point is that the 1965 crisis was, in fact, resolved not entirely within the Community institutions, but by consultation and bargaining between the national governments. The Commission would still retain the power of policy initiation and the ability to place proposals before the Council of Ministers. But more and more, major proposals and initiation would emanate from national governments, with differences between them being negotiated in the first instance within COREPER. In particular, the nature of the relationship between France and West Germany would become especially important. What this meant was that the Commission could not so easily make a decisive move without the groundwork already having been prepared by one or more of the national governments. The Commission therefore became less a policy formulator, Jean Rey being a more tactful and cautious president than Hallstein, and more a broker, whose primary tasks were to strike a balance and compromise between national viewpoints and to implement packages that were acceptable to the six capitals, though it would nevertheless remain a supranational element within the institutional framework, with the potential for significant influence. The popular view at the time was that the Luxembourg Compromise, through accepting the right of member states to use a veto, had institutionalised the superiority of the Council of Ministers and the national state: it was a view which remained unchallenged for 16 years.

To some extent, many of the Community's problems as it completed its first decade of operation were due to the fact that the Treaty of Rome in general provided only a broad framework for action: in particular, it had not resolved the ultimate issue of political responsibility. This inevitably affected the more gradualist functional approach which still lay at the heart of the Community's progress, and meant that the organisation was replete with contradiction. The paradox of the EC can be indicated by two antithetical pictures. On the one hand there was the inability to agree on a single location as the centre of its operation. Jean Monnet and others in 1957 had urged the establishment of a special 'European' district on the lines of Washington or Canberra. The ECSC had faced a similar problem, and locating its executive in Luxembourg had only been a provisional arrangement. In 1957 the premier of Luxembourg, Joseph Beck, did not wish the EEC to be located there, but nevertheless wanted to retain the ECSC. No agreement was possible, and in 1958 the Six accepted the retention by Luxembourg of the ECSC for a further two years, placing the administrative centre of the EEC in Brussels, with its assembly joining the others in Strasbourg. The temporary arrangement became permanent, with neither Belgium, France nor Luxembourg willing to give up what they possessed. The end result has been that ministers, officials and parliamentarians, along with support materials, must commute on a regular basis between three locations, a practice reminiscent of the ancient royal progression from castle to castle rather than being typical of a modern political system. On the other hand, there was perhaps the greatest and most underrated success of the Six, the establishment of a genuinely supranational court. The Court of Justice had been steadily building up a body of case law. In its judgements it repeatedly upheld the superiority of Community law over national law across a steadily increasing number of sectors of activity; and its position and role had been accepted and applied by national courts.

If intergovernmentalism was the major characteristic of the post-1965 EC, then ultimately it implied that if the EC wished to reach its declared goals in economic and political integration, the national governments would have to play a larger and more positive role. For this to succeed, the Council of Ministers and COREPER might not be enough: they could collate, collaborate and coordinate, but in the end they were only representatives. Decision making might be much easier if the heads of government themselves met to plot out future actions, passing on agreed instructions to both their representatives and officialdom in Brussels. But summit meetings had not been common practice. It was de Gaulle's successor as French president, Georges Pompidou, who took the initiative very soon after assuming office in 1969 in calling for a summit meeting of the six heads of government in order to address directly the problems and issues facing the Community. Not only did the Community seem to have lost some impetus and sense of purpose, France regarded such a meeting as a matter of some urgency also because of worries about West Germany. As the latter's economic strength and political confidence grew, its interest in the EC, while still strong, had been matched by a growing desire to reach an agreement with Eastern Europe, particularly of course with East Germany. The 1969 West German election resulted in the Christian Democrats losing power for the first time. The new coalition government of Social Democrats and

Free Democrats was headed by Willy Brandt, who had long argued for a new approach to the East. It was clear that a new eastern policy, or Ostpolitik, would be Brandt's first priority. The possibilities of a rapprochement between the two Germanies revived some of the old spectres and phobias about German power. In part, therefore, the French initiative was intended to seek movement within the EC in order to lock West Germany into an even more binding western commitment.

Pompidou's call was answered by the other five, and the heads of government met in The Hague in December 1969. With the exception perhaps of de Gaulle's dramatic press conference vetoes of British entry, the Hague summit was the most significant event within the Community since its inception. It opened the way to enlargement of the club, set down pointers for the development of common policies, reaffirmed a faith in ultimate political integration, and was an augury of the new style of decision making that would develop in the 1970s. The fact that the green light was given by the collectivity of the heads of government symbolised where power in the Community essentially lay, and indicated how institutionalisation within the organisation would develop in the years to come.

More specifically, the Hague meeting finally approved proposals for financing the CAP, switching Community funding from direct national contributions to a system of the EC's own resources. The summit agreed to an extension of the budgetary powers of the European Parliament (EP), a move blocked in previous years by France. Some note had to be taken of the EP, which had seen its plans for direct elections, worked out between 1958 and 1960, simply ignored by the Council of Ministers. Earlier in 1969, however, the EP had threatened to take the Council to the Court of Justice unless it reacted to the proposals. Future policy was also advocated by the Hague summit. It agreed on the principle of monetary union, in the short term through cooperation in a European Reserve Fund, with full monetary union to be reached by 1980, and it commissioned Pierre Werner, the premier of Luxembourg, to head a committee to explore and plan the timetable. A further committee, led by the Belgian diplomat (and future Commissioner), Étienne Davignon, was established to explore ways of achieving closer political coordination. In all this Pompidou was backed by his fellow leaders: most importantly, Brandt was forthright in his support, keen to demonstrate that his Ostpolitik plans would in no way weaken West Germany's commitment to the EC. These Hague decisions and their consequences will be explored in the next chapter. Here we will concentrate on one further crucial decision taken by the Hague summit. The Six agreed not only on the principle of enlargement, but also that the question would have to be resolved before all these other decisions could be put into effect.

ENLARGEMENT AT LAST

Immediately upon de Gaulle's resignation from the French presidency in 1969, the Action Committee, which by then included members from all three British political parties, launched a new campaign for British entry. Any reconsideration of Britain's second application, lying dormant since 1967, had to await the summit meeting at The Hague. The key still lay with France. While Pompidou showed some sympathy, he still had reservations about British entry, certainly displaying less enthusiasm for it than his five colleagues. It was Willy Brandt who took the lead in calling for a commitment to enlargement. This Pompidou was willing to accept, but the French price was EC commitment to what France wanted: the completion of the transitional phase and an agreement on a new system of financing the CAP. It is probable, as we have seen, that France was now more willing to consider Britain as a potential ally against West Germany. Not only was Brandt, determined to push his Ostpolitik, expected to be less amenable to French interests, even his Christian Democrat predecessor as Chancellor had declined a request from France in 1968 for a revaluation of the Deutschmark in order to relieve pressure on the ailing French franc. Indeed, West Germany was soon to strike out on its own by allowing its currency to 'float' on the exchange markets in 1970, one of the acts which heralded the collapse of the international monetary system established 25 years earlier at Bretton Woods.

Following the decision at the Hague summit that negotiations should be reopened with the four applicant states, discussions began within the Commission on the points to be raised and how the applicants would be fitted into the institutional and representative frameworks of the Community. Negotiations did not begin until mid-1970, with Britain being represented by a new Conservative government, victors in the 1970 general election. The main phase of the negotiations took one year to complete. Even so, satisfaction was reached only after France had changed its position on several key issues: it is perhaps indicative of the true power relationships within the EC that influential in that change was a personal meeting in May 1971 in Paris between Pompidou and the new British prime minister,

Edward Heath (who had headed the negotiating team in Britain's first application). The latter half of 1971 was taken up with resolving some outstanding items, all relatively minor bar the common fisheries policy of the EC which had come into force in February. Britain, along with Ireland and Norway, felt that it should have been consulted about a policy which came into force after the negotiations on accession had commenced.

The terms thrashed out in the negotiations would have to be ratified by the six members, in France also by popular endorsement through a referendum. But it was the first time that the choice lay with Britain. Given the past record, if this application had been turned down, it probably would have been the last one. Alternatively, if the terms had been rejected by Britain, it might well have drawn the final curtain on the search to make Britain part of Europe. In the event the British Parliament ratified the terms, although the Labour Party had reverted to opposition to entry, at least on the terms in front of it. Attacking the terms for the 'unacceptable burdens arising out of the CAP, the blows to the Commonwealth, and any threats to our essential regional policies', Harold Wilson pledged that a future Labour government would seek to renegotiate the terms and hold a referendum on whether Britain should remain in the EC. The Treaty of Accession was signed in Brussels in January 1972 by Britain, along with Ireland, Denmark and Norway, and one year later Britain formally became a member of the European Communities after a decade of perseverance. It was, however, to be a Europe of only nine states, not ten.

The other three applicants had more or less pursued the same path as Britain, and their renewed negotiations proceeded in parallel with Britain's. Despite not being a member of NATO, Ireland did not allow worries about a possible compromising of its neutrality to overcome the reality of its very close and dependent economic linkage with its giant neighbour: Britain was the market for some 70 per cent of Irish exports and the origin of around one half of Irish imports. Indeed, one of Ireland's hopes was that with both states inside the Community it might be able to develop a more diversified trading pattern and economic structure. The Irish negotiations proceeded smoothly, and the proposal to enter the EC received an overwhelming popular endorsement in a 1972 referendum, with 83 per cent voting in favour. The referendum had been necessary in order to ratify amendments to the constitution that had to be made in order to permit Community membership.

Denmark and Norway did not experience such a smooth transition. For both, their links with Britain meant that economically they would be advised to go where Britain went. On the other hand, there were stronger suspicions about European involvement; both had remained aloof from all but a minimal participation in all developments since 1948. Even their membership of NATO remained a domestic political issue. Indeed, NATO was opposed so strongly by elements of the political left that it had tended to dominate foreign policy debates, leaving little space for the consideration of Europe. Moreover, they had to reconcile their move with the identification with the cultural concept of a Nordic community, which since 1952 had been sponsored by the Nordic Council.

Since its formation, and despite its lack of any formal structure, the Nordic Council had achieved a great deal in the harmonisation and coordination of a wide array of policies: in many ways it had been more successful than the EC in establishing common ground and practices. It had been strengthened in 1956 when Finland, after taking soundings in Moscow about the Soviet Union's views, felt able to join on condition that neither defence nor foreign policy would be discussed by the Council. The one area where progress by the Council had been virtually non–existent was in economic policy. The discussions in the 1950s on a Nordic customs union had been overtaken by events, and abandoned with the establishment of EFTA. The question of a Nordic alternative had not arisen during the first two submissions to Brussels, though under a convention signed in Helsinki in 1962 the Nordic states had agreed that in any negotiations with the EEC the future of Nordic cooperation should be safeguarded.

Sweden was the state which seemed to be most interested in a Nordic alternative. In 1961 it had been sharply critical of what it regarded as Denmark's hasty declaration of an intention to follow Britain. Worried that it would be left isolated if Denmark and Norway joined the EEC, Sweden's first preference in 1961 had been for EFTA to negotiate as a unit with the Community, even though the latter had already made it clear that this option was unacceptable. What was left was Nordic economic collaboration, but this was not taken up during the first round of applications to the EEC. The Nordic alternative emerged more visibly after de Gaulle's second veto in 1967. At the Nordic Council meeting in April 1968, the Danish prime minister, Hilmar Baunsgaard, argued for more intense Nordic economic cooperation. His proposals went beyond a simple customs union to imply some kind of economic union. In Denmark's eyes, the time was ripe for such an initiative. The possibility of EC membership seemed to be ruled out for some time. On the other hand, it did not seem possible for more trade between the Nordic states to occur under the EFTA umbrella. In the recently completed Kennedy Round of GATT discussions, the Nordic states had agreed to provide but a single delegation and had negotiated as a unit. It seemed logical to pursue that unity further. The proposal fitted in with some of Sweden's preferences, and also appealed to Norway whose approach to the EC had always been a rather reluctant one.

The Nordic Council agreed to an interim report on the proposal by January 1969. Further meetings led to the four countries agreeing to a Nordic customs union (NORDEK) which would be submitted to the national parliaments for approval by April 1970. However, the institutional framework was still to be essentially intergovernmental. There would be nothing like the EC Commission, and in the NORDEK Council of Ministers progress would be only by unanimous agreement. Even though it was proposed to set up a customs union, a common agricultural policy, and various other trappings of a common market, NORDEK was not to be a facsimile of the EC. There were far too many differences of opinion for that. Sweden, for example, supported the idea of a common external tariff, but this was opposed by Denmark and Norway. Denmark, with its important agricultural sector, backed a Nordic version of the CAP, but Norway feared that this would have severe consequences for its own rather uneconomic farm sector. Finland too had several worries about NORDEK, not least of which was the possible effect upon the country's delicate relationship with the Soviet Union.

NORDEK was ostensibly killed by President Urho Kekkonen of Finland in March 1970, when he announced that because of worries already expressed, Finland would not be able to sign the treaty. Instead, he proposed to seek a separate trade agreement with the EC, provided that it could be achieved without compromising Finland's neutrality. For the next two years Finland was to concentrate on persuading the Soviet Union that an association with the EC was not inconsistent with the 1948 treaty between the two countries. While further meetings on NORDEK were simply abandoned after Kekkonen's statement, the real death blow to the project had, in fact, been the retirement of President de Gaulle. The level of Nordic commitment to NORDEK could not be described as enthusiastic: for those who sought it, the hope had been that NORDEK would be set up and in operation before the EC option became available again. Once it again became possible for Britain to consider EC membership, it was more than likely that Denmark and Norway would want to follow suit. The decision of the Hague summit in December 1969 effectively meant that it was only a matter of time before NORDEK was abandoned. None of the three other states attempted to persuade Finland to change its mind after March 1970. The Scandinavian states settled in 1971 for the more modest aim of reforming the Nordic Council to provide for a more formal Council of Ministers to coordinate intergovernmental cooperation, backed up by a permanent secretariat (which was set up in 1973) based in Oslo.

Opposition in Denmark to a further approach to the EC was primarily restricted to left-wing elements. But this opposition failed to generate much mass support. EFTA had not been an entirely satisfactory alternative for Denmark, especially because agriculture had been excluded from the liberalisation programme. Britain and West Germany were its major export markets: if both were in the EC, then economic logic dictated that Denmark must also join. The debate therefore was primarily upon the economic virtues, or otherwise, of joining the EC. The Treaty of Accession easily passed through the Danish Parliament. However, because the vote fell just short of the stiff five-sixths majority required by the constitution for permitting the delegation of sovereignty to international bodies, a referendum had to be held. Here too, the Treaty gained considerable popular approval, with 63 per cent voting in favour.

Norway was not so fortunate. Its approach to the Community had been more lukewarm. It feared any kind of international involvement, including Nordic cooperation where it was concerned about its economy being dominated by Sweden. On the other hand, the loose form of Nordic cooperation was politically preferable to the EC. But as in Denmark the government was persuaded by economic factors and the importance to it of the markets of an enlarged EC. There had been some domestic opposition to EC entry in both 1962 and 1967; while the emotional content was high on both occasions, the issue had not acquired a very high political profile, mainly because discussions had still been at a very preliminary stage by the time of the French vetos. The opposite was true in 1969. The issue of EC membership aroused such deep feelings that it almost ripped the country's fabric apart. Between 1969 and 1973 the European issue generated the rise of a huge popular movement which, despite the lack of any coherent organisation and the pro-EC stance of most of the country's elites, captured the agrarian sector of society and, in its crusade against entry, effectively hijacked the symbols of independence in a rhetoric of chauvinistic nationalism. It caused the fall of a coalition government in 1971, ostensibly over the leakage by the prime minister of the contents of a confidential document relating to the accession negotiations to a leader of the anti-EC movement. It deeply divided the dominant

Labour Party, caused a near fatal split in the Liberals, and helped to stimulate two new political formations, one on the far left and the other on the far right.

The minority Labour government which took over in 1971, while willing to sign the Treaty of Accession, had decided to hold a consultative referendum. Given the vocal opposition and his own minority position, the prime minister, Trygve Bratteli, stated that, even though it was only consultative, his government would treat the referendum result as binding, and that if the vote went against membership, the government would resign. The campaign was very bitter and the end result, in September 1972, perhaps unsatisfactory: a narrow majority (53 per cent) against Europe. Bratteli immediately fulfilled his promises: the government halted all discussions with the EC, and resigned. The imbroglio left a deep scar on Norwegian politics. From our perspective, because no political party wished a repeat of the acrimonious atmosphere of the early 1970s, it meant the deliberate removal of the question of EC membership from the Norwegian political agenda. It was only in 1988, with the prospect of the 1992 common market looming on the horizon, that the Community emerged again as a matter for debate.

The Norwegian referendum result shocked the Community. It was the first time since its formation that it had been rejected by any one. Sicco Mansholt, now President of the Commission, admitted that it was 'a step back for Europe'. However, the Norwegian decision neither politically nor constitutionally prevented the application of the Treaty of Accession to the other three potential entrants: the Treaty had allowed for such an eventuality. Hence, only Ireland and Denmark joined Britain in January 1973 as full members of the European Communities.

One further topic consequent upon the decision to enlarge the EC remains to be mentioned: the relationship of the EC with EFTA. During their negotiations with the EC, Britain, Denmark and Norway had stressed the need for a special Community agreement with the non-applicant EFTA states which by 1970 had come to include Iceland, as well as Finland which had become an associate member of EFTA. Discussions between the two sides opened in November 1970, and the following June the Commission published a document outlining what it thought should be the principal features of any such agreement. Formal negotiations were begun towards the end of 1971. After some hard bargaining they were completed in July 1972, with an agreement on a free trade area of 16 countries covering both the enlarged EC and EFTA. Under the agreements there would be gradual progress towards free trade in most industrial goods over a transitional period of four and a half years. Special arrangements would apply to some products, and to some countries, particularly Iceland and Portugal. The Special Relations Agreements obviously were different from those reached with the applicant states. They related to specific commercial agreements under which the six EFTA states would have no voice in EC decision making, and their institutional participation would be limited to a joint executive committee designed to meet at twice yearly intervals to oversee the free trade agreements. A similar deal had to be struck with Norway after the 1972 referendum, with ratification of this further Special Relations Agreement occurring in mid-1973. Of the other EFTA states ratification occurred very quickly in the four founder members – Austria, Portugal, Sweden and Switzerland. Finland and Iceland ratified the following year. The Special Relations Agreements were a new structure for the EC, differing in the degree of their provision of trade reciprocity from other agreements struck for example with Turkey or the Yaoundé states. These agreements sealed the breach which had opened in Western Europe in the late 1950s. They endorsed the centrality of the EC in Western Europe. And hopefully they might provide a stepping stone towards further enlargement in the future: all the agreements, bar that with Finland, left open the possibility of further collaboration beyond strictly commercial activities.

CHAPTER ELEVEN
The Revival of Ambition

While the European Community had made steady, if slow, progress throughout the 1960s in implementing some of the provisions of the Treaty of Rome, for example on tariffs and the common agricultural policy, by the end of the decade there was a widespread feeling that new stimuli were needed to prod the organisation into more effective activity. It was the Hague summit meeting of December 1969 which was credited with generating a renewed sense of ambition. The summit not only opened the way to enlargement of the Community, it also debated and provided guidelines on the initiation and development of policies, especially on how closer political cooperation and economic union might be achieved. The discussions on advancement within the EC that were set in motion by the government leaders of the Six took place over the next few years simultaneous with the negotiations between the EC and the four applicant states. Obviously, the potential members of the Community followed these discussions very closely, as they would be affected by them, indeed bound by them if their findings were implemented before enlargement. To some extent, this factor lay behind the urgency that pervaded the Hague summit. The desire was not just to get the EC moving again, but to place it firmly on a particular path of development that could not be blocked or diverted when enlargement did occur. This period of exploration can be said to have ended with the next two summit meetings, in Paris in 1972 and Copenhagen in 1973. That in Paris also marked the beginning of a new phase since, in anticipation of their countries' formal entry into the EC in January 1973, the government leaders of the applicant states were also in attendance. While the EC would have variable success during this period in seeking political cooperation and a variety of policy objectives, it was the question of economic integration which increasingly dominated as the international economic outlook steadily darkened.

THE SEARCH FOR POLITICAL COOPERATION

Perhaps the most ambitious decision reached at The Hague, and strangely the one which achieved the most success, related to the ultimate goal of the EC: political integration. In order to revivify this goal after its derailment in the 1960s, the six foreign ministers were charged with the responsibility of studying 'the best way of achieving progress in the matter of political unification, within the context of enlargement'. Perhaps mindful of the arguments this had caused in the past, the government leaders did not try to be specific, deliberately leaving as an open question the route such political progress might follow. Several alternatives, not entirely mutually incompatible, were available for the foreign ministers to explore. In terms of the political objectives of the Treaty of Rome, it would have been most logical to take the institutional framework of the EC as a starting point and seek its political enhancement. Such a course of action could undoubtedly have strengthened the EC, but inevitably it would also increase the supranational characteristics of the Community, with a reinforcement of the powers of the Commission and Parliament. That route would almost certainly reopen the wounds of the past by arousing the ire of France. Indeed, France made it clear that route could not be an option. From the sidelines, Britain also made known its dislike of this possible alternative. A further option would have been to take up again the question of coordinating and ultimately unifying national policies. This too was an old chestnut. In any case, it would be even more difficult to pursue that route in the Europe of the Luxembourg Compromise, and at best would perhaps be a long–term programme devoid of any dramatic and immediate effect. Since there seemed to be an agreement at The Hague that policy coordination could and should develop within the existing institutional framework of the EC, this alternative also was set aside by the foreign ministers. A third alternative would be to explore ways of reinforcing political integrity among the states outside the EC framework. This was the way forward chosen by the foreign ministers.

Their arguments were set down in a report compiled by Étienne Davignon, a Belgian diplomat and future EC Commissioner. If political cooperation was to be the preliminary step towards political unification, then it should ideally begin in a policy sphere where the member states already had an identifiable commonality of interest. The Davignon Report of 1970 recommended that it should be in the coordination of foreign policy 'that the first concrete efforts should be made to show the world that Europe has a political vocation'. This was both a sensible objective and realistic goal. It fitted with a growing perception that West European needs and aims were not necessarily the same as those of the United States. As the superpowers continued to discuss détente, there were constant worries that a West European voice was not present in the dialogue, and indeed that matters intimately affecting Western Europe might be decided upon by the two superpowers without the countries in the area being consulted. Many European politicians would tacitly have agreed with several of President de Gaulle's strictures about the United States. In addition, by the opening of the 1970s Western Europe had become more uneasy, even alarmed, by American involvement in Vietnam, a war of which most European governments disapproved. Indeed, foreign policy cooperation had been raised earlier in WEU, as a way of tying Britain to the Community, and in 1968 the premier of Belgium, Pierre Harmel, had argued in WEU for intergovernmental cooperation not just on foreign policy, but also on defence and security, technology, and even currencies. But like many other things, its prospects of success, given the relative weakness of WEU, had to await upon settlement of the enlargement issue.

The recommendations of the Davignon Report were quite specific. It proposed a regular consultation process among the foreign ministers, with meetings being held quarterly. These would be backed by a support group meeting monthly; this group, called a Political Committee, would consist of the political directors of the national foreign ministries supplemented by working groups specialised by both regions and specific problem areas. The Davignon Report also called for an ongoing liaison of ambassadors from EC states in foreign capitals, and for the issuing by the EC states of common instructions on certain matters to their ambassadors abroad. The report was widely welcomed, and its main recommendations were put into effect more or less immediately. As a means of strengthening foreign policy cooperation, West Germany and France both raised the possibility of establishing a permanent political secretariat. Logically, this ought to have been located in Brussels, where it might well have aided further institutionalisation of the EC; on the other hand, if it did become part of the official EC structure, it might in the longer run have been less effective because of the risk of it inducing national arguments and institutional sclerosis. In any case, France proposed that a permanent secretariat be based in Paris, a suggestion opposed by the others, particularly the Benelux states, for being too far removed from Brussels – and perhaps also because it might have generated a rival centre of power in France.

Implementation of the Davignon Report therefore occurred outside and independent of the institutional framework. It was in that way both an augury of future developments and a reflection of the reality of the importance of the national states. On the other hand, since it involved meetings of the foreign ministers who would also meet in the EC Council of Ministers, there would be a strong link with, and input into, the institutional system. The important point, however, is that this cooperation would be essentially intergovernmental, voluntary, and without a rigid institutional base.

The first ministerial meeting under the new regime was held in Munich in November 1970, and the EC made its first joint policy declaration, on the Middle East, the following May. The process was an immediate success, and a second Davignon Report in 1973, presented to the EC summit meeting in Copenhagen, recommended its continuation. This second report stressed the non-binding aspects of political cooperation; its aims were 'to ensure a better mutual understanding of the major problems of international politics through regular information and consultation; . . . to promote the harmonisation of views and the coordination of positions; . . . to attempt to achieve a common approach to specific cases'.

The process of cooperation proved resilient to the vicissitudes of international politics, rapidly acquiring a distinctive appellation, being referred to as European Political Cooperation (EPC). Intensive collaboration between national ministry officials provided a base from which the member states could not only issue a joint declaration on an international issue, and so be regarded by the rest of the world as an important and single actor in the international political system. It also enabled the EC states to be represented as one participant in international organisations and at international conferences. It enabled the EC states to speak with one voice in bodies such as GATT. Politically, one of its earliest fruits could be seen in the negotiations during the Conference on Security and Cooperation in Europe, held in Helsinki in 1975: setting a tone and standard for the future, the Helsinki Final Act which resulted from the conference was signed by Aldo Moro 'for Italy, and in the name of the European Community'.

POLICY OBJECTIVES OLD AND NEW

At the end of the 1960s the process of tariff reductions undertaken by the EC constituted a programme, but hardly a policy. Of items mentioned by the Treaty of Rome, only in agriculture had the Six developed anything that resembled a common policy. The Hague summit took the opportunity to review a wide array of policy proposals and objectives, as well as finalising the CAP. The most important policy arena was that of monetary and economic union, a topic that merits separate discussion in the following section. Seeking further common policies, the summit agreed to supplement the CAP with a parallel policy in the other major primary sector activity of fishing. A common fisheries policy had, in fact, been proposed by the Commission in 1966, but this was not followed up by the Council of Ministers. It might not be too cynical to say that the Six were spurred into action on this front by the prospect of enlargement bringing into the EC four countries with major fishing interests. The policy was discussed and drafted within six months, with final approval being given in June 1970. The core of the policy was that all EC fishermen should have the right of equal access to all EC waters. Since the policy was approved only one day before negotiations with the applicant states were due to begin, it was widely regarded in the latter as a hurried manoeuvre to set up a system to the advantage of the Six before enlargement. Fishing was raised by all four applicants in their negotiations with the EC, and indeed the issue was regarded as an important factor influencing the negative referendum vote in Norway. In the event, the other three applicants did win some concessions at the last minute. Until 1982 they were to be permitted to restrict the access of fishing vessels from other EC states within the six mile limit (or in certain areas, a 12 mile limit) to those which had traditionally operated in those waters. The whole issue became rather academic as states elsewhere, at about the same time, unilaterally expanded the reach of their territorial waters to 50 and then to 200 miles, with the latter limit finally being ratified by the United Nations Law of the Sea in 1973. The EC itself reacted slowly, agreeing to impose its own 200 mile limit only in 1976. The new world had serious implications for the deep sea fishing industry, excluded as it was from its traditional fishing grounds off Canada, Iceland and Norway. Although the 1970 arrangements remained in force until they were, as had been agreed, reviewed in 1981, the EC in effect did not have a common fisheries policy. The extension of limits was one factor contributing to overfishing in EC waters, for which the EC would have no easy answer, and in any case states were still prepared, as Ireland did in 1977, to resort to unilateral action to protect their own stocks and industries. A new common fisheries policy was not to appear until the mid-1980s.

The Hague summit did not necessarily use the directives of the Treaty of Rome as the basis of its discussions on future integration. For example, although a transport policy was mentioned in the treaty, and although it is reasonable to see transport as central to economic integration – including the Six's great interest in economic and monetary union – it still remained a non-subject for discussion.

By contrast, the possibility for a common regional policy was raised in 1969. Regional policy was not mentioned in Rome, although a special protocol did list the Italian Mezzogiorno (the southern half of the country and easily the poorest area within the Six) as a European responsibility; and it was because of Italy that a European Investment Bank had been listed in the treaty. During the 1960s the dominant view had been that regional disparities were not a problem; they would be overcome by the general economic growth of the EC. The darker world economic picture at the end of the decade had cast doubts on that scenario. Italy was particularly enthusiastic about a common regional policy, and Britain and Ireland would also press hard for such a scheme. Indeed, Edward Heath, believing that Britain would eventually become a net contributor to the CAP scheme agreed upon at The Hague after the transitional period of grace was over, and knowing that the EC was by and large unpopular in Britain, hoped that the financial costs that would come from entry would be offset by tangible aid through a regional policy: Britain would be the poorest country after Ireland and Italy in the Europe of the Nine. In 1969 and the next few years, a regional policy with an EC fund available for investment in poorer regions was opposed by West Germany which, already concerned about the cost of the CAP to which it was the largest contributor, objected to the open-ended nature of the scheme proposed. Despite having poor regions of its own, France also was less than enthusiastic. Pompidou, still relying upon Gaullist support within France, did not wish to be accused of giving up even more national sovereignty. In addition, recent French growth rates had been so substantial that it could well become a net contributor to any regional development fund. Very little progress had been made when a common regional policy, like so much that came out of the optimism of 1969, fell victim to the worsening international economic crisis that climaxed with the oil shock of 1973. The Community would have to start again on developing a regional policy.

What is meant by a European social policy has changed over the years. In the Treaty of Rome social policy was not something that referred to welfare state issues, but was essentially about opportunities and equality in employment. The Social Fund that had been established was based upon the experience of the ECSC. It was primarily concerned with employment opportunities and retraining, contributing up to one half of the costs of the retraining and relocation of workers affected adversely by EC policies. The limitations of the fund had been widely accepted. However, at The Hague its expansion was seen as not going into broader welfare policies, but was discussed in conjunction with the plans for monetary union. Insofar as those plans were also to be partly dashed, the European social policy would also have to wait a while longer for reform.

Inevitably, much of the summit discussion focused upon agriculture. France had made it clear that its endorsement of enlargement was conditional at the least upon a satisfactory solution to the financing of the CAP. This in turn was dependent upon resolving the issue of the EC budget, including the longstanding demand of the European Parliament for a greater budgetary responsibility.

By 1969 the system of common prices for agricultural products had been complicated by the introduction of a scheme of 'green' or artificial currencies. The change was forced upon the EC because common prices depended upon fixed exchange rates. The latter were disturbed by the French devaluation and West German revaluation of 1969, acts which were a step towards the world of floating currencies in the 1970s. However, despite their monetary policies, neither France nor West Germany wished to abandon the common price scheme. France wanted to avoid the inflationary input that devaluation would have on its consumers, while West Germany worried about the adverse effect of revaluation upon its agricultural exports. The net result was a decision to retain the common agricultural prices at their original level. These prices would form the new green currencies. As a temporary arrangement it was agreed that the difference between prices based upon the new exchange rates and the original price levels would be made up by Monetary Compensation Amounts (MCAs), which would be used to compensate those countries which were losers in the exchange rate game.

Like so much else in EC history, the temporary MCAs would become permanent. By 1973 the responsibility for them had passed from the national governments to the EC, as part of a change in the means of resourcing the CAP. The MCA system rapidly became exceedingly complex, varying over time because of the introduction of floating currencies and between different types of products. At the extreme, for example, because sterling had been floated, in 1973 the MCAs for Britain and Ireland (whose currency was tied to sterling) were liable to change from week to week. When they were introduced, perhaps MCAs were meant to be temporary only until the EC arranged a definitive financial system for the CAP and established a coherent monetary policy for the whole Community.

When the CAP was set in operation in the 1960s, its financial costs were operated through the European Agricultural Guarantee and Guidance Fund (EAGGF), set up in 1962. The Guarantee element of the Fund was to deal with prices, the Guidance section with the structural elements of the CAP. The main problem about the EAGGF was that because the scale of national contributions to it were not fixed, being subject as it were to the requirements of the moment, no national government could know in advance what its contribution would be. Notwithstanding this absence of information, a government still had to allow for it when drawing up the annual budget. Not surprisingly, it was an arrangement with few friends in the national capitals. This problem lay at the heart of the Hague discussions on the CAP, and the decision to draw up 'the definitive financial arrangements' for the policy. The scheme decided upon was very similar to that put forward by the Commission which was defeated in 1965. Contributions from national governments were to be replaced by a system based upon the EC's own resources: the ultimate purpose was to provide for the 'integral financing of the Community's budget'.

What the EC's own resources were to be had also been clear for some time. They were to be achieved by handing over to the EC the agricultural levies and customs duties collected at the Community's borders as well as a small proportion of receipts from national VAT revenues. The whole financial system was to be in place by 1975. The final details were agreed by the Council of Ministers in April 1970, and enshrined in the Treaty of Luxembourg in the same month. In the transitional period up to 1975, the own resources would come from all levies on agricultural imports into the EC along with a rising proportion of the tariffs placed on imported manufactured products. Thereafter the levy system would be supplemented by VAT revenue, to a value not exceeding 1 per cent of the VAT receipts raised by the member states. In wishing revenue of its own, the EC was looking for a regular and predictable source of income. Whatever the level proposed for the levy on EC imports, it was felt that trade fluctuations would make the sum available less easy to predict. In order to have the ability to forecast revenue so as to plan and budget for the future, something more reliable was required: the VAT element was to provide that.

The establishment of the EC's own resources was not just for the CAP; they were to provide the EC with an income for all the expenditure administered by the Commission on the basis of an annual budget. This inevitably raised the question of how the budget was to be vetted. Consequently, the Treaty of Luxembourg was formally an amendment of the Treaty of Rome in that it extended the role of the European Parliament in budgetary procedures. The importance of all this was that, by enlarging the role of the Commission and Parliament, it increased the supranational possibilities of the EC: the control that national parliaments had been able to exercise over contributions made by the national states would be replaced by one of European Parliament influence over a budget financed from the EC's own resources. The shift in CAP funding also made it desirable for the EC to have a more efficient monetary instrument. The discussions at The Hague on economic and monetary union were perhaps the most ambitious ones of the summit.

ECONOMIC AND MONETARY UNION

The idea of Economic and Monetary Union (EMU) fitted with the desire to extend the customs union, was in keeping with the notion of spillover, and was central to EC development. Monetary union was the most fundamental policy required for a true economic community, since monetary policy decisions have a pervasive influence on the whole of society. Politically too, it had its virtues since with it would come supranational decisions on fiscal policy, tax harmonisation, a single economy, and even a single currency – in short, many of the prerequisites of a political entity.

Up to 1969 the Community's development had benefited from monetary stability as a condition of policy coordination. It acquired a particular urgency at The Hague because of the recent turbulence in the international monetary system. The readjustments that had occurred in some European currencies, forcing the EC for instance to introduce the notion of green currencies in order to maintain a common price structure for the CAP, were but one consequence of the underlying international problem: the fraying of the Bretton Woods structure and the weakening of both its reserve currencies, with the dollar joining sterling in trouble. The faltering of the United States as an economic power, contributing inter alia to its suppression of the gold pool in 1968 with convertibility of the dollar into gold being limited to central banks, along with both involvement in the Vietnam war stoking inflation and the continuing large American payments deficit, posed a serious threat to monetary stability and economic growth.

There was a difference of opinion within the Six as to whether economic coordination or monetary union should be the first step. On the one side stood France, backed by Belgium and Luxembourg, which wished monetary cooperation to be given first priority, with the belief that economic coordination would inevitably follow in its wake. The reverse position was adopted by West Germany, the Netherlands, and to some extent, Italy, with the argument that monetary integration could only be achieved through the harmonisation of economic policies. Although there was very little dissent among the Six as to the virtues of EMU, they were not able to resolve this 'Monetarist versus Economist' debate: indeed, the two leading antagonists enshrined their positions the following year when their respective finance ministers, Raymond Barre of France and Werner Schiller of West Germany, spelled out their objectives in detailed plans.

The task of reconciliation was passed by the government heads to the Council of Ministers which in March 1970 appointed an ad hoc committee headed by Pierre Werner, the premier of Luxembourg, to explore the issue and propose a detailed plan and timetable. The committee reported back to the Council in October. In essence the Werner Report attempted to enforce a marriage between the two schools of thought. It stressed the need to move forward simultaneously in coordinating and harmonising policy, and in narrowing exchange rate margins, the integration of capital markets and the establishment of a common currency and single central bank. There needed to be a decision-making centre within the EC for monetary policy, with the European Parliament providing the necessary political supervision. The goal of EMU would be reached in 1980 after a sequence of stages, with the first stage to be completed within three years. The Council of Ministers discussed the Werner Report in early 1971, finally adopting a modified version which, upon the insistence of France, omitted the institutional elements of the plan. Three decisions were taken: to increase coordination of short-term policies, to improve coordination between central banks, and to develop a means of providing medium-term financial aid. However, without ever actually stating the criteria that would be necessary to bring the first stage to fruition, the Council nevertheless optimistically set January 1974 as its completion date.

The ink was barely dry on the Council's decision when all plans for EMU were dented severely by a dramatic downturn in the international climate. The EC had scarcely come to grips with the economic and monetary problems of 1971 when it was confronted with the even starker consequences of the 1973 Yom Kippur war between Israel and the neighbouring Arab states, which pushed the western world into recession and high inflation. However, the monetary crisis of the 1970s began with an old problem, the evergrowing American payments deficit and the promise of an even more dire situation in the future. The fixed-rate system obliged all participants bar the United States to discipline their currencies. While all other countries were pegged to the dollar, the latter was linked to gold. Sustaining dollar parity was the duty of the country concerned, sometimes occasioning difficult soul-searching; the dollar itself had no responsibility.

It was West Germany which first directly challenged the fixed exchange rate system, unilaterally deciding to 'float' the mark in 1970. By itself, this was insufficient to correct the growing strains within Bretton Woods. A revaluation of all major currencies might have provided a solution, but that was a pipe dream. It was the United States which held the answer, and when it came shortly after the West German action, it was that the Bretton Woods system was no longer viable. This was the implication of President Richard Nixon's unilateral decision to suspend the convertibility of the dollar against gold, as well as imposing an import surcharge in order to avoid devaluation. The United States saw the responsibility lying elsewhere, blaming in particular the protectionism of the EC and Japan. Effectively, however, it meant that the fixed exchange rates of Bretton Woods would ultimately be replaced by a more uncertain world of floating currencies.

It was not until late 1971 that the Western world managed to come to an agreement on how to handle this new situation. In the compromise of the Smithsonian Agreement, the United States definitely divorced the dollar from gold and agreed to a slight devaluation. In return, there would be a loosening of fixed exchange rates, with wider margins than had been allowed previously of permissible fluctuation around a mean: floating would be permitted only within parameters set at 2.25 per cent of the new par value of the dollar. Even this degree of flexibility was deemed a threat to EC stability and EMU. With the EC states playing a prominent role, the West European countries agreed to reduce the maximum permissible fluctuation from 4.5 per cent to 2.25 per cent. This European agreement became known as the 'snake' that would wriggle within the broader Smithsonian 'tunnel'.

Neither was very successful. The Smithsonian accord failed to cope with further financial and dollar crises in 1972 and 1973: its failure persuaded more countries to join the floating world. The snake suffered similar problems. Britain, for example, along with Ireland and Denmark left it in 1972 even before thcy had formally joined the Community. The fact that Denmark felt able to rejoin the snake later in the year simply underlined the problematic nature of the whole structure. Western Europe was soon divided into hard and soft currency groups, each with different problems and looking for different salvations.

While the decision to float by West Germany (along with the Netherlands) was not entirely responsible for this chain of events, it was a challenge to EC monetary stability. Even before European unity was put on an even greater rack by the economic crisis of 1973, the problems of the preceding years had been such that states had to struggle just to sustain existing levels of cooperation, let alone look forward to a bold new future. EMU was conceived at the worst possible moment. In some ways it symbolises the true impact of the Hague summit rather than enlargement. Despite the euphoria surrounding EMU and the plaudits given to it, perhaps the one undisputed success of the summit was enlargement. While it proposed political cooperation, the development of the latter would largely occur outside the EC framework. The decisions on financing and the CAP were to store up problems for the future, and EMU was a wilting reed. Nor did the summit launch any major institutional changes that would make the EC better able to fulfil its existing commitments, let alone propose new ones. That would be a political decision. At the Hague summit it would be fair to say that the Six had been willing to grasp the economic nettle, but perhaps were too ambitious in doing so; the political one remained untouched. As a serious topic for discussion, political issues had to await a further summit. The next one was not to be until 1972.

THE MOMENTUM FALTERS

Despite the decisions taken in 1969, the government leaders were content, once they had issued their general statements, to lcave the guidance of future progress in the hands of their subordinates or EC officials. While some progress had occurred, it was not as satisfactory as might have been the case. Although the possibility of a further summit was mooted on several occasions, no meetings were arranged: the Six even declined a summit proposal put by Pompidou at the height of the international monetary crisis of 1971. But partly perhaps because of the aftermath of that crisis, and partly because the EC was due to be enlarged in January 1973, with several important decisions needing to be taken, 1972 saw a renewed interest in a summit meeting. This was duly held in Paris in October, with the government leaders of Britain, Denmark and Ireland in attendance. The leaders had agreed to advance to discuss three major topics: the further progression of EMU; the strengthening of the institutional framework of the EC as a prerequisite for political union; and the international role of the Community.

Despite their general agreement, each country had particular points it wished to raise, and the construction of an agenda that would satisfy all proved to be very difficult. Indeed, the haggling was such that in June Pompidou, the designated host of the summit, felt compelled to warn that unless the preparations improved substantially, the meeting would have to be cancelled. Given this background, it is perhaps not surprising that it was only towards the end of the summit that attention was turned to the matter of priorities. Each country had arrived in Paris with a shopping list of demands and proposals; these pre-empted most of the available time. The end result was a series of bland declarations of intent: the establishment of a European Monetary Cooperation Fund in 1973 in order to launch the second stage of EMU by January 1974, and keep faith with the target of full EMU by 1980; the establishment of a Regional Development Fund by the end of 1973, action to be taken on an environment policy by July 1973, and on social policy and on science and technology by January 1974; agreement on a common commercial policy towards Eastern Europe by January 1973; a decision on EC policy for the next round of GATT talks by July 1973, and towards Third World countries by the end of 1973. The final communiqué from the summit concluded with the leaders pledging 'to transform the whole complex of their relations into a European Union before the end of the present decade'.

This very impressive list of objectives, perhaps even more heady than those enunciated three years earlier, concealed the fact that the leaders were simply passing responsibility elsewhere. There was still, despite the Werner Report, the underlying and unresolved problem of whether economic or monetary union should be the first step towards EMU. And EMU was the key to so much else of these proposals for the future: in particular, the creation of a regional policy, strongly supported in Paris by Britain, Ireland and Italy, hinged upon progress on EMU. Very little was decided in the way of institutional reform and improvement. Several ideas had been put forward, including making summit meetings a regular and integral part of the EC, establishing a permanent secretariat for EPC, and having all national governments appoint a 'Minister for Europe'. The summit simply referred the question of EPC to the foreign ministers for further consideration, and agreed to seek an improvement in the decision-making procedures of the Council of Ministers. Some useful decisions, however, were taken on the international front, including constructing a Mediterranean policy and concluding a free trade policy with the remaining EFTA states.

In short, the final communiqué of the Paris summit was a political construction that could be accepted by everyone. It was perhaps a rhetorical statement first and foremost, with very little in the way of real commitment. Nowhere was this more obvious than in the dramatic declaration on European Union. The concept was not a new one: it had been in circulation for some time. This, however, was the first time that it had been applied specifically to the EC itself. The initiative for the declaration came from the Benelux states, which had held their own mini-summit prior to Paris. European Union was a phrase with little content. Since no details had been supplied, its very vagueness meant that all could agree to it. At best, it was merely a symbol pointing to the way ahead. But Paris offered no guidance on what was meant by European Union, nor on how it was to be achieved. However, since it had been made a declaration of intent, these would be questions which would continually preoccupy the EC in the future. In the end, however, if European Union were to be achieved, the EC should ideally have some form of EMU, and that proved to be the stumbling block for almost everything else. There was little progress on the EMU second stage; prospects for it were to become even more gloomy during the next twelve months.

In 1973 the condition of the EC became more difficult. In the main deterioration was due to international developments, which affected the EC both directly and indirectly through their impact upon national governments and their domestic problems. One set of political problems were raised by a downturn in relationships with the United States. The West European states were deeply suspicious over the call by the American Secretary of State, Henry Kissinger, for a new Atlantic Charter: many feared this would unleash renewed American demands for a greater European financial and manpower contribution to NATO, as well as feeling that it might be an attempt to undermine the cohesion of the EC as an actor on the international stage – particularly as a contrast was drawn between the 'global interests and responsibilities' of the United States compared to Europe's regional interests. Further annoyance was generated by Kissinger's declaration, without consulting his European allies, of 1973 as the 'Year of Europe'. This issue opened up divisions within the EC on what their relationship with the United States should be. By itself, it was perhaps a minor issue, but it was linked to others that were more serious.

Economically, the monetary snake had run into immediate trouble, with Britain, Ireland and Denmark leaving it almost at the moment when it began to operate. Though Denmark rejoined the snake a few months later, this was counterbalanced in 1973 by the departure of Italy which decided to let the lira float without any EC restrictions. The new floating world served to make the CAP, still the only operating EC policy, even more complex. While floating was attractive to national governments because it gave them a certain flexibility in financial policy and a greater ability to determine their own domestic economic priorities, it could not shield them entirely from the growing shadow that was enveloping the international economic climate. Most EC economies had been slowing down for several years as the great postwar boom gradually weakened. In short, most economies were not entirely in good health when they were plunged into even greater crisis in 1973.

As a response to the Yom Kippur war between Israel and the Arab states, the Organisation of Petroleum Exporting Countries (OPEC), a cartel dominated by the oil producing states of the Middle East, especially Saudi Arabia, used its economic hegemony over a product upon which the industrialised states of the West had become heavily dependent as a political weapon. They cut back production and quadrupled the price they were charging for crude oil. In addition, a complete embargo was placed on the export of OPEC oil, directly or indirectly through intermediaries, to those countries which the Arabs regarded as giving unequivocal support to Israel: the major victims were the United States and the Netherlands. The immediate result was economic chaos in the Western world. There was panic in the oil market as each country scrambled to preserve its own economic interests, seeking to strike some accommodation with OPEC. Not too much thought was given to the problems of other states: its EC partners were not strikingly disposed to come to the assistance of the embargoed Netherlands. The major attempt at coordinating a response was in fact made by the United States, which invited other

Western countries to join it in an International Energy Authority (IEA) to plan and develop contingency plans for sharing oil. Most of Western Europe accepted the invitation. Britain and Norway, on the verge of becoming major producers of North Sea oil, reserved the right to take independent action as they saw fit. At the extreme, France refused to join the IEA, arguing that it would aggravate relations with OPEC and reduce the possibility of a satisfactory agreement between oil producers and consumers.

In short, 1973 was not a good year for the EC. It failed to develop a concerted economic or political response to the crisis, indicating perhaps how easily narrower national interests could uproot the common structure. EMU seemed further away than ever, as did the other aims proclaimed at Paris the previous year. In addition, political and electoral trends in several member states might indicate a less positive input into the EC. In France the Gaullists had lost their overall parliamentary majority: while Pompidou could still rely upon a majority, there were signs that the Communists and rejuvenated Socialists could mount a serious challenge for power. With the Ostpolitik negotiations approaching a satisfactory conclusion, the West German coalition government under Willy Brandt seemed to be running out of steam. In the third major country, Britain, Edward Heath and his Conservative government were entering a prolonged and bruising industrial conflict with the miners' union, a conflict which was to cost Heath, a dedicated supporter of the EC, both the premiership and the leadership of his party. Elsewhere, a political and electoral earthquake in Denmark had doubled the number of parties in the legislature, making government formation and survival much more difficult; while in Italy an increasingly shaky Christian Democrat hegemony was confronted with the further, and seemingly inexorable, electoral advance of the Communist Party to a point where a Communist presence in government in the near future did not appear at all fanciful.

With this background of mounting problems and the failure of the EC to build upon the Paris decisions, in October 1973 Pompidou proposed a further summit. Meeting in Copenhagen later in the year, the government leaders were, not surprisingly, preoccupied by the oil crisis. The events of the year had reinforced the potential value of political cooperation by the EC states, and indeed the Copenhagen agenda embraced EPC as much as it referred to more specific EC points and issues. This was confirmed by the final communiqué, which reinforced the view that in EPC at least it was possible for the EC states to make some progress. The summit commented upon

EMU, social policy, energy policy, and the creation of a regional fund. But at heart these several statements did not make any advance upon the positions taken at Paris, failing to make it clear how these objectives could be implemented.

While the summit meetings up to 1973 had not been complete failures, the EC did in the early 1970s seem to be in danger of drifting without too much purpose and direction. The major problem was the lack of leadership. It took the prolonged economic crisis of 1971–73 to force the government leaders to accept the fact that given the EC structure as it had emerged, it was only they who could take the initiative. If this was the case, and if the EC was to mean something, then it was not enough for the heads of government to meet sporadically and content themselves with issuing grand statements and bland communiqués: more preparation was needed before summits, more detailed discussion required, and more precise guidance given. Pompidou, at least, had recognised this failing, and in calling for the 1973 summit he had argued for regular summit meetings. On the other hand, he envisaged them dealing only with matters of political cooperation rather than the EC itself. While the Copenhagen summit agreed to hold regular meetings in the future, no frequency was indicated; the future sessions were to be held 'whenever justified by circumstances, and when it appears necessary to provide a stimulus or lay down further guidelines for the construction of a united Europe'.

That was still not an entirely adequate response: at worst it might mean that summitry was no more than a crisis mechanism. Someone would still have to take the initiative in deciding when circumstances were appropriate or when the necessity had occurred. The point was that the member states had accepted the principle of the EC as a relevant location for discussion and problem solving. If they wanted to resolve the problems, then the government leaders had to be more involved. European political cooperation could not be strictly divorced from the EC, as Pompidou had initially preferred, and it was not enough just to pass declarations over to the Council of Ministers for consideration. Ultimately, only the heads of government could take decisions on the EC, and that required a greater commitment from them than their ad hoc responses of the past. It was therefore only a short step towards holding summits at regular and frequent intervals. The move towards institutionalised summitry was aided by a change of leadership in the three major states within a short space of time. Pompidou died, Brandt was obliged to resign over a spy scandal involving one of his personal assistants, and Heath went down to electoral defeat. Britain became more remote from the EC as the new Labour premier, Harold Wilson, was more concerned about seeking to honour his party's pledge to renegotiate Britain's terms of entry. That opened the way, if suitable candidates were forthcoming, for a reconfirmation of a Franco–German axis within the Community. What was important was the arrival on the summit scene of Valéry Giscard d'Estaing of France and Helmut Schmidt of West Germany, two men who saw the need to utilise and develop the EC as an instrument of pragmatic political and economic integration, and who were central to the operationalisation of what had become the true reality of the EC as an institution.

CHAPTER TWELVE
The Emergence of Summitry

For the ardent federalist, the Treaty of Rome had provided the foundations of a European political system. The Commission would be the nucleus of a European government which would be answerable to a European Parliament as represented by the Assembly. According to the extreme version of this scenario, the Council of Ministers would be an executive body that was merely necessary during the transitional phase that had to be endured before the desired goal was achieved. From the outset the Assembly, which optimistically adopted the title of European Parliament for itself, was not given any opportunity to develop as a true legislature: its watchdog function was limited, it had very little ability to develop as a true legislature, and it remained indirectly appointed by the national parliaments without any popular base of its own. On the other hand, under the vigorous presidency of Walter Hallstein the Commission did seem to be taking the powers given it by the Treaty of Rome as building blocks on the way to becoming a European executive.

That structure, or rather the hopes for it, ended with the Community crisis of the mid-1960s. Any faint dreams about its revival that might have lingered on were finally dashed by the prospect of enlargement. The first summit meeting of the Nine in Paris in 1972 simply confirmed that the institutional matrix of the EC had undergone a fundamental shift in structure, with the Commission being more obviously treated at best as a partner of national governments rather than as a supranational entity. This new matrix was far removed from the federalist dream; it was to endure until at least the mid-1980s.

THE CHANGED INSTITUTIONAL MATRIX

While the Commission, along with the European Parliament (EP), might continue to see itself as the motor of the Community (a view it repeated to the prime minister of Belgium, Leo Tindemans, in 1975 when he was compiling his commissioned report on the state and future of the Community) its ability unilaterally to initiate cooperation and impose direction steadily weakened during the 1970s. It may still have been the motor, but something else was in the driving seat. Its influence was seemingly weaker not only because of a less aggressive role within the EC framework, where nevertheless it still had an ability perhaps to influence the course of events, but also because the institution of regular summit meetings that emerged after 1974 effectively meant that many important decisions were taken outside the province of the Treaty of Rome. The Commission had to struggle to ensure that its president would have a right to participate as a representative of the EC in the several intergovernmental forums that had sprung up, a right that was granted, by some member states rather grudgingly, only towards the end of the 1970s during the presidency (1977–81) of Roy Jenkins.

In addition to the changed institutional balance of the EC, it was perhaps only inevitable that enlargement would adversely affect the Commission's ability to act as a collegiate body. It too had to grow in size to accommodate appointees from the new member states. It grew to 13 members in 1973, and to 17 by 1986: of the newcomers Britain and Spain would be each allotted two commissioners, the others one each. This would make agreement more difficult, even though Commission decisions are normally taken on a majority vote with the principle of collective responsibility applying thereafter. In addition, each extra commissioner had to be given an area of responsibility: the uneven development of EC policies inevitably meant that some portfolios are much less important than others. While the Commission was able to maintain some continuity of practice because typically about one half of the commissioners have been reappointed every four years, thereby enabling it to develop some kind of collective memory, this did not entirely offset these disadvantages. On the other hand the Commission has benefited from the fact that most appointees have been senior politicians, almost invariably drawn from the governing party or coalition in the member states. Britain is unusual in that, although the appointment of its two commissioners is the province of the prime minister, one of the nominees has always come from the ranks of the major opposition party.

To a not inconsiderable extent, the vitality of the Commission has depended upon the personality of its president. Along with Hallstein, Roy Jenkins and, after 1985, Jacques Delors have been regarded as activist presidents. But even in Hallstein's day the president had little of the control over his colleagues enjoyed by a national premier. They are not appointed by him, and his lack of appointive power is matched by an inability to dismiss individual commissioners. Nor, although a president can wield some influence, does he ultimately determine the allocation of portfolios: that is done by the commissioners en bloc, if necessary by a majority vote. And although the commissioners are supposed to be politically neutral, taking an oath of allegiance to the Community, undertaking not to be influenced by or accept instructions from their own national governments, inevitably the distribution of portfolios is affected by national interests, as commissioners jostle to secure a portfolio which is important to their own state.

It would be misleading, however, to downgrade the Commission too much. It still enjoyed significance in those areas where under the Treaty of Rome it held exclusive powers; and in the province of coal and steel it had inherited substantial decision-making authority from the old ECSC. Furthermore, its tasks grew further as the government leaders and the Council of Ministers placed further demands on it, especially in administering the 'own resources' of the EC and channelling their distribution across the various funds and policies which the EC established in the 1970s and early 1980s. It continued to hold a watching brief on the implementation of the Treaty of Rome, by delivering an 'opinion' when a member state was believed to have infringed the commitments of the Treaty, in the last resort reporting the transgressor to the European Court. However, all of this activity, important as it was, could not disguise the fact that the Commission had much more obviously become an administrative rather than a political executive. Many of the major economic and monetary issues that came to dominate the EC agenda in the 1970s fell outside (or were kept outside) the provisions of the Treaty of Rome. It was the collectivity of the national government leaders, acting in unison, which emerged in the 1970s as the 'political executive' of the EC.

The European Parliament had never been satisfied with its secondary role. It had very early on taken the title of Parliament for itself, and asserted its right, like any legislature, to meet whenever it wished. To circumvent the Rome Treaty's provision of an annual session, it simply divided its annual session into several distinct periods spanning a whole year. It had always hoped that its disadvantaged position within the EC structure would be rectified. A slight change came with the 1970 Treaty of Luxembourg when it achieved some increase in powers, especially in influencing the budget; its budgetary powers gained a further modest increase in 1975, and two years later it was granted the right to reject the EC budget in its entirety. But given the fact that most Members of the European Parliament (MEPs) wished to strengthen not only the EP's own role, but also the overall structure and performance of the EC, this was a blunt weapon that perhaps could be used effectively only in the most dire circumstances – since rejection of the budget would simply result in EC expenditure being frozen at its existing level.

The EP believed that higher status and influence might be achieved if it could secure a more democratic base through the direct election of its membership. Provision for direct elections had been included in the Treaty of Rome, but throughout the 1960s its implementation had been delayed – in reality, blocked – by the Council of Ministers. The Parliament had also hoped that with the entry of British members, which along with representatives from the other two entrant states boosted its size in 1973 from 142 to 198 members, its stature would also be enhanced because of their experience of the more cut and thrust atmosphere of the House of Commons.

The Council of Ministers did not bend to the pressure for direct elections until 1974; even then Britain and Denmark 'reserved' their position. In 1975 and 1976 the Council reconfirmed its 1974 decision, including the setting of 1978 as the date for the first elections, with future elections thereafter occurring at fixed five-yearly intervals. The size of the Parliament was also to be greatly increased from 198 to 410 MEPs: the representation of the four largest states was fixed at 81 each, which effectively meant that the smaller states would be over-represented. No decision, however, was taken on a common electoral system. Instead, each state was free to decide upon its own system: in practice, this meant that each chose to apply its own national electoral system. Despite these decisions by the Council of Ministers, opposition still raged against the proposals, most prominently in Britain and France – though in the latter much of the force of the campaign against direct elections was eliminated by a 1976 ruling of the French Constitutional Court that as long as the EP's powers were not increased, the scheme did not present a challenge to national sovereignty. While Gaullists in France and British Conservatives continued to express concern about the whole idea, and while France and Luxembourg threatened to block the schedule unless the proposals to relocate the whole EP operation in Brussels were abandoned, the real threat to the election timetable came from Britain. As time went on, James Callaghan's Labour government insisted that at the summit meetings it had not entered into a binding commitment to direct elections in 1978, but that it had merely promised to attempt to meet the deadline. In the end the tardiness of Britain meant that the schedule had to be postponed for a further year.

At one level the first direct elections to the EP in 1979 were a milestone in the history of the Community. On the surface they appeared to mark the emergence of something that could be a real legislature. However, within the member states there remained significant opposition to this concept among both governments and parliaments, where it was common to find the view that a distinction had to be made between electoral base and political power. The governments in Britain and France were particularly opposed to the EP having any supranational powers or legislative competence; and in 1979 the national parliaments of both Denmark and France reiterated the view that the popularly elected Parliament should not necessarily acquire any expansion of powers.

Hence, the revised format of the EP scarcely seemed to disturb the way in which the organisation worked in practice. The effectiveness of the new expanded parliament of full-time deputies barely rose above that of its predecessor of appointed part-timers. What increases in power it gained were given in trickles, and by themselves often seemingly minor, such as the practice since 1981 of the national government head currently serving as host of the European Council to appear before the EP to give a 'state of the union' address. Yet they did slowly provide the EP with an accretion of responsibilities, albeit not enough to dispel either its feelings of frustration at its exclusion from effective decision-making authority or the inevitable conflict between it and the Council of Ministers. The EP eventually 'rebelled' in 1982, utilising the budgetary powers it had been granted in 1977. It successfully deferred the discharge of the budget as an expression of dissatisfaction over the way in which, in the implementation of the 1980 budget, the Commission had deviated from EP amendments and suggestions. While this did force the other institutions into discussions and negotiations, deferring the budget was essentially, as has been said, a negative act that could more likely have unfortunate consequences for the EC should the EP dig in its heels. For where the EC enters a new calendar year without an approved budget, its expenditure is simply restricted each month to one twelfth of the budget for the previous year.

The 1982 budget revolt was perhaps indicative of what the EP could achieve. Short of a direct campaign to amend the treaties so as to increase its competence, MEPs could only seek to increase their influence through maximising the advisory and supervisory functions they did possess, or by creatively interpreting, within the boundaries of the treaty provisions, their right to possess their own rules of procedure. The budget, lying at the heart of the EC, illustrated the limited role of the EP. Since the Treaty of Luxembourg in 1970, a distinction has been drawn within the budget between compulsory and non-compulsory elements. The former, constituting some four-fifths of the total budget, relate to expenditure (in practice, mainly on agriculture) stipulated by the treaties: here the EP effectively has little or no influence. Its possibilities to amend the non-compulsory elements of the budget submitted to it by the Commission via the Council of Ministers have been much greater: even so, it is constrained within a ceiling that is predetermined by the Council of Ministers. The major point, however, is that EP budget modifications and amendments were not absolute; they could be overturned by the Council of Ministers.

None of this prevented the EP remaining the poor relation of the Community, far from being a true legislature. The very size of the directly elected parliament (and with the accession of Greece, Spain and Portugal it had grown by 1986 to 518 members) inhibited its effectiveness as a debating chamber, as perhaps did the plethora of languages employed. Certainly, attendance during its first decade was rather disappointing, even allowing for the fact that much of its work was done in committees behind the scenes. But to mention committees draws attention to another weakness of the EP: its continued peripatetic existence. The fact that the EC has no single home is glaringly illustrated by parliamentary life. The plenary sessions of the EP are normally held in Strasbourg, while of necessity the committees must meet in Brussels so as to be near the Commission and its bureaucracy. By contrast, the vast army of assistants that constitute the EP secretariat is based in Luxembourg. There is in short a continual movement of people and of documents translated into nine languages that inevitably inhibits the effectiveness of the EP. France and Luxembourg continued to resist the removal of all branches of the EP to Brussels, which is where most MEPs would wish it to be, even taking their resistance to relocation to the European Court. By contrast, despite its probing and complaints at the limitations placed upon it, the EP did not directly challenge this view and take what would have been an extremely important and symbolic act, that is to hold plenary sessions in Brussels.

The degree of national commitment to the EP remained rather limited: no government or national parliament seemed to be unambiguously in support of strengthening it. Among the national contingents to the EP, that from Britain seemed to be somewhat dubious about the whole exercise, while that from Denmark included a party (the People's Movement against the European Community) which consistently won around one fifth of the Danish vote in all three Euro-elections (1979, 1984 and 1989) and which, as its name indicates, was dedicated towards securing Denmark's withdrawal from the EC. In the Parliament itself, MEPs continued the practice of arranging themselves in transnational party groups which sat together in the sessions. The cohesion of each group, however, was variable, and prone to splintering when the issue under consideration was of especial importance to one or more countries. While it might be fair to say that there was a slight increase in cohesiveness over the first decade of operation, to some extent these party groups had not shaken off the characteristics of a marriage of convenience.

The relative peripherality of the EP was reinforced by the second round of elections in 1984. The level of popular interest was lower than in 1979, perhaps partly because the novelty of direct elections to a supranational body had worn off. The election was not fought on European or Community issues, except perhaps in Denmark where, because of the People's Movement, continued Danish membership of the EC was an issue. Generally, the parties contested it as national parties, debated national issues, and treated it as an evaluation of the effectiveness and popularity of national governments. It was, in short, a series of national contests. The deep linguistic conflict between Walloon and Fleming dominated in Belgium, while in France the election was regarded more as a test run for the 1986 parliamentary and 1988 presidential elections in which the aspirants for the premiership and presidency could show their paces. At the extreme, Luxembourg even arranged to hold its own general election on the same day, something which made it merely inevitable that national concerns would dominate. By the time of the third direct elections in 1989, despite the significance of the Single European Act of 1986, there was nothing to suggest that this ambivalence had changed significantly.

Rather than enhancing the role of the Commission and Parliament, enlargement gave the Community an even greater intergovernmental character. It reaffirmed the centrality of the Council of Ministers in the institutional framework. As the mainspring of the EC, the Council became an even more complex structure, with a multitude of committees. The membership of the Council and its committees became more variable, depending upon the issues and national ministries involved. For example, when agriculture constituted the agenda, it was ministers of agriculture who formed the Council. Central to the whole edifice were the regular monthly meetings of the foreign ministers, which became known as the General Affairs Council. The foreign ministers had to hold a watching brief over the whole complex operation and its various agendas and committees, as well as having to tackle those urgent, delicate or broad matters that did not clearly fall directly within the brief of specific national ministries. Inevitably, this evolving structure required considerable auxiliary support, and this meant an increase in the workload and potential influence of COREPER, the national delegations headed by an individual with senior ambassadorial status which each country had to maintain in Brussels as an essential link in the chain of information. Partly because of the volume of work, but also for political reasons, the Council of Ministers rarely discussed a topic without extensive discussions and analyses having already been performed by COREPER. Remembering perhaps the conflict of 1965 and mindful of the fact that with an enlarged Community the possibility of disputes between states (as well as the complex arithmetic of qualified majorities) was even greater, the Council of Ministers in its initiatives showed a reluctance to call for a vote wherever it could be avoided. The preference of the Council to search for unanimity meant in practice that it was rare for states to feel it necessary to invoke the Luxembourg Compromise, and that a huge array of issues, many of them quite minor, were therefore treated as having a significant effect upon important national interests.

While COREPER could attempt to bring some order to this complexity, it could not give direction; nor could it prevent the emergence, on occasions, of a European version of interdepartmental rivalry. In addition, despite the coordinating role of the foreign ministers, the Council could, in its various manifestations, pull in several different directions at once. At the end of the day each foreign minister was following the instructions and policy of his own national government. If after 1973 the structure was not to decay into some kind of institutional anarchy, it would be necessary for the heads of national governments to become more directly involved in the affairs of the EC. This was one important reason behind the emergence in the mid-1970s of the institutionalisation of summitry with the creation of the European Council, a body whose existence definitively meant that as the 1970s progressed, the evolution of the EC would not occur along a dominant Commission–Parliament axis.

Finally, it might be noted that in the new intergovernmental atmosphere of the EC that seemed to be consolidating itself in the 1970s and early 1980s, one body that would help the survival of supranationalism, and so aid the Commission and the EP, was the European Court. However, the Court's role was still confined to ensuring that EC law was uniformly applied throughout the Community. In other words, the Court's major concern in the cases brought before it, whether by the Commission or a member state, was to ensure that governments were complying with the provisions of the various treaties. It did not have any direct sanctions that it could bring to bear upon states, nor did it participate in the decision-making process. But along with a further body, the Court of Auditors, founded in 1977 and based in Luxembourg, which was charged with certifying that EC revenue had been legally received and expenditure legally incurred – so providing a check on the financial soundness of EC management – the Court could still be a useful corrective to the greater strength of intergovernmentalism. On the other hand, in no way could it block or even reverse that development, for the power of the latter essentially lay outside the legal and institutional framework of the EC.

THE EUROPEAN COUNCIL

In 1974 the man, who in so many ways was the godfather of the Community, Jean Monnet, commented that 'What is lacking more than anything else in European affairs . . . is authority. Decision is organised; decision is not.' The European Council, set up in 1974, was to provide the missing authority by institutionalising the practice of summitry. French political leaders had always liked the idea of summits. It was the logic behind de Gaulle's concept of the 'Europe des Patries', and it was Pompidou who had taken the initiative for the summit meetings of 1969 and 1972. It was not surprising therefore to find that after enlargement it was Pompidou's successor, Valéry Giscard d'Estaing, who urged the holding of further summits. On the other hand, some of the smaller states were suspicious of such proposals: Belgium and the Netherlands in particular were concerned that regular summits would have an adverse effect upon EC developments. The Vedel Report on institutional arrangements in the EC sponsored by the Commission to consider in particular the position of the EP reported in 1972 that if summits became a regular occurrence, they would lose much of their effectiveness.

Indeed, many national governments had become somewhat disillusioned with summits. The recent sessions in Paris and Copenhagen were widely regarded as having been failures. Yet in 1974 the member states responded to a call for a further summit, again pushed by France. However, the new French President, Valéry Giscard d'Estaing, had a rather different view of the utility and objectives of summitry, and in this he found strong support from the new West German Chancellor, Helmut Schmidt. The commonality of shared attitudes which these two men had towards the EC, European issues and world affairs was of great significance in placing summitry at the centre of the political map of the EC. In so doing they brought to an apogee the notion of Franco-German cooperation, the principles of which had been laid down in the 1963 treaty between the two countries, and re-emphasised the significance of this axis for the EC.

Schmidt and Giscard d'Estaing, both with a background in economics and experience as national finance ministers, were sceptical of the exuberance which seemed to sweep the EC when it came to laying down guidelines for the future. In that sense they both were concerned about the role played by the Commission – not just perhaps that it ought not to be too powerful, but also that it perhaps tended to have an image of future developments that was visionary rather than practical, and hence less than useful. Similarly, they had both been sharply critical of the two previous summits for their declaration of goals and target dates that were unrealistic rather than ambitious. Both had a pragmatic view of government and a preference for personal intervention which they sought to impose upon the EC.

It was Giscard d'Estaing who took the lead in 1974 in calling for a further summit, winning over the doubtful smaller states. Once the principle had been agreed, the normal round of bilateral and multilateral trading began among the states to decide upon an agenda. These talks culminated in a hastily arranged meeting of the heads of the nine governments on 14 September in Paris. This brief meeting was significant in two respects: it was able to discuss and reach broad agreement on the policy matters that should be debated at greater length at the summit proper in December; and the government leaders individually declared a readiness to take greater responsibility for European affairs. Nevertheless, each state had its own solo it wished to perform at the summit. Italy and Ireland still argued vehemently for a regional policy, and indeed threatened not to turn up in Paris in December if agreement on a regional policy seemed improbable. Britain supported their argument, although the Labour government was more concerned about its demands for renegotiation of the British terms of entry. The Benelux countries wanted a definite commitment to direct elections to the EP by a specified date. On the other side stood West Germany. As the richest member of the Community, it would have to make the largest contribution to a regional or any other kind of EC policy, and so was more concerned about the financial commitments that would be implied. What was needed was not just to weld the various national interests into a package acceptable to all, but create one that would rest not on grand rhetorical declarations but rather on at least some detailed costings of the exercise.

In the event, despite some disagreements and even strong clashes between individual leaders, that kind of detail could be found in the Paris summit of December 1974, which was accepted as having been both realistic and profitable in its review of and decisions on several institutional items such as direct elections to the EP, on satisfying the British demand for renegotiations by offering a 'corrective mechanism' which Harold Wilson could claim as a success but without threatening the Community in any way, and on several policy issues including a regional policy. The summit also took steps to strengthen EPC and commissioned the prime minister of Belgium, Leo Tindemans, to produce a report on European Union. Inevitably, many things remained undiscussed and several policy areas untouched; but the 1974 Paris summit set the tone for the future in its combination of reviewing general future progress in conjunction with a discussion of policy details, and in its blurring of the divide between EC-specific items, national problems, and broader questions of international politics.

In terms of the future development of the EC, undoubtedly the most important decision taken at Paris was that to regularise the practice of summitry in a European Council (a term popularised by Giscard d'Estaing). The Council would be composed of the heads of the national governments, with the President of the Commission having the right to be in attendance, and it would meet three times a year (amended in December 1985 to twice annually), that its presidency would rotate across the national capitals every six months, and that each meeting would take place in the country which currently held the presidency or in Brussels. The first meeting of the European Council would be in Dublin in March 1975. The principle of rotation emphasised that all member states were equal: it would be particularly important for the smaller states since it offered them, despite the heavy workload which presidency of the Council would involve, the opportunity to become centres of European, and even world, diplomacy once every few years.

With the establishment of the European Council, the EC acquired a central powerful body that could set new targets and lay down the guidelines for future progress, modify or abandon existing programmes, and resolve disputes between the members at the highest level. Its emergence confirmed that the EC had become, more than anything else, an intergovernmental organisation leavened by an element of supranationalism. The European Council made no collective pretence at supranationalism: what came out of it, usually after long and intense arguments derived from national interests, was compromise among those interests. The new picture was perhaps well summarised in 1981 by Margaret Thatcher when she said, 'there is no such thing as a separate Community interest; the Community interest is compounded of the national interests of the Ten member states'. Most importantly, since the European Council stood outside the Community treaties, it could not be bound by their provisions and hence could not formally be subjected to the influence of either the Commission, the EP or the European Court. Despite the aspirations that might exist in Brussels and Strasbourg, there was never any intention of seeking to adjust all members to some Community norm, but rather to seek to adjust the several national interests closer to each other in order to achieve some minimum overlap. This fitted with the primary objectives of Giscard d'Estaing and Schmidt who saw the Council as a vehicle for handling not just EC questions, but also both national problems, especially in economics, and broader EC issues of international cooperation. For a decade the European Council operated at the heart of the EC without formally being part of it. It was only with the adoption of the Single European Act of 1986 that it received legal recognition, though significantly that recognition did not entail any attempt to define its powers.

Throughout all the summit sessions since 1974 the European Council has concerned itself with a variety of topics. It has not confined itself to EC institutional or constitutional matters; discussions on the EC have not been divorced from EPC, the general economic and social situation within the member states, or broader international and monetary issues. Nevertheless, the EC has been the focal point of its deliberations and has remained its raison d'être. In many ways the success of the European Council has depended upon the degree of compatibility between French and West German interests. On Community matters, if the two states have been in accord, then generally the EC has advanced further. Nowhere was this more apparent than in the years between 1974 and 1982 when the close relationship between Giscard d'Estaing and Schmidt dominated the Council. Neither had an emotional commitment to the EC, but both regarded collaboration on Europe as the best means of maximising returns from membership for their countries. In particular, under Helmut Schmidt West Germany more obviously came of age and began to flex its muscles within the EC, reviewing proposals for policies and future developments in the light of their possible impact upon West German national interests. For Schmidt this meant two things. First, as the largest contributor to the EC budget, West Germany was resistant to any proposal that would incur additional expenditure unless it was convinced that it was impossible to reduce the cost further or was persuaded that it would benefit from the proposal. Second, it meant that West Germany had joined France in being wary of allowing the Commission to accumulate too many powers or to attempt to push the Community too far too quickly. While this more functional approach of the Giscard d'Estaing–Schmidt partnership may have been beneficial in the shorter term, it did store up problems which the European Council eventually had to wrestle with in the 1980s.

In a sense, the two leaders had few alternatives to collaboration with each other. Most of the other states were too small to be treated, as it were, as equals: prime ministers in Italy came and went; and for much of the period Britain had to be regarded as almost a provisional member of the EC. Schmidt himself put it more brutally, albeit in commenting specifically on the policy area of defence, in a newspaper interview in 1984 when he said, 'Italy is notorious for its lack of government. Britain is notorious for governments, Labour or Conservative, that think the Atlantic is narrower than the Channel. That leaves only the French and the Germans'. For Giscard d'Estaing and Schmidt, the primary value of the European Council was as a meeting place for informal exchanges of views. But because they also met each other more frequently in bilateral talks under the provisions of the 1963 Treaty of Friendship, they could not, even though they did attempt to keep their partners informed of their ideas and plans, always succeed in dispelling suspicions about an exclusive two-man club. By the end of the 1970s criticisms of their behaviour began to mount. It was perhaps Margaret Thatcher who, arriving as British premier in 1979, most directly challenged the Schmidt–Giscard d'Estaing axis in her arguments over the CAP and the British contribution to the budget. While she perhaps underestimated the value which both France and West Germany attached to their relationship, it is also correct that at times Giscard d'Estaing and Schmidt gave the impression that they regarded the Council as their private preserve. Certainly they found Mrs Thatcher's forthrightness and persistence difficult to tolerate, and seemed willing to test her resolve in a trial of strength.

The arrival of Mrs Thatcher in 1979 marked a more persistent British voice in the European Council and the EC after the relative lack of interest of the previous Labour governments. The joint departure of the European Council's two senior statesmen within the space of a few months brought to an end in 1982 a distinctive period in the operations of the Community and European Council. It was not until the mid-1980s that, with the new French President, François Mitterrand, taking the traditional lead, one can say that France and West Germany came closer together again. However, because of the personalities involved and because by 1986 the EC had grown to 12 members, the cooperation that developed between Mitterrand and Helmut Kohl of West Germany did not – and it would have been unreasonable to expect it – reach the peaks of the late 1970s. That pinnacle of consensus arose from both a specific combination of political and personal circumstances, not least of which was the close personal friendship that developed between Giscard d'Estaing and Schmidt. Nevertheless, their collaboration in the 1970s set a definite mark upon the European Council and through it upon the EC: the Franco–German understanding became central to the development of the Community, and will probably continue to be so. Under their leadership the two states, despite differences of opinion over some policies, consolidated a community of interest, the preservation of which was important for the future course of the EC.

Between 1974 and 1979 the summits, reflecting the international problems of the decade and perhaps also the personal concerns of the government leaders – especially of Giscard d'Estaing and Schmidt – concentrated more on world problems as they affected the EC. Two themes were important. First, there were international political questions and the role of EPC. Here the Council was quite successful in encouraging an intensification of a Community line on a host of issues – for example, in the 1975 Conference on

Security and Cooperation in Europe at Helsinki and the follow-up meetings. The Council was also able to develop a common line on some non–European issues such as the Middle East. Second were problems created by the international economic and monetary crisis. The most obvious fruit of these discussions was the decision at the Brussels summit of 1978 to establish a European Monetary System (EMS).

After 1980 European Council sessions turned to matters more directly pertaining to the EC: further enlargement, new policies and modification of existing policies, and institutional and procedural amendments to the EC framework. Between 1980 and 1984 the most prominent theme of debate was probably the CAP and its soaring costs. With the signing of the Single European Act the Council entered a new phase, at least insofar as its relationship with the EC institutions are concerned. Of course, these periods are purely arbitrary. The EMS has remained a subject for debate after 1979, primarily because not all member states chose to join. The CAP was inextricably intertwined with the British budgetary contribution, a topic presented at virtually all Council sessions until its resolution at the Fontainebleau summit in 1984. And the question of political union was also a theme of Council and EC discussions from the 1974 Paris summit through to the Single European Act.

Not all summits have been decisive. Indeed, James Callaghan, the British premier, could at the end of the 1977 London summit paraphrase Jean Monnet by dismissing the Council as 'strong on discussion, not so strong on decisions'. Callaghan's comment contains more than a grain of truth. Council meetings have been characterised as much by argument, and not only between Britain and the rest, as by decisive action. One difficulty with the Council has been that of implementing the policies agreed upon: there is no Council medium for following up its decisions. Another is that because ultimate authority does rest only with the government leaders, more minor or more technical problems which could be dealt with by their subordinates have been passed up to the Council for decisions which those subordinates were unwilling or unable to take themselves. This practice turned the Council almost into a court of appeal.

Such problems have imposed limits upon the effectiveness of the European Council as a decisive actor. But in a sense this has suited its members. The member governments (with the possible exception of those from Britain, especially Mrs Thatcher) have constantly been caught in the cleft stick of needing to demonstrate both their ability to defend national interests and their commitment to further European progress. Governments cannot readily abandon the national interest, if only because their own future depends upon re-election. And the more they were prepared to discuss the fine detail of further EC progress, the more they might run the risk of falling foul of entrenched national interests. Nowhere has this been more noticeable than in the field of political union where commitment to the cause has often been restricted to general declarations of support that politically were without cost. The dichotomy between rhetorical principle and the problem of practical measures and their implementation made the Council a constantly shifting body. While this gave the EC a certain flexibility, it also endowed it with some degree of incoherence: it typified the tendency whereby the important changes and decisions occurred outside the formal structure of the treaties, almost in an ad hoc manner. Nevertheless, the cumulative effect of the European Council upon the EC has been a positive one, extending the policy instruments of the Community and its institutions. With the Single European Act of 1986 the ground shifted towards a possible new relationship between the EC and the European Council. The following chapters will look at the development of common policy formulation in the EC after 1974, the problems it faced with members and prospective members, and the perennial issue of political union.

CHAPTER THIRTEEN

The Internal Policy World of the EC

It was almost inevitable that with enlargement policy development in the EC would become more difficult. The new members would have different policy concerns and look for Community action in different areas. The interest of Britain and Ireland in regional policy and the dislike of the three new members to the common fisheries policy rushed through by the Six in 1972 have already been mentioned. In the 1980s the accession of three Southern European states meant that Mediterranean products such as olive oil and citrus fruits would become a greater bone of contention, as well as raising in a more pronounced form the question of regional disparity and the issue of the redistribution of Community resources from the richer north to the poorer south.

All issues, ideas and proposals had to jostle for attention on a crowded agenda. On the one hand, national interests were strongly expressed in those Community institutions populated by government representatives. On the other, the Commission and its bureaucracy, backed by the EP, sought to keep in focus the longer term commitment to political integration, and endeavoured to achieve harmonisation and standardisation across a range of economic and social policy areas. In this interaction no member state was entirely satisfied, yet all, including those like West Germany and Britain which were net contributors, received something of value from the Community. The major problem was the seeming lack of any overall strategy or rational degree of coherence. Because of this the EC gave the impression during the 1970s of stumbling forward from suggestion to suggestion without really sitting back to contemplate a grand design. To some extent, this was due to national reluctance to consider experimentation, and to some extent to the innate conservatism of institutionalisation – an unwillingness to consider reform of the CAP in the light of experience and the other needs of the EC. In addition, the EC could not look so much to the Treaty of Rome for help in the same way as it had in the 1960s where the Treaty had provided a quite precise timetable (with details of the constitutional elements) for the first decade of development.

A further important factor which in a sense froze the EC was the Yom Kippur war and the consequent oil crisis. The member states were plunged into an economic downturn with inflationary and unemployment pressures. Many saw their balance of payments slide into deficit. Paradoxically, this both helped and hindered EC collaboration. On the one hand, all governments were obliged to introduce austerity measures to aid their ailing economies: this in turn made them look more askance at demands for further EC common policies as something which, if adopted, would inevitably require additional resourcing. On the other hand, the economic problem was international in scope, and insofar as there was a convergence of economic policy it was as a consequence of the similarity of national reactions to world economic pressures.

Given the gloomy economic background of the 1970s, as well as the fact that enlargement had made decision making more difficult, if only because it simply involved more people sitting around the table, the degree of agreement that was achieved, especially in EPC, was quite creditable. Within the EC itself the first post-enlargement period culminated in the decision in 1978 to establish a European Monetary System. After 1980 the member governments, through the European Council and the EC institutions themselves, turned their attention more intensively to the establishment of common policies and the harmonisation of existing ones. But the EC faced problems similar to those experienced by any modern state: the demands made upon its resources were almost infinite. The adoption of common policies had budgetary implications. The size of the EC budget and, for some states, of the national contributions to it were recurring themes in the 1970s and 1980s. To increase or change the budget meant first that the question of control tended to be linked to the institutional structures of the EC and the role they played or ought to play in budgetary affairs. Second, it meant that the member states would have to grapple with both the problem of monetary policy and standardisation and the burden of the Common Agricultural Policy. This interrelated set of issues, in one form or another, never left the political agenda.

FROM EMU TO EMS

A monetary policy had been a long-standing Community aim. In the balmy climate of the 1960s, however, with all economic omens looking positive, very little attention had been paid to it. As has been reviewed, the first serious moves in that direction were made towards the end of the decade. The EMU that emerged out of the Werner Report floundered in the wake of the widespread economic disruptions of the early 1970s. The attempt by the EC to improve upon the Smithsonian Agreement of 1971 with the adoption of the snake never worked effectively as a Community instrument or policy. Britain participated for only two months. Italy left in 1973 when at the same time the snake actually floated outside the tunnel, which was itself in any case almost in a state of terminal collapse. French behaviour was more erratic. France abandoned the snake in 1974; it rejoined the following year, only to leave again in 1976. To some extent the problems of EMU were due to the broad divergencies in economic performance. West Germany, with its powerful economy, insisted that the restraint of inflation must be the top priority, while other members with weaker economies, though accepting this as a vital consideration, were equally insistent that it should not involve the sacrificing of adequate growth rates. Only some EC states – West Germany, Benelux and Denmark – were to find it possible to stay within the set margins of fluctuation, and in effect the snake was soon confined to a small group of currencies, not all belonging to EC members, clustered around the pivot of the West German mark.

By the second half of the decade there was a growing disillusionment in Europe with the new floating world. While the flexibility it permitted governments might have its desirable aspects, experience of it had suggested that it encouraged overreaction to problems by governments, which in turn contained the risks of even greater fluctuations. With floating it was even more imperative for the EC to have a monetary instrument. The snake and EMI, it was felt, had attempted to impose too rigid a framework that was all too easily susceptible to fracturing under stress. The idea for a European Monetary System was first raised by the newly elected President of the Commission, Roy Jenkins, in October 1977. The argument was taken up by Helmut Schmidt who, backed by Giscard d'Estaing, placed it on the agenda of the meetings of the European Council in 1978. At Bremen in July the European Council agreed to pursue closer monetary cooperation through a European Monetary System to be set up the following year. However, the EMS was not to be the full-scale monetary union of the Werner Report. Schmidt, Jenkins and Giscard d'Estaing did not see it as primarily an instrument for political union. While the EMS could well evolve into a monetary union, it was first and foremost a means of strengthening the EC in the medium term through introducing a kind of flexible Bretton Woods system for the member states: some degree of predictable exchange rate mechanism, it was felt, was necessary to buttress the EC in the uncertain monetary world, especially *vis-à-vis* the dollar and American monetary and exchange range policy.

The EMS would provide an exchange rate mechanism linking the currencies of the member states with, as in the snake, limits on how much each currency would be permitted to fluctuate against its partners. The exchange rate mechanism (ERM) would be paralleled by the establishment of a European Currency Unit (ECU) that would stand alongside the national currencies. The ECU would be guaranteed by a European Monetary Cooperation Fund, a large reserve to which the states would contribute 20 per cent of both their gold reserves and their dollar reserves. Under the ERM element of the EMS, each country was to have a central rate against the ECU, and from this bilateral central rates would be calculated for each pair of currencies. If a currency hit the floor or ceiling of its permissible range, the central banks would have to intervene on the foreign exchange markets to keep it within its agreed range. Such intervention was designed to assist participants which ran into short-term difficulties. If these persisted over time, then the EMS rules provided for the Council of Ministers to approve a realignment of the currency within the EMS.

All of this was meant to work for three broad EC objectives: to make exchange rate adjustments less traumatic and a matter of common concern so as to reach both exchange rate stability and the level of monetary stability necessary to regenerate EC and world trade; to present a common monetary and exchange rate policy towards the rest of the world, with a European currency gradually emerging to match the American dollar as a world currency; and to pave the way for full-scale monetary union. Of these objectives, the final one scarcely left the drawing board. It was only in the late 1980s that pressure came, most importantly from the Commission under the activist Jacques Delors, for a start to be made on those building blocks, such as a single central bank and a single currency, that would be necessary for the achievement of the goal. In addition, although the ECU became established in financial markets outside the EC as well as an internal means of accounting, few deliberate efforts were consciously made to secure the second objective. In practice the EMS was primarily restricted to the first objective. It did reduce exchange rate volatility, certainly from the levels of the 1970s, and it made this a collective action. Similarly, it had some success in permitting a realignment of currencies in difficulties without the problems associated with the sudden devaluations of the past. In 1983, for example, the Council of Ministers agreed to allow France and Italy to realign their currencies in order to resolve national budget and inflation problems: the continued EMS support for the franc and lira after realignment effectively reduced the possible negative impact of further speculation against the two currencies.

The member states varied in their attitudes towards the scheme, and to some extent have continued to do so in the extent of their commitment to it. Italy and Ireland were originally nervous about joining the EMS; though they eventually did so, along with Belgium they wanted to retain the right to impose some restrictions on the free movement of private funds within the system. West Germany debarred its citizens and financial institutions from accepting deposits or liabilities in the new currency unit. Italy retained an exchange rate margin twice as wide as those of its fellow members, and later introduced a system of exchange controls. Most importantly, however, the EMS lacked a Community-wide scope. Britain had remained unconvinced of its virtues, and while allowing sterling to be part of the basket of currencies that would form the new ECU, declined to join the exchange rate mechanism. The British decision was based upon a view of sterling's role as both a petro-currency and an international investment currency. Though the justification for staying outside the ERM became less valid as the 1980s progressed, Britain remained only a partial member of the EMS. While Mrs Thatcher continued to assure her European colleagues that Britain would join the ERM when the time was appropriate, it seems difficult to conclude that it was economic factors which constituted the major reason for the British decision: political implications, especially as the EMS was believed to affect national sovereignty, were probably more important. Of the later entrants, Greece followed the British example by not accepting the exchange rate mechanism, while Portugal and Spain preferred to remain completely outside. In 1989, however, Spain reversed its position and joined the EMS.

The EMS was an important step on the road to integration. On the other hand, while it has worked satisfactorily by fostering a significant degree of cooperation among its participants, it remained perhaps less a system than a set of mechanisms for currency adjustment that were born of political compromise and economic necessity. It was less ambitious than EMU and therefore not a substitute for it. For full-scale monetary union the EC would have to consider not just a common monetary policy, but also a single currency and a central bank – two things that, were they to occur, would directly challenge national sovereignty. It was not until 1989 that the EC seriously began, with the acceptance in Madrid by the European Council of the Delors Committee report on how full monetary and economic union could be achieved, to consider moving decisively beyond the limitation of EMS.

THE BUDGET AND THE BURDEN OF THE CAP

If Europe lacked a coherent monetary policy, the same could not be said of agriculture: indeed some cynics might find it reasonable to claim that the Common Agricultural Policy, consuming some two-thirds of the EC budget, has been the Community. On the other hand, until at least the late 1980s, when the EC began to bite the bullet of reining back the CAP, most farmers would perhaps regard the policy as an outstanding success. Set in motion in 1968, the CAP quickly became a fully developed Community policy in that the vast bulk of agricultural produce was subject to the CAP regime. While it has been the subject of a great deal of satisfaction for many keen supporters of European integration, it has also been, ever since the first days, at the heart of almost every internal Community dispute – as well as being a source of contention between the EC and both traditional food exporting countries such as the United States and developing countries which have felt threatened by the EC practice of subsidising the export of its own food surpluses.

By the beginning of the 1980s the CAP had consolidated itself as a social rather than an economic policy. The restructuring element of the policy was paltry, and welfare (and electoral) considerations far outweighed any concern for a rational and efficient agricultural sector. To some extent, this may have been inspired by the changed economic world of the 1970s. It might have been reasonable in the 1960s to expect surplus agricultural manpower to be absorbed by the industrial and service sectors. With rising unemployment after 1973, this scenario became implausible, and in many ways the major aim of the CAP became the maintenance of agricultural employment. The high levels of industrial employment, peaking in the first half of the 1980s, made it appear perhaps even more grotesque. The CAP became a classic study, not only of how difficult it is, at the international level, to set priorities and allocate resources, but also of how, once decisions have been made and structures established, inertia sets in to make any reform extremely difficult.

One major problem with the CAP has been that it came to be dominated by national interests, with each state being fundamentally interested in what it could extract from the policy for itself. This alone virtually ruled out the possibility of reaching an overall balance within the CAP. Several states also were less than enthusiastic about entertaining the possibility of restructuring. France, for example, wanted the states each to retain responsibility for their own restructuring programme, while West Germany was opposed to any scheme that would involve additional costs. On the other hand, West Germany was in line with almost all the member states in not being willing to accept a transfer of CAP resources from the support programmes towards restructuring. The most vociferous, indeed almost the only, opponent of the CAP was Britain, and it was the CAP which lay at the heart of the prolonged British complaints after the mid-1970s about the budget. While Britain, especially after Mrs Thatcher's accession to power in 1979, linked its budgetary complaints and the CAP firmly together, its partners preferred to see them as separate questions.

While all states eventually came to agree upon the necessity of reform in the 1980s, none wished any reform procedure to disturb whatever benefits it was already receiving. West Germany illustrated the schizophrenic attitude of most states towards the CAP. Helmut Schmidt accepted that there was much that was wrong with the CAP, and by implication therefore also the need for reform. Yet the West German agricultural ministry contributed as much as anybody to the escalating prices and surpluses. While West Germany may have disliked the inefficiencies of the CAP, its farmers were major beneficiaries, and hence in the last resort political and electoral considerations tended to be given priority. Over and above all this, for the original Six the CAP had become an almost holy object: it had been one of their first objectives, it still remained the only complete Community policy, and criticisms about it tended to be dismissed almost as statements of heresy.

As a result the overall imbalances in the system were permitted to continue, with a consequent escalation of both the costs of the programme and the massive surplus produce it generated. The butter mountain and wine lake became symbols of the wasteful nature of the policy. The core of the problem lay with the guaranteed price system which, totally insulated from market conditions, provided a permanent stimulus for over-production, especially in dairy farming. Although milk production was less than one fifth of the EC's total agricultural output, by 1980 it was consuming more than two-fifths of CAP funds. Quite simply, the price mechanism was unselective and quite automatic. For farmers, in fact, it was a double-edged sword: while it did not encourage them to be economic, all its resources did not go to the benefit of farmers. In addition, the way in which the transfer of income to farmers was carried out tended to benefit the wealthier farmers and the richer regions of the EC.

In 1960 over 15 million people in the original Six had worked on the land. In the mid-1970s the agricultural population of the enlarged EC was only 14 million, falling to 10 million by the mid-1980s. Yet during the same period the relative position of farm incomes did not improve – indeed, there was a decline in real farm incomes. The difference was the huge administrative cost of providing storage for the surplus produce that the policy encouraged. Within the European Agricultural Guidance and Guarantee Fund (EAGGF), very little resourcing was available for the Guidance segment, which consumed less than 5 per cent of the CAP budget. And the CAP itself ate up the bulk of the revenue available to the EC. The latter's budget was not large: 0.5 per cent of Community gross domestic product in 1974, it was only 0.9 per cent by 1985. But the CAP share of the budget inexorably increased. If the amount spent on agriculture is set to one side, then what was left to be made available for other programmes was equivalent to only 1 per cent of the total spending of national governments. If the EC wished to develop a coherent economic strategy or to pursue other common programmes, then either the states would have to agree to an increased EC budget or accept the need to tackle the voracity of the CAP. The costs of the CAP rose steadily in the 1970s and with no end in sight of the ratchet effects on costs, it was the CAP which plunged the EC into a series of budget crises in the 1980s.

As we have stated, the EC budget was quite modest. By 1985 it had risen to only some 2.8 per cent of the sum of the national budgets. Yet the implication of 'own resources' was that the EC had to live off its own. It could not amass budget deficits or borrow to meet shortfalls. As the CAP remorselessly consumed more of the budget, the EC had moved by the end of the 1970s to the brink of insolvency, where it was to hover throughout much of the 1980s. Between its meeting in Luxembourg in 1980 and the 1984 sessions at Fontainebleau and Dublin, the European Council was obliged to discuss the challenge presented by the budget and the CAP. Most debates were acrimonious, with national positions being determined by national economic concerns and farm interests. Those members which were net exporting countries – Denmark, France, Ireland, the Netherlands – were hostile to proposals put forward by the net importing states of Britain and West Germany for some form of price restraint. By contrast, where suggestions were raised that might penalise the more efficient farm sectors, they were resisted by an alliance of Britain, Denmark and the Netherlands.

The problem was that EC income was in relative decline. Revenue coming from customs duties had been less year by year as the EC's external tariffs were adjusted downwards. Simultaneously, because a byproduct of CAP overproduction had been an increase in Europe's self-sufficiency in food, the yield from agricultural levies had also declined. The one remaining source of EC income was revenue from VAT contributions: that too, fixed at a ceiling of a 1 per cent rate throughout the EC, would soon be exhausted. Either the budget had to be cut or Community income had to be increased – and that could come only from raising the proportion of VAT revenue accruable to the EC. Those who supported the latter route pointed to the boost it would give not just to other EC plans and policies, but also the development of a 'real' common market which, because of the many barriers to trade that still prevailed, was almost as far away as it had been at the time of the Treaty of Rome. The opposing viewpoint was expounded vigorously and almost solely by Britain, which even indicated that it was prepared to exercise its right of veto unless the EC put its house in order, remedying Britain's own complaints about the budget and embarking upon a root and branch overhaul of the CAP.

The debate limped on for a number of years, though insolvency never actually materialised. Eventually, at the 1984 Fontainebleau summit the European Council was able to agree upon a formula for budget contributions that satisfied Britain. In return, Mrs Thatcher agreed to a raising of the VAT limit to 1.4 per cent. Earlier in the year the EC seemed to have taken an important step in curbing the CAP by imposing quota limits on the worst offender, the dairy industry, and by 1985 the call which milk products made upon the EAGGF had declined by one third. Fontainebleau also pointed in the same direction, agreeing that spending on agriculture would in future increase at a lower rate than EC expenditure as a whole, thus reducing the dominance of the CAP within the EC policy world.

The relief which greeted the Fontainebleau decisions was short-lived. Partly because of events beyond its control, such as the declining value of the dollar (which automatically entailed a rise in the cost of export subsidies), the CAP continued to plague the Community. The 1984 summit had not involved any radical restructuring of the CAP, and its demands, backed by the several influential national farm interests, continued to press hard on the EC and its budget. A year after the VAT limit was raised, the threat of insolvency returned, and shortfalls in the budget had to be met by non–refundable grants from the member states. Yet most of the states still displayed a marked reluctance to grasp the nettle of the CAP – still over–producing and still consuming some two–thirds of the budget. In 1987 the Commission put forward a package of proposals (the so–called Delors package) intended to place the EC budget on a more secure footing while providing more control over CAP spending. In the following debates on the budget Britain, for the first time, found an ally, in the shape of the Netherlands, for its argument that budget reviews must involve much more than a cosmetic tinkering with the CAP. At Brussels in 1988 the European Council eventually proved able to concur on a set of proposals based upon the Delors package. Insolvency was again averted, and in 1989 it was agreed that the budget would be further augmented by a contribution from the member states, each contribution being in proportion to the state's share of the total gross national product of the Community, up to a ceiling of 1.2 per cent of EC gross national product. Even so, in the long run the EC could well continue to find it difficult to achieve a satisfactory budgetary position without undertaking a more thorough and realistic revision of the CAP.

POLICY DEVELOPMENTS

The policy world of the EC embraced more than the CAP and the EMS. Yet few other policy sectors have received a similar amount of attention in debates as monetary policy on the same level of resourcing as the CAP. While the latter has absorbed some two–thirds of the EC budget, the next largest item of expenditure, on regional policy, has amounted to only some 6 per cent of expenditure. Nevertheless, if the EC wished seriously to pursue its long–term goals of economic integration and political union, and if the Commission wished to be taken seriously as a prototypic European government, then there was a need to develop other common policies and a greater harmonisation of existing national policy areas. This section will review briefly some of the most important of these other policy areas which have been raised within the EC.

Perhaps the most important of these other policy sectors has been regional policy. Apart from the Italian Mezzogiorno, little in the way of a regional policy had been discussed by the Six. During the process of enlargement in the early 1970s it became an important topic of debate. The European Council decision in 1974 on regional policy, despite some resistance by a West Germany worried by the potential costs, was turned into the European Regional Development Fund of 1975, whose grants to regions would normally be made on the basis of matching contributions from the member state involved. It would not, however, be the totality of regional policy. The European Investment Bank, the Social Fund and even the ECSC would have a role to play since the objectives of the regional policy were threefold: not just to give support for the development of poorer regions, but also to provide for a better coordination of national regional policies and to ensure that regional questions would be considered within the context of other EC policies.

Unfortunately, the effectiveness of regional policy and the Regional Development Fund was hindered by two problems. The first was that it was designed as a supplement to, not a replacement for, national regional policies. Coordination would always have been difficult, but this perhaps made it more so, since the Regional Policy Committee associated with the Fund would be directly confronted with entrenched national positions. The second problem, related to the first, was that the national states entered into the question as intervening variables. Each state received a quota from the Fund. In practice, this meant that while the poorer countries received the largest quotas, the funds did not necessarily go to the poorest areas of the EC. In 1977 and again in 1981 the Commission, complaining that regional policy needed to be more effective in its targeting and better resourced, produced further guidelines which were duly discussed by the European Council, but without any agreement on fundamental change.

On the other hand, in national terms it is fair to say that the policy has been quite successful. Between 1975 and 1985 some 90 per cent of development money went to only five countries: Britain, France, Greece, Ireland and Italy. In per capita terms Ireland was the major beneficiary, followed by Greece (despite the fact that it entered the EC only in 1981) and Italy; and about one half of the grants awarded from the Fund went to high priority regions – the whole of Ireland and Greece (bar the Athens area), the Italian Mezzogiorno, Northern Ireland, Greenland (which took the whole of the Danish quota), and the French overseas regions. A decisive step in regional policy reform came only in 1985, partly as a result of an evaluation of the way it had worked, and partly because of the imminent accession of Portugal and Spain. The EC and the European Council accepted the need for a more flexible policy, and agreed to eliminate the system of fixed national quotas. In its place each state was given a percentage range, with the lower figure being the minimum amount guaranteed to it from the annual European Regional Development Fund budget – assuming, of course, that the state put in bids to the EC for regional money. As part of the new look, the European Council agreed in Dublin in 1984, after strong pressure from Greece, for a more coordinated regional policy for the poorer southern areas of the Community. The following year the Council of Ministers adopted the Integrated Mediterranean Programmes, a seven-year package of projects to develop and modernise the socioeconomic structure of these regions in order to aid their integration into the broader European economy. Regional policy was finally given official EC status when it was incorporated into the Single European Act.

Unlike regional policy, the EC was committed to a social policy by the Treaty of Rome. This too, however, really only developed with enlargement. The European Social Fund, financed from the EC's own resources, was launched in 1974 as a consequence of the 1972 Paris summit decision that the EC should seek to improve the quality of life of its citizens. While the Commission has constantly striven to ensure a harmonisation of the social welfare policies of the member states, the terms of the fund were much more specific. It was to be primarily concerned with employment and retraining, especially insofar as these were needed because of the effects of other EC policies – though as unemployment worsened in the late 1970s and early 1980s the Fund assumed an importance greater perhaps than that originally envisaged. As the states began in the 1980s to come to grips with at least some of the problems of mass and structural unemployment, the EC decided to use the Social Fund for even more specific targets. In 1983 the Council of Ministers directed that the fund should have two major priorities: youth employment, and job creation in the most disadvantaged regions. At least three-quarters of grants from the Fund were to go on the training and employment of people aged under 25, channelled through schemes run by the national governments. About one half of the Fund has gone to seven regional blackspots: the whole of Greece, Ireland and Portugal, the Italian Mezzogiorno, the south of Spain as well as the province of Galicia, Northern Ireland, and the French overseas departments.

The first common fisheries policy of 1972, unlike regional and social policy, had been a complete failure, collapsing more or less immediately as an effective policy instrument. Despite stock exhaustion through overfishing, along with the new international regime of 200 mile national limits, the EC was slow to seek some new form of agreement and to react to Commission proposals first made in 1976. In self-defence it imposed its own 200 mile limit in 1977, but this did nothing to disguise the severe internal disagreement that existed within the EC. The European Council discussed a Common Fisheries Policy in some depth at Luxembourg in 1980, Maastricht in 1981, and Copenhagen in 1982. Eventually, after some bitter opposition from Denmark, agreement on a Common Fisheries Policy (CFP) was reached, with the EC committed to an annual review of resources and permissible catches, surveillance of fishing vessels, and imposing standards on the marketing of products. In general the CFP made EC waters open to all EC fishing vessels within a 200 mile limit, except in the Mediterranean and Baltic where lower limits were accepted. In addition, each member state was allowed to pursue its traditional practices of exclusion within up to 12 miles from its shoreline. Fishing was an important element in the discussions on entry with Spain, whose fleet outnumbered that of the EC of the Ten. In the end, however, Spain, along with Portugal, had to agree to adapt its fishing policies to the CFP.

Another policy area where the EC proved to be quite effective was the old ECSC responsibility of steel. Like many industries it suffered severely in the post-1973 recession as world demand slumped. Governments, concerned about unemployment, intervened to such an extent that national subsidies were soon spiralling out of control. It was only in 1977 that the Commission was able to persuade the industries to set up a voluntary cartel (EUROFER) which would seek to end the chaos through a rational programme of production cuts and minimum quota prices for virtually all steel products. EUROFER worked quite well for three years, but then fell victim to the economic dislocation caused by the second massive increase in oil prices in 1979. The Commission reacted swiftly, imposing more draconian controls on the industry: some four-fifths of all steel production was made subject to compulsory controls, with the remainder having to operate with voluntary quotas, and heavy financial penalties were introduced for transgression of the rules. The medicine was austere, but it led to a much slimmer and healthier steel industry. In 1982 the Commission attempted to speed up the process of rationalisation, aiming for a more or less complete end to state subsidies by 1985. However, the world market was still problematic, and in 1985 the EC had to agree that state subsidies should be phased out gradually over three years, a programme that again had to be extended in view of the difficulties that some steel concerns were still facing.

Steel is perhaps an exceptional case of action, since the Commission had inherited more decisive powers for itself from the ECSC than were available to it under the Treaty of Rome. It stands in strong contrast to the EC performance in other industrial sectors and in industrial policy in general. Despite the centrality which the oil crisis of 1973 gave to the energy question, the EC found it difficult to formulate an effective energy programme other than adopting a general strategy put forward by the Council of Ministers in 1974, and modified in 1980 and again in 1986, to reduce the EC's dependence upon oil imports – especially from a single source of supply. On the more general industrial front, the EC objectives were to help the older declining industries to adapt to the modern world and to invest in the development of the new technological industries. It was only in the 1980s, however, that the EC, spurred by fears of the technological lead of Japan and the United States, seriously began to urge more research and development, setting up a plethora of new agencies and committees which as yet still have to yield much fruit.

Overall, then, while there is a policy world within the EC, it is a world of uneven topology. The EC developed one fully operable policy in the CAP, but paradoxically its very success was one factor inhibiting the extensive development of common policies in other areas. And while the EC created a monetary instrument in the EMS, something that would be crucial for economic union and a common market, it was not able before 1986 to attempt to push that instrument to its logical conclusions, nor to persuade all the member states to participate fully in it. In addition, some items listed in the Treaty of Rome still remained unfulfilled by the late 1980s. Perhaps the most striking example is transport, a policy area which as much as anything else was fundamental to the dream of a common market. The EC and the Commission focused most of their attention upon road transport where they found well-entrenched national systems of regulations and specifications which effectively prohibited any easy development of a common policy. During the 1980s it began in earnest to deal with these discriminatory regulations, against some considerable national resistance, but it was clear that the road ahead would be long and tortuous. By contrast, until the EC took its dramatic step in 1986 to finalise an internal market by 1992, it had barely considered sea transport: a Council of Ministers agreement on a common shipping policy was reached only in 1986. Air transport proved equally difficult, bound as it was by a world network of intergovernmental agreements. A possible breakthrough did occur in 1986 when the European Court ruled that air transport (including which carriers could serve which routes, and fare levels) was subject to the EC's general competition policy, though it would undoubtedly take time for the EC to erode national influence in this area. Transport policy was indicative of how far the EC still had to go in the world of common policies, the difficulties it faced, and the degree of commitment and harmony displayed by national governments. The EC had had some partial successes, but it also had had some failures. The goal of economic integration was still a distant one.

CHAPTER FOURTEEN
Problems of Territorial Assimilation

By the mid-1980s the Community had grown from 6 to 12 members. Following in the 1973 footsteps of Britain, Denmark and Ireland, Greece became a member in 1981 and Portugal and Spain in 1986. The applications from the three southern European states and their acceptance by the EC had been occasioned by revolutionary political change within each country. With the exception of the difficult case of Turkey, which also had expressed a desire to join the Community, it seemed in 1986 that the EC had, for the foreseeable future, expanded to its territorial limit. The remaining West European states, with the possible exception of Austria, appeared to be quite content with their involvement in EFTA, with the question of EC membership being either not seriously entertained or firmly rejected as an option. Further east, the countries of Eastern Europe were still firmly within the Soviet orbit and under Soviet tutelage. The suppression of the free trade union movement, Solidarity, in Poland in 1981, though carried out by the Polish army and not Soviet intervention, seemed to follow the pattern of events in East Germany in 1953, Hungary in 1956, and Czechoslovakia in 1968. There was to be no unravelling of the Soviet Union's defensive structure, ideological hegemony and economic direction in Eastern Europe. Few, if any, at the time could have forecast the dramatic events of 1989 as one by one the Communist regimes of the east fell within the space of a few weeks.

At any rate, 1986 seemed to mark an end to the enlargement of the EC, and one factor that could distract the EC from the business of further integration appeared to have been eliminated. Yet the sequences of enlargement had not been easy. As we have seen, it took 12 years for the first expansion to be completed. Even without de Gaulle, the process of further enlargement still proved to be awkward and protracted: six years in the case of Greece, and nine years for Spain and Portugal. Admittedly, not all of the delay could be laid at the EC's doorstep. Nevertheless, the time taken did, to a certain extent, reflect the difficulties and worries expressed about the effect of enlargement upon a going concern, and also about the EC taking on board, in the second round of applications, three states with a rather different kind of economy and without a strong tradition – or indeed any kind of tradition – of democratic government. To that extent it is valuable to look at the progress of the negotiations with Greece, Spain and Portugal. If the first enlargement was any kind of guide, then the worries were, in many ways, justified. It was simply inevitable that new members would be less European-orientated, less familiar with and less prepared to tolerate the, at times, byzantine mode of operations of the Community. In that sense they might also be expected to be less attuned to the need to accept a certain loss of national independence with its implied diminution of national prestige and government authority.

The tone had been set by Britain which, from the decision of Harold Wilson's 1974 Labour government to seek renegotiation of the terms of entry through to Mrs Thatcher's battles over the budget, seemed to dominate Community headlines. Yet the British position was only a symptom of a more general problem. Quite apart from the substance of its complaints, Britain acquired notoriety mainly perhaps because of its size: it was a country that was, as it were, too important to be ignored. In a more quiet, yet equally persistent, way, Denmark also attempted to assert a distinctive position for itself. With very weak coalition governments and a parliament which, wary of European developments, had been able effectively to secure full control of European policy decisions, if what Denmark wished to establish as the modus operandi of the EC had been successful and adopted as a general principle, the character of the Community would have been changed radically. After 1981 Greece followed the British precedent. Immediately after entry, the new Socialist premier, Andreas Papandreou, submitted a demand that the terms of accession, approved by his Conservative predecessor, be renegotiated. What he was, in effect, presenting to the EC was a shopping list of further concessions and financial aid to Greece. In the years after accession Greece continued on occasions to pursue an idiosyncratic line.

This chapter will look briefly at the accession negotiations of the EC with the three southern states as well as reviewing its arguments with Britain. The British dispute was in many ways far more important than any complaint that might be raised by another entrant in that it struck at the heart of the EC operation – its budget and the CAP. Even so, despite the travails, the new members or at least their governments, including those of Britain (even perhaps the 1974 Labour government) did not seriously seem to entertain the option of leaving the EC. Moreover, the longer the new members stayed in, the more difficult it would be to consider withdrawal as a possibility. Hence, while the EC might remain relatively unpopular in countries such as Denmark and Britain, being conveniently placed to be blamed as the scapegoat for all national ills and the ultimate symbol of bureaucratic triviality and intrusion, and while political parties in opposition could seek to utilise the disillusionment for their own advantage, the possibility that governments would terminate membership steadily became a more remote prospect. However, the EC did suffer one departure, its first 'failure' since its rejection by Norway in 1972.

THE DEPARTURE OF GREENLAND

Greenland, a Danish colony since 1721, had been incorporated into Denmark as an integral part of the state in 1953. As part of Denmark, the huge island, remote from Europe and sparsely populated, automatically became part of the EC in 1973, even though in the referendum of the previous year, membership had been opposed by some 70 per cent of the Greenland electorate. In 1978 Denmark accepted, after years of agitation, the possibility of home rule for Greenland, a proposal which was endorsed by a consultative referendum in January 1979. Under the consequent legislation, Greenland was given full autonomy over its own affairs except in foreign, defence and monetary policy, and provision was made for the island, if it wished, to leave the Community – possibly to seek a relationship with the EC similar to that enjoyed by the Faroe Islands, another Danish territory but one which had possessed internal autonomy since 1948. The Faroes had rejected the offer of EC membership and under the 1973 Treaty of Accession were linked to the EC only in its free trade arrangements.

Elections in April 1979 gave a majority in the new Greenland assembly to the anti-EC forces. However, it took a further two years of campaigning by the new government to persuade Denmark in August 1981 to hold a referendum in Greenland on the issue of withdrawal. Denmark's resistance was based on the arguments that gaining independent control over fishing, Greenland's major industry, might not be sufficient to offset the financial losses that might be incurred by withdrawal, that the loss of EC aid might not be compensated by the granting of external associate status to the island, and that it should not be assumed that Denmark would automatically cover Greenland for the loss of this aid. Perhaps it was because of these arguments that in the referendum of February 1982 the huge anti-EC vote of 1972 was pared down to a bare majority of 52 per cent. Nevertheless, the Greenland government took the view that a verdict had been delivered, that withdrawal had been endorsed by the electorate.

In May 1982 Denmark had proposed to the Council of Ministers that the relevant treaties should be revised, and that in the event of withdrawal Greenland should be granted Overseas Country and Territory (OCT) status, in which it was supported by the Commission. OCT status would be extremely favourable to Greenland, in effect involving very little change in its relationship with the EC other than institutional adjustments. However, the proposals met with resistance in the Council of Ministers during the course of 1982: the other states, and particularly West Germany, were concerned about the effect of withdrawal upon fishing interests. What they did not wish to see was the adoption by Greenland of a line similar to that of the Faroes, whose fishing agreements were negotiated outside the Common Fisheries Policy which the EC had eventually managed to construct. It was, however, accepted by the Council that negotiations should be completed by March 1984 so as to allow Greenland to leave the EC by January 1985. It took the whole of this timetable before agreement on the final terms was reached by the Council of Ministers in February 1985. The agreement conceded OCT status to Greenland, giving its fisheries products duty free access to EC markets. In addition, there was to be a 10-year fisheries agreement with the possibility of automatic renewal thereafter at six-yearly intervals. In February 1985 Greenland formally left the EC, the first contraction of Community territory. The lengthy negotiations over withdrawal for what was a remote and small population, albeit one which was important to the fishing industries of the EC, were indicative perhaps of the difficulties that would be encountered were any of the member states to contemplate withdrawal.

BRITAIN AND THE BUDGET

Although Britain had not joined in the movement towards European integration in the 1950s, the European debate had nevertheless revolved around the British position to a considerable extent. Once Harold Macmillan had reversed British policy in 1961, it again returned as a central theme. The view that had coalesced in the 1950s, and one reiterated by de Gaulle a decade later, that Britain was a European maverick seemed to be confirmed after the Community's enlargement in 1973. For the next decade at least Britain was to be the problem child of the EC.

The terms of entry had been negotiated by the strongly European Edward Heath in the face of a growing popular rejection of the Community. The Labour Party had also rejected the terms, if not the principle, of entry, promising that a future Labour government would not only demand renegotiation of the terms, but would also – a revolutionary step for British politics – if the renegotiations proved successful, test the public mood through a referendum on whether Britain should remain in the EC. Two months after Labour returned to power the foreign minister, James Callaghan, launched the attack in April 1974, criticising the CAP, the plans for EMU, and the British contribution to the budget – in short, pulling back completely from the concept of European Union announced at the 1972 summit. Although irritated by the demand for renegotiation, Britain's partners conceded the point, and discussions between the two sides began later in the year on the series of demands and conditions which Britain had placed before the Council of Ministers. In January 1975 the Commission put forward proposals that proved to be acceptable to the British government: at any rate the prime minister, Harold Wilson, could tell the House of Commons in March that 'we had now taken our discussions within the Community on renegotiation as far as they could go', and that the government would arrange a referendum on continuing membership, to be held in June. On what was perhaps the core British complaint, its budget contribution, the Council of Ministers had accepted that British financial contributions would be related to the relative value of gross national product in the Community, with a clawback if the contributions exceeded a certain level. This corrective mechanism, designed to prevent excessive British payments into the budget, was to prove ineffective. For the moment, however, Britain seemed appeased: with all party leaderships urging acceptance, the subsequent referendum provided a comfortable majority in favour of continued membership.

That, however, was not the end of the matter – and not only because the Labour Party, from the grass roots right up to Cabinet level, remained badly divided on the question of Europe, with a vocal minority resolutely hostile to membership. In the new gloomy economic climate, the EC was to be an easy scapegoat blamed by large sections of the British population for at least some of the country's economic ills. It is true that the picture had changed dramatically from the pre-entry assumptions that Britain would derive concrete benefits from the EC, especially, as one of the poorer members, from the projected Regional Development Fund, something for which Heath had been a passionate advocate. That optimism had been dashed in part by the 1973 economic crisis. Events had placed pressure upon West Germany which, as the major paymaster of the EC, was reluctant to go along with an expansionist regional development programme until the issue of EMU was settled. In addition, West Germany, among others, was unhappy about what was widely seen as Britain's nationalist oil policy.

Although opposition to membership from within its own ranks made life difficult for the Labour government, it consistently adopted a negative stance over a whole range of EC activities. In particular, many in the EC found it difficult to understand how some British ministers, for example John Silkin and Tony Benn, could simultaneously attend meetings of the Council of Ministers in Brussels and continue to conduct a vociferous anti-EC campaign. While the Wilson government, like its successors, was able to receive sustenance in its arguments in Brussels over financial issues from popular disenchantment with the EC, arguments which were to continue until at least 1984, it was a reluctant European participant. In not actively arguing the case for developing EC policies, for example in regional aid and energy, that might offset Britain's budget position, it was very much an unwilling partner, giving Britain the worst possible start as a participant in the EC.

On the other hand, there were perhaps grounds for complaint. The essence of the British dispute with the EC was the perception by Britain that, though the fact that it was one of the poorer members of the Community had been conceded by its partners, it bore an unfair share of the EC budget. During James Callaghan's spell as Labour prime minister between 1975 and 1979 attitudes hardened as the prospect loomed of Britain becoming an even greater contributor, despite the 1975 agreement, once the transitional period of adjustment to the EC was completed in 1980. This led to the second part of the British case, that the return it received from the EC was inadequate, the reason being that as an important importer of food on the one hand Britain had to pay into the EC a large amount of import levies, while on the other hand, as a relatively small food producer, it received less than what it considered its due under the CAP.

The roots of the dispute lay in the 1970 EC decision to have its own resources. Since the CAP was by far and away the most expensive expenditure item, the 'own resources' had always been essentially a way of funding the CAP. It was in this way that the two British complaints were interrelated. Britain argued that its budget contribution was too great compared to what it received under the CAP compensatory system. The resentment was all the greater because the outcome affected, as we have seen, one of the weaker members of the EC. Only part of the British argument was correct. In terms of its gross national product, and in comparison with the overall pattern of payments by the member states, the British contribution was not excessively out of line. The real problem was not what Britain paid, but what it received in return through the CAP which dominated EC expenditure. It was the gap between payment and receipt that produced a conviction in Britain that it was being discriminated against.

The question of adjusting the budget mechanism, first raised by the Labour government during the renegotiations of 1975, rumbled on acrimoniously throughout the 1970s. The 1975 agreement soon proved to be ineffective, partly because the particular conditions necessary for triggering the mechanism did not occur, and partly because Britain shifted its ground somewhat to argue that the difficulties arose less from the gross British share of EC resources and more from the negative difference between its contribution and receipt of expenditure. By 1978 the Labour government had moved on from arguing for a reduction in the scale of the British contribution, something which had fitted with its more minimalist view of EC participation, to a threefold strategy. It insisted that there must be an immediate reduction of the net British contribution pending an agreement first to reform the pattern of EC expenditure more in Britain's favour, and second to put strict limits on the costs of the CAP.

The issue did not disappear with the election victory of the more pro-European Conservatives in 1979. Instead, it became an even more dominating problem. Margaret Thatcher made it clear that she was not interested in any kind of token or cosmetic agreement, bluntly informing the European Council in Dublin in 1979 'I want my money back'. Under the Conservative government the British approach therefore concentrated upon the returns that the country received from the EC. After 1979 European Council meetings were plagued by confrontation on the British demand for a more just return on what Mrs Thatcher insisted on calling 'our money'. The arguments raged on until 1984; it was almost the only item certain to be on the agenda of the European Council. The EC also re-emerged as an issue in British politics as the Labour party lurched to the left after its 1979 defeat and, inter alia, called for British withdrawal, a position it was not formally to reverse until after its third successive electoral defeat in 1987. Mrs Thatcher's phraseology annoyed many in the EC. It was particularly rejected by France which held the view that the 'own resources' belonged to the EC as of right: the member states were merely collecting agencies acting on behalf of the EC.

When Mrs Thatcher raised the issue again in 1980, the European Council eventually agreed in May to an interim rebate formula that would limit the British contribution up to 1983. The Council of Ministers constructed a package for application during the coming year, and promised a further agreement for the medium term. This was not entirely satisfactory for Britain, but it did mark a concession by the other eight members. Matters became further complicated the following year when Helmut Schmidt declared that he wished limits to be placed upon the West German contribution. The strongest attempt to cut the knot was perhaps made by the Commission in 1981, with the suggestion that net beneficiary countries should return some of their receipts for redistribution to Britain. West Germany and France, however, were insistent that rebates, if any, should come from the EC budget and not be paid directly by other members. It might be regarded as a first British penetration of its opponents' armour. In 1982 the principle of a British rebate was conceded: the rebate would be linked to the difference between the British share of the EC's gross national product and the proportionate value of its share of the budget. This, however, was not enough for Britain. The acrimony became more bitter and the voices more strident. Yet despite all the pressure and her isolation within the European Council, Mrs Thatcher remained unmoved. She continued to insist upon a better deal, linked to a curb on what she regarded as the profligacies of the CAP, something strongly resented by many members. Denmark, France and Ireland in particular rejected any idea of placing a ceiling on agricultural expenditure.

The long-simmering row eventually erupted in May 1982. The issue was a new farm settlement of target food prices that was being drawn up by the Council of Ministers. After agreeing to each of the elements in the discussions, Britain exercised a veto on the overall package, invoking a vital national interest. The move was a transparent tactical action designed to pressure the other nine in the concurrent negotiations on budget contributions. In exasperation, the other Council members set aside the Luxembourg Compromise of

1966, refusing to accept the veto on the grounds that fixing the level of CAP prices was a matter of regular Council business that could be decided by a qualified majority vote. Despite the angry words, the shock of what had happened forced the two sides to withdraw somewhat from the brink. The British reaction was muted and philosophical, possibly in part because of its need for EC support for its Falklands policy. For the other side, the foreign ministers hurriedly agreed in principle a temporary financial compensation to Britain for the current year, with the additional costs being borne by West Germany. In addition, Britain was promised a review for subsequent years within a few months.

Finally, at the Fontainebleau summit of 1984 a long–term annual corrective mechanism for a budget rebate for Britain was accepted and immediately implemented. Much of the credit for the resolution of the long–running saga must go to President François Mitterrand of France. To some extent, his moves were determined by self-interest. By 1983 France had come to believe that it was moving towards a net deficit position, and that unless the rules were changed French costs would rise substantially after the impending admission of Spain and Portugal into the EC. Britain had found an important ally, as France began to argue that the budgetary issue needed to be resolved in a way that limited the problems of those countries which were in deficit under the current rules. In addition, the presidency of the European Council had passed to France for the first half of 1984, and Mitterrand wished to stamp his presidency with some effective action. This was the background to why the British issue, along with other problems of long standing such as the applications from Spain and Portugal, was satisfactorily resolved at Fontainebleau. Under the terms of the settlement, Britain would receive an annual rebate based upon 66 per cent of the difference between its VAT contributions and its share of EC expenditure. In return, Mrs Thatcher agreed to a rise in the level of VAT contributions to the EC.

In terms of the effort and time which Britain devoted to its budget grievances, it is questionable whether the cost was worth it. Certainly the 1984 settlement was widely regarded as a British victory, which it undoubtedly was in terms of the concessions made by either side. On the other hand, it did little to lessen the negative image of Britain that prevailed in much of the Community. Moreover, Britain had known before entry that a deficit of this order was probable; in terms of total British expenditure, the amount of money involved was not very great; and British farmers did receive some benefits from the CAP. It is a moot point whether the gains compensated for the forfeiture of a great deal of goodwill through its aggressive diplomacy, especially under Mrs Thatcher. Britain failed to appreciate, or chose to ignore, the great significance which most of the other states, especially France, attached to the CAP. The programme was regarded by France as the major economic benefit it derived from Europe, and had been a major French policy objective since the early 1960s. West Germany, the major EC paymaster, was the other key actor that Britain had to win over. West Germany was willing to consider some adjustments, but on the other hand, it was annoyed by the British position on the EMS, while governments in Bonn were not willing to sacrifice the Franco–German relationship.

Within the other member states there was perhaps a lack of appreciation of the British mood: the British public was cynical about, even fearful of, the EC, and the British economy was much weaker than that of most of its partners. To stand up to the EC may have been for Margaret Thatcher a further tactic for the regeneration of British pride. At a more individual level, the possibility of a satisfactory settlement was also hindered by the clash of personalities involved. Given their leading roles within the European Council, Schmidt and Giscard d'Estaing could have been more positive towards Britain, especially with the return to government of the Conservatives in 1979. Instead, it was clear at the first European Council meeting attended by Mrs Thatcher in November 1979 that they were not willing to compromise at all. In turn, Mrs Thatcher was perhaps irked by what she saw as the dismissive and patronising treatment of her by the two senior European leaders, something which only made her more determined not to give ground.

While on one level the British issue may have been rather trivial, on another it was very important since the budget question was inextricably bound up with the CAP. The Common Agricultural Policy had become, if one mixes metaphors, both white elephant and sacred cow. Despite its cost and relative inefficiency, it was one of the few concrete symbols of what the EC had achieved. As such the commitment to it among the original members and the Commission was very high, as it was to the need to fund it even though it threatened EC solvency throughout the 1980s. A more common critique of Britain was that its argument was merely utilitarian and concerned only with national interest. That was a reasonable point: certainly the terms upon which entry had been sold to the British electorate were highly utilitarian. Though in the longer run it may have been the weakness of its industries which prevented Britain from taking a fuller advantage of membership, British governments would still have to be seen to be securing something from the EC. On the other hand, Mrs Thatcher was right about the imbalance in the budget and without her the CAP may not have had a stricter regime imposed upon it in the 1980s.

In pursuing such a policy, Britain was not in fact behaving very differently from other member states. Utilitarianism had always been a prominent characteristic of the EC. It had always been a necessary element of French policy and of French conflicts with other members, such as the 1975–1976 wine war with Italy when, in response to a wine surplus and protests from its own farmers about wine imports from Italy, France closed its frontier to Italian wine, later switching to adopting an additional tax upon it: both moves violated EC rules. Under Helmut Schmidt, West Germany also adopted a protectionist stance in many areas, while Denmark consistently pursued a minimalist and self-interested policy towards the EC. In 1984 the prime minister of Ireland, Garret Fitzgerald, walked out of the European Council in protest against a decision on milk quotas that would adversely affect Ireland. In short, governments have to combine cooperation within the EC with fighting for their own national corner – and must be seen to be doing so.

Britain's reputation as a maverick may have been due in part to the fact that governments in London, unlike many of their partners, rarely chose to cloak national self-interest with the rhetoric of outright commitment to full union. Second, it may have arisen from the not altogether concealed suspicion, even hostility, which the Labour governments of Harold Wilson and James Callaghan displayed towards Europe in the 1970s. Finally, there was the personality of Mrs Thatcher, the issues on which she chose to fight, and her earthy scepticism of ambitious political plans. Perhaps the essential point is that Britain was too important to be ignored or to be simply dismissed as a 'new boy'. This last point is a major distinction between Britain on the one hand, and France, West Germany and Italy on the other. That each member state was tempted towards utilitarian attitudes, protecting national interests and refusing to concede true sovereignty, is corroborated by evidence from the one area where a Community viewpoint prevails. Every member state has been subjected to investigation by the Commission and the European Court for infringement of EC regulations. All have been found wanting on numerous occasions, yet Britain has never been the worst offender: that 'honour' has gone to the leading 'pro-European' protagonists of France and Italy. At any rate, with the Fontainebleu settlement, the EC could hope that its problem child would be content, that the British issue had been finally resolved, and that attention could be focused, without risk of distraction, upon future developments, one of which was the further enlargement of the Community.

THE SOUTHERN ENLARGEMENT

Throughout the postwar period three non-Communist countries had remained on the periphery of, even outside, the mainstream of West European politics. The two Iberian states of Spain and Portugal and, to a lesser extent, Greece all seemed to stand apart from the commitment to liberal democracy and the evolving patterns of international cooperation. Admittedly, Portugal was a founder member of NATO and EFTA, while Greece joined NATO in 1952 and became associated with the EC in 1962. Even Spain eventually joined OECD and GATT in 1960. While all three were therefore linked in some way to the rest of the continent, these ties were insufficient to deny their peripherality, in Spain and Portugal because of their long-standing authoritarian dictatorships. Greece was in a rather different situation: at least until 1967 its political system had been semi-democratic, though political competition historically had tended to revolve much more around personalities than durable political parties and programmes, with the left and the right denying each other legitimacy. In 1967 the frail democratic system finally collapsed with a military coup. For the next seven years a military junta pursued a particularly brutal form of oppression. Yet, remarkably, within months of each other, these three authoritarian regimes disintegrated in the mid-1970s. The first regime change occurred in Portugal with the revolution of April 1974. Three months later, the military regime in Greece collapsed almost without a whimper. Finally, the death of Francisco Franco in November 1975 effectively brought to an end a long frozen period of modern Spanish history. The new regimes were to be democratic, and all three declared a desire to join the EC.

The 1962 agreement between Greece and the EEC was in practice suspended during the lifespan of the military government. In November 1974 the new civilian premier, Konstantinos Karamanlis of the liberal-conservative New Democracy party, indicated to Brussels that Greece would shortly be applying for full EC membership, with provisions rather like those granted in the first enlargement for both a transitional period of adjustment and special arrangements. The Association Agreement was immediately restored and Greece formally applied for full EC membership in June 1975. Surprisingly perhaps, the Commission's reception of the application was rather wary: given the economic problems which membership would entail for both Greece and the EC, the Commission suggested that there should be an indefinite pre-accession transition period during which the necessary economic reforms could be implemented. In February 1976, however, this cautious approach was rejected by the Council of Ministers, which decided that negotiations on admission should begin immediately.

The negotiations overlapped with the opening of talks with Spain and Portugal, raised once again the question of the EC's relationship with Turkey, and meant that the EC would have to consider very carefully the balance between northern and southern European economies. Greece, however, successfully argued that its application should not be linked to these other questions, and negotiations continued to maintain a strong momentum in order to meet the decision by the EC foreign ministers that the process should be completed by the end of 1978. The Treaty of Accession was finally signed in Athens in May 1979, with entry to the EC scheduled for January 1981. Greece would be granted a five-year transitional period, with an additional two years for the elimination of tariffs on some agricultural products and for the full implementation of free movement of labour.

The Greek application proceeded quite smoothly. One reason was the anxiety of Karamanlis and his government to obtain EC membership as an additional bulwark for the fledgling Greek democracy. Consequently Greece did not take a very strong line in the negotiations: Karamanlis took the view that membership would subsequently give it a much stronger bargaining position. For its part, the EC was concerned about the anti-EC and rather anti-western stance of the opposition PASOK Socialist party and the instability that might ensue from a PASOK electoral victory. To some extent these fears appeared to be justified. PASOK strongly, though unsuccessfully, opposed the ratification of the Accession Treaty. And when the party won the expected victory in the October 1981 election, the new government of Andreas Papandreou immediately launched a sustained attack on the terms of entry, demanding renegotiation and further concessions. Otherwise, he said, Greece 'would not hesitate to adopt the measures necessary to protect the workers and the producers and to develop goals independent of Community obligations'. It is a moot question how far Papandreou was prepared to push his arguments: certainly, he did not pursue his threat of a referendum on Greece's continuation as a EC member. On the other hand, his stance was perhaps instrumental in winning in 1983 a package of proposals from the Commission to cope with 'the special economic and social problems faced by Greece and the difficulties which these create in the process of integrating Greece into the European Communities'. Greece's aims were to a considerable extent met by the Integrated Mediterranean Programmes outlined at the European Council meeting in Brussels in March 1985. Greece had insisted that only if this package was endorsed would it approve the entry into the EC of Spain and Portugal, whose nego-tiations with the Community had only recently been completed.

The EC's problems with Greece came after entry rather than during the negotiations. By contrast, the negotiations with Spain and Portugal, though occupying only slightly more time than those with Greece, proved to be more difficult. On the one hand, these two applicants were not so prepared as Greece to concede their position in the negotiations. On the other, their applications, especially that of Spain with its large population, generated some not inconsiderable opposition within the EC. Two issues seem to have been particularly important. One was the fisheries question. Spain had a giant fishing fleet almost equal in size to that of the whole Community, and this posed a severe threat to EC states still struggling to come to terms with the fisheries problems of the past decade. The other important issue was agriculture, where Iberian Mediterranean production would pose a particular threat to that in France and Italy. Certainly, France under Giscard d'Estaing showed little urgency to resolve the issue, and its stance did slow down, though not wreck, the negotiations.

Spain had asked the EEC to consider associate status, as a step towards full membership at an unspecified date, in 1962. A drawn-out series of talks which began in 1964 eventually resulted in a preferential trade agreement in 1970. Because of Spain's lack of democratic creden-tials, the EC was unwilling to go any further. With the enlargement of the EC, plans were drawn up to renegotiate the agreement. In 1975, however, the EC broke off the discussions in protest at the trial and execution of five men accused of murdering policemen and civil guards. It was not until January 1976, two months after the death of Franco, that the EC foreign ministers agreed in principle to a resumption of the trade negotiations. Events then speeded up. After the election of 1977, the first in Spain for over forty years, the prime minister, Adolfo Suárez, announced Spain's application for full EC membership. During the course of the next year, Spain's application, along with that from Portugal, created dissent within the EC. Britain led those countries which argued for an extension of the Community from nine to twelve members, whereas in France and Italy there was substantial opposition to accepting the two Iberian states because of the adverse effect this would have on their own agricultural sectors. Because of this opposition, formal negotiations with Spain did not begin in earnest until the autumn of 1979. In the meantime, Spain had by December 1978 successfully concluded a free trade agreement with EFTA, the first multilateral agreement that body had signed with a non-member state.

When the two sides had eventually agreed to begin formal negotiations, it had been hoped that Spain and Portugal could enter the EC by the beginning of 1983. This hope was dashed by Giscard d'Estaing who in June 1980 suggested that any further enlargement should be postponed until the EC had resolved problems that still hung over from the first round: he said, 'it is necessary that the Community should give priority to completing the first enlargement before it can be in a position to undertake a second'. His remarks clearly referred to the arguments raging between Britain and its partners over the former's contribution to the budget and the May 1980 agreement to introduce a revised budgetary system for 1982. In addition, there is little doubt that worries about what might happen to French agriculture also lay behind the speech. Giscard d'Estaing's statement angered both Spain and Portugal and the other EC states, although his fellow *éminence grise* on the European Council, Helmut Schmidt, seemed to accept some of the logic of the French argument, saying that 'without the indispensable adjustments to its agricultural policy and without a more balanced distribution of burdens, the Community cannot finance the tasks which face it in its expansion southwards'.

The next few months witnessed a flurry of diplomatic exchanges and activity between the capitals of Western Europe, but not to much avail. In the light of the French position, the Council of Ministers in July did not endorse the Commission proposal of January 1983 as the official entry date, merely promising 'uninterrupted negotiations' for entry 'as soon as possible'. An attempted military coup in Madrid in February 1981 had, however, given rather more urgency to the problem of Spain, as there were few dissenters from the view that EC membership would strengthen the young Spanish democracy. Despite continuing favourable comments from the European Council and the Commission, and despite continuing diplomatic activity, any acceleration of negotiations in 1982 and 1983 ran foul of internal EC problems, most particularly the long-running sagas of budgetary contributions and discipline and soaring agricultural spending. Satisfactory progress with Spain and Portugal simply had to wait upon the EC putting its own house in order. Towards the end of 1983 the new Socialist premier of Spain, Felipe González, felt obliged to write to each government leader in the EC to ask where he or she stood on the question of Spain's membership. Behind González's action lay not only the frustration of the past few years, but also an increasing resentment and anti-EC mood among the Spanish electorate.

Even so, some progress had been made. By 1984 only three, admittedly very large, issues remained outstanding: agriculture, fisheries and the reduction of trade barriers for Spanish industrial goods. During the first six months of 1984 the presidency of the European Council was held by France. President Mitterrand sought to use this term of office to speed up negotiations. The Fontainebleau summit saw not only a seeming resolution of Britain's problems, but also a hopeful end to the Spanish and Portuguese negotiations. A deadline of September 1984 was set for the conclusion of negotiations along with, for the first time, the setting of an official date, January 1986, for formal accession. Agriculture and fisheries still proved to be thorny problems, with both sides vigorously defending their own corner. A final agreement on agriculture was not reached until February 1985, although under insistence from Greece any agreement was made conditional upon the establishment by the EC of a general Mediterranean policy; one month later the two sides agreed on the fisheries issue.

Like Spain, Portugal had had no prospect of joining the EC as long as it remained an authoritarian dictatorship, although it had been a founder member of EFTA. The first approach to the EC, which did not however specify the kind of relationship desired by Portugal, came in the wake of Britain's 1961 application. By the time of de Gaulle's 1963 veto the two sides had only got as far as agreeing upon a planned schedule of talks: these were abandoned with de Gaulle's decision. Discussions were only resumed after the 1969 Hague summit when the EC agreed to talks with the non-applicant EFTA states, including Portugal, with a Special Relations Agreement being signed in July 1972.

The total collapse of the authoritarian regime in April 1974 brought with it a wish for a closer relationship with the EC. However, the continuing political turmoil of the next two years, which at times seemed to be on the verge of sinking into anarchy, meant that no progress was possible on the EC front. With the slow return of political stability, Portugal formally applied for full membership in March 1977, four months before Spain. Portugal's position was less problematic than Spain's. One factor was the concern in the rest of Western Europe about the possibility of a Communist coup in 1975. This is one reason why the EC, in advance of the completion of the negotiations, was willing to advance substantial pre-accession aid to Portugal in 1980. A further reason for the less problematic nature of the Portuguese application was, paradoxically, the backwardness of the country. While this meant that Portugal would require substantial help from the EC, it also meant that, because of its small size, it would not constitute much of a threat to the economies of the other members. Even so, the negotiations dragged on for several years, not being concluded until 1985. The lack of progress was to some extent due to differences of opinion between the two sides on a few issues; more important, however, it was Portugal's misfortune to see its negotiations occur in parallel with those between the EC and Spain. The delay in Portugal being accepted as a full member of the EC was ultimately due to the difficulties in achieving a satisfactory resolution of Spain's application.

By 1985, however, the negotiations with both states had been completed, and were accepted by the European Council in March; the Treaty of Accession was signed in June, and in January 1986 Spain and Portugal formally became members of the EC. The new president of the Commission, Jacques Delors, could state, 'All the family quarrels have been sorted out. The family is now going to grow and we can think of the future.' His optimism was endorsed by Mitterrand who said that the next European Council meeting would be 'considering what Europe will become'. But that had been a theme of European meetings for the past two decades.

CHAPTER FIFTEEN

The Search for Political Integration

The essential political objective of the Treaty of Rome had been spelled out in its preamble: to achieve 'an ever closer union among the European peoples'. Earlier chapters have traced how during the first decade of operation progress on this political front was limited and painful, with de Gaulle and the issue of enlargement as stumbling blocks. It was the Hague summit of 1969 which prepared the ground for further advances, with its momentum and enthusiasm carrying through to the Paris summit of 1972. By the time of enlargement the EC had, through its adoption of the Davignon Report, accepted a framework for European Political Cooperation that was to bear some immediate results. As for political movement on the domestic front, the capstone of progress was to be EMU, with the commitment by the member states to a transformation of 'the whole complex of their relations into a European Union before the end of the present decade'.

Despite the rhetoric, there was little indication of how economic cooperation would transform itself into political union. The overarching concept of political union remained undefined, sufficiently vague to be acceptable to all the member states without presenting a threat to any. As we have seen, the 1970s proved to be difficult years for the EC. In particular, the EMU structure quickly unravelled; its replacement by the EMS in 1979 did not by itself necessarily advance the political cause. Nevertheless, the EC persisted with the notion of political unity. On the international stage the EC steadily grew in stature as an important actor both in terms of its formal relationships with other states and through EPC, both activities benefiting greatly from the involvement in this aspect of EC affairs of the national government leaders through the European Council. Progress in terms of the political unification of the EC was to be more hesitant, if not almost non-existent. Yet the EC states had committed themselves to an ultimate union where the several threads of the past and the members' hopes for the future were to be interwoven into a seamless garment. In terms of the various forays which the EC was to make after 1973 into the field of political union, one can almost talk of them as forming a quest for a holy grail. This chapter will explore both the development of EPC and the various EC initiatives on political union that eventually culminated in the Single European Act.

EUROPEAN POLITICAL COOPERATION

Political cooperation is something that has constantly been urged upon the Community since its creation. Insofar as the EC has involved a continuing relationship between several national governments, it has achieved a not insignificant degree of political cooperation. Unlike the 1950s, the decisions in the 1970s and 1980s to advance further were built upon a foundation, no matter how anarchic it may have seemed at times, of a persisting lattice of interaction, something which has locked the member states ever closer together. While the internal debates of the EC on its institutional structure, economic and monetary integration, and political union often seemed to demonstrate that there were at least as many voices as members, externally the EC has been quite successful in presenting a united front to the outside world. It has done this through negotiating bilateral treaties with other world actors, through opting for a single representation at international meetings, and through the evolving process of EPC.

Before 1973 the EC's formal relationships with other countries or groups of countries had not progressed much beyond the Yaoundé Conventions. Within the space of just over a decade the EC's external relationships had expanded to agreements with well over 100 countries and some 30 multilateral agreements. As a result the EC had become the world's leading trader, with almost 20 per cent of world trade. This, however, was little more than a reflection of the fact that the EC needed to import much of its energy and most of its raw materials which in return required it to export finished goods. The problem which the EC has had to face in the 1980s, and will probably continue to have to face, is that despite the flourishing internal market its share of world trade was in gradual decline. This alone was a spur to external action. In general, EC policy in its formal external relationships was based upon the concept of free trade, though obviously with some exceptions. Agriculture, for example, is an area where EC protectionism has ruled supreme. The EC also rejected free trade in those declining industries such as steel, ship-building and textiles. In the latter case, the EC was a partner to the international Multifibre Agreement (MFA) of 1973 whereby cheap textile imports from Third World suppliers were strictly regulated.

Perhaps the centrepiece of the EC's bilateral trade policies have been the several Lomé Conventions. The first Lomé Convention of 1975 was essentially a renegotiation of the Yaoundé agreements to incorporate the former British colonies. During the negotiations the 58 Third World countries involved (since the mid-1970s known as the ACP, or African, Caribbean and Pacific states and which by the late 1980s had expanded in number to 66) displayed a surprising degree of coordination, with the result that Lomé was a more balanced and less neocolonialist agreement than Yaoundé. One valuable innovation was the introduction of a stabilisation fund to compensate the ACP states in the event of a collapse in their export revenue earnings due to natural disasters or huge falls in world prices. To last for five years, the Lomé Convention permitted free access to the EC market for most ACP agricultural products without any insistence upon reciprocity. In return the ACP states had to allot most-favoured nation status to many EC products. The net effect was the reproduction of something that looked very much like a free trade area that fitted reasonably well with the GATT programme of tariff reductions.

A second Lomé Convention was signed in 1979, after some considerable disagreement between the two sides. The EC view, which eventually prevailed, was essentially for the retention of the status quo; the ACP states had wanted an expansion of the level of aid outlined in Lomé I. The third Lomé Convention of 1984 shifted focus more to the development aspects of the agreement, stressing the role of the European Development Fund for rural and agricultural development and the financing of more comprehensive and interrelated programmes rather than isolated, individual projects. Lomé III was to last until 1990, and in the late 1980s negotiations began for an extension of the programme in a fourth convention.

The Lomé conventions were paralleled by a series of agreements with non-associated countries. In Asia, for example, the EC signed more limited agreements with Sri Lanka (1975), Bangladesh and Pakistan (1976), and India (1981) which included an important component of development aid; further east a cooperative agreement with the six-country Association of South-East Asian Nations (ASEAN) was effected in 1981. In Latin America the EC signed agreements with Uruguay (1973), Mexico (1975), Brazil (1980), and the five states of the Andean Pact (1983). The oil crisis of 1973 and the rise of Arab and Islamic nationalism helped focus EC attention on its southern flank and there slowly began to emerge, albeit randomly rather than as the consequence of a deliberate strategy, an EC Mediterranean policy. Agreements on trade and development aid were struck with the Maghreb states of Algeria, Morocco and Tunisia in 1976, followed by one with the Mashreq states (Egypt, Syria, Jordan and Lebanon) in 1977. Bilateral agreements were made with Israel in 1975 and Yugo-slavia in 1980. These supplemented the association agreements the EC made with Cyprus, Malta and Turkey. In effect, the EC developed a network of arrangements with all the Mediterranean states except Libya and Albania, something which it hoped would help promote political stability in the area and its peaceful economic development.

Nearer to home, relationships between the EC and EFTA became more amicable. In 1977 EFTA had become linked to the EC in a wide free trade area for industrial goods. Importantly, the agreement looked forward to further cooperative efforts. In 1984 the two bodies concluded a further agreement in Luxembourg whereby they under-took to go beyond the existing free trade arrangements to develop cooperation in a host of policy areas. The net effect was to pull EFTA ever more closely into the EC orbit, with EFTA states consulting and informing the EC about policies they proposed to introduce. On the other hand, Europe also represents the most conspicuous failure of the EC: its inability to arrive at an effective agreement with Eastern Europe. While the 1972 summit had agreed to work for a common commercial policy towards the east, the first approach was, in fact, made by COMECON the following year. Limited sectoral agreements were made with individual East European states, but all attempts to forge a more overall relationship fell victim to the more icy political climate of the late 1970s and early 1980s. The talks that began in 1977 were abandoned in 1980 without anything to show for the effort. They were not to be restarted until 1986, after Mikhail Gorbachev's accession to power in the Soviet Union. The collapse of the Communist regimes in Eastern Europe in 1989 would offer the EC new and important opportunities in the area, while simultaneously creating a huge challenge of how the EC should react to the political and economic earthquake.

The net effect of these trading agreements was to offset the exclusivity of the EC's common external tariff and to raise its economic and political profile in the world. These developments paralleled the need for the EC to find a niche for itself in the world of international organisations. Earlier practice was followed in the Tokyo Round of GATT talks that began in September 1973, when the EC participants negotiated as one, aided by a standing committee of representatives which had been briefed and instructed by the Council of Ministers. Similar practices were developed for participation at the four-yearly UNCTAD meetings. Perhaps the most important breakthrough came in winning separate EC representation in the western economic summits. The first such summit was held at Rambouillet in November 1975, with six heads of government in attendance. During the preparations for the second meeting in 1977, the smaller EC states, backed by the Commission, argued for a distinctive EC representation, a move that was strongly opposed by Britain and France. A compromise was reached in time for the summit, with Roy Jenkins, as President of the Commission, being allowed to attend some discussions as the EC representative, while being excluded from others. Even such a partial victory was significant in its recognition, if only symbolically, of the political importance and potential political unity of the Community.

The rules surrounding the Conference on Security and Cooperation in Europe (CSCE) precluded a separate EC representation, but as we have seen the member states collaborated closely during the exercise and the Helsinki Final Act was also signed 'in the name of the European Community'. To the dislike of most of the other participants, the EC continued to pursue a common line in the subsequent CSCE meetings in Belgrade in 1977 and Madrid in 1982. The EC states also proved able to collaborate more closely on defence. With France still absent from NATO the EC could provide a defence link between it and NATO. On the other hand, Ireland rejected defence as being a development not included in the founding treaties. The Irish line was backed by Denmark and Greece, the former because of its view that EC activity should be strictly limited to matters specifically mentioned in the Treaty of Rome, the latter because the 1981 Socialist government pursued a distinctive security policy that was less inclined to be critical of the Soviet Union. However, given European unease about both American and Soviet intentions after the late 1970s as the two superpowers moved from a renewed cold war to bilateral talks on armaments, the four major states of the EC in particular found it useful to share their views on defence and security. This was one reason for the relatively successful activation of WEU in the 1980s which effectively made WEU an appendage of the EC, while still protecting the sensibilities of some of the member states.

All of these developments were but some of the fruits that came out of the Davignon Report and the establishment of EPC. Of course, the member states had their own foreign policy interests, and common ground was not always possible. The important point, however, was the greater willingness to seek the common ground and, once attained, to sustain it. As part of this process, some practices became more or less completely institutionalised. By 1976, for example, ambassadors from the EC states to the UN were meeting on a regular weekly basis, while the practice has developed for the foreign minister of the country currently holding the presidency of the European Council to speak on behalf of all the EC states in the general debate which opens each annual session of the UN General Assembly.

EPC, however, also involves the taking of common actions and the launching of common initiatives. During the first years of operation, EPC was very much a reaction to events and pressures from outside, for instance on the issue of European security or the Middle East. In the latter instance, as we have seen, EPC was not particularly successful in handling a response to the 1973 oil crisis. Indeed, during the 1970s the network of discussions did not, on balance, lead to much in the way of common positions or actions. It was only towards the end of the decade that the states began more seriously to extend the range of EPC – on, for instance, the Soviet invasion of Afghanistan in 1979, the suppression of Solidarity in Poland in 1981, the Falklands War and Argentina in 1982, and South Africa in 1986. While the level of EPC has been gratifying, it has not been an unqualified success. Quite often, general statements of policy have been left hanging without serious attempts to follow them through. Where sanctions have been employed, it has been all too easy for one or more countries to break ranks: Greece, for instance, refused to join in the condemnation of and sanctions applied to Poland and the Soviet Union in 1981. Britain remained an unhappy participant in the EC's South African policy, while Italy and Ireland abandoned the sanctions policy against Argentina while the Falklands War was still raging. All of this draws attention to the fact that while EPC may have been a success in increasing the level of cooperation, there still remains some way to go. The Commission may have been accepted into the meetings on foreign policy in 1981, and the EP may have won the right to be informed, but the fact remains that EPC remains outside the EC structure as an essentially intergovernmental and voluntary operation. As such, it does not in the end involve any erosion of national sovereignty where the member states, most of whom have to reconcile EPC with other foreign policy concerns, do not wish to be associated with any EPC action. In the end this has probably been satisfactory for most states, large as well as small. All have perhaps gained benefits from the continuing liaison, and in the last resort it has allowed for a possibly greater effect for one's own national foreign policy without, in the last resort, imposing restraints and binding commitments on the latter.

THE QUEST FOR POLITICAL UNION

Under the aegis of Giscard d'Estaing and Helmut Schmidt, the important Paris summit of 1974 had been intended to breathe an air of realism back into EC plans after the ambitious declarations of recent years. Political union, however, was not ignored, and the task of exploring how it might realistically be achieved was entrusted by the summit to Leo Tindemans, the prime minister of Belgium. Tindemans embarked upon a series of consultations across the national capitals and in the EC's institutional heart in Brussels. This took a year to complete. Tindeman's report, issued in 1976, illustrated some of the difficulties of matching reality with rhetoric. It fell far short of the expectations of ardent Europeans, though perhaps reflecting the mood of the times as expressed by the European Council. Tindemans himself stressed that the cautious tone of the report was because he had wanted to be realistic and because he felt that the EC should not encroach upon the powers of the national governments: utopianism, he argued, was not particularly useful if it tended airily to dismiss the very real obstacles that did exist.

The report put forward several specific proposals: a common foreign policy and defence system, economic and monetary union, European social and regional policies, joint industrial policies. None of this was new: as essentially a list of guidelines on which Tindemans hoped to secure governmental agreement, it did not go much beyond the declarations of recent summits. On the other hand, Tindemans did have something positive and contentious to say about the institutions of the EC. He came down unambiguously on the side of a strengthened executive body independent of national governments and focused around the Commission, which would in terms of its functions replace both the existing Commission and the Council of Ministers. This executive body would be accountable to and elected by a more powerful legislature. His parliament was to be bicameral, a popularly elected Chamber of the People (similar to the EP) being supplemented by a Chamber of States appointed by the national governments. This was clearly a return to the principles of federalism. A further contentious idea was the suggestion that the EC might accept a rate of integration in economic and financial areas that would vary from country to country, that the end goals might be more easily achieved if the EC did not insist that all members, in all policy areas, should move in tandem with each other. While this was something that was in fact to occur later with the EMS, the notion of a two-speed (or multi-speed) Europe was something that was viewed with deep suspicion by the less committed states of Denmark and Britain. While the idea was never formally adopted and quietly disappeared, Tindemans had, in fact, produced a weapon that some members might be tempted to wield against recalcitrants such as Britain, and it was to resurface again in 1984 in the notion of a Europe of 'variegated geometry'.

On the whole, the Tindemans Report did not advance the cause of union very far. While it reaffirmed the Paris decisions, it was marred by two paradoxes. First, the stress which Tindemans laid upon concentrating on the minimum concrete steps that might be possible was more than counteracted by the much more drastic overhaul proposed for the EC institutions: the latter was highly unrealistic given the recent emergence of the European Council as a powerful actor and the characteristics of the dominant personalities on it. Second, if the institutional reforms had been approved, it is difficult to see how they would not have encroached upon the powers of national governments. Indeed, while the European Council had endorsed the development of a popularly elected EP, many member states had been insistent that the question of representation be divorced completely from that of the powers of the EP: quite simply, strong views had already been expressed that an increase in EP powers would not be acceptable. In a sense, therefore, the Tindemans Report seemed to pull in several different directions, and in so doing it may well have helped diminish further whatever momentum still remained from the hopes of 1972.

In the end nothing came directly of the Tindemans Report. Despite the fact that it appeared without fail upon the agenda of every session of the European Council between 1975 and 1978, it was never discussed by the national leaders, the very people who had commissioned it. It perhaps says something for the attitude of the national leaders that even though they had this document available for discussion, Giscard d'Estaing found it necessary in 1978 to propose that the Council should launch a further review of the operation of the

EC machinery. His specific proposal was that a 'number of eminent persons' should be appointed to investigate the current institutional state of affairs in the EC, if necessary to suggest those 'adjustments' in procedures and organisation that would make the institutions more effective, and – once again – to ponder whether any progress could be made towards European Union. At Brussels in December 1978 the European Council accepted Giscard's proposal and duly appointed an investigating committee.

The committee consisted of 'Three Wise Men': Barend Biesheuvel, a former prime minister of the Netherlands, Edmund Dell, a former British government minister, and Robert Marjolin of France, a previous member of the Commission. In their report published in 1979 the 'Three Wise Men' pinpointed the cumbersome nature of policy making as the major source of ineffectiveness within the EC framework. In particular, they commented adversely on the negative role of the Council of Ministers. The report concluded that the Commission should be reorganised and endowed with more authority, and that majority voting should be used more widely in the Council of Ministers. The 'Three Wise Men' therefore followed Tindemans in arguing that greater effectiveness would come through more supranationalism, something which was not exactly music to the ears of the European Council where their report was politely welcomed at the Luxembourg summit as a 'rich source of ideas and suggestions'. But it was obviously not a source from which the Council was willing to drink. No action was taken, and the report followed that of Tindemans into the archives. Despite its earlier declaration of intent, the European Council did not seriously advance the cause of political union: the 'end of the present decade' came and went without any obvious progress on the issue.

The Commission and Parliament may also still have had union as their major ambition, but they remained relatively muted on the topic for much of the 1970s. Indeed, the Commission and its presidents, despite the occupancy of the presidency by such distinguished people as Sicco Mansholt and François-Xavier Ortoli, adopted a rather low profile after the Hallstein years. Hopes were raised for a new Commission dynamism with the appointment of Roy Jenkins as president in 1977. Jenkins had been a persistent and committed advocate of the EC within Britain, and it was hoped that under his regime a new injection on integration would be forthcoming, particularly in terms of healing the breach between Britain and the rest. The Jenkins presidency was widely regarded as a success: two major achievements, for example, were the creation of the EMS, of which Jenkins was one of the major architects, and his 'victory' in gaining the right of the Commission president, as the representative of the EC, to attend the world economic summits. On the European front, however, the expectations were not realised, and he failed to receive firm backing from the British premiers, James Callaghan and Margaret Thatcher.

The next initiatives were to come from outside the Commission and the European Council. That some positive action was required was widely felt in the EC in the early 1980s. The EC was faced with a series of interrelated problems that demanded action, some of which have already been reviewed: the unlimited expansion of the CAP and the threat of budget exhaustion; the problem of Britain; the need for industrial rejuvenation to meet the technological challenge of the United States and Japan; the further enlargement of the Community to embrace Spain and Portugal; the continued struggle to eliminate internal barriers. Behind several of these issues lay the institutional structure of the EC itself, a problem highlighted by both Tindemans and the 'Three Wise Men'. While what could be done might have been debatable, there was a general consensus that institutional reform was necessary to make decision making more effective and less time-consuming. More contentious was the argument advanced by some that this entailed making the EC institutions more accountable: accountable to whom was the tricky issue. And institutional reform could not be disentangled from the broader issue of political integration.

The first major push of the 1980s came out of an individual initiative sponsored by the foreign ministers of West Germany and Italy. Known as the Genscher–Colombo Plan, it was perhaps less of a plan than an attempt to spur the EC, and especially the European Council into action. Without a brief from the Social Democrat-led government of Helmut Schmidt, the West German foreign minister, Hans-Dietrich Genscher, argued for a new initiative at a national congress of his own small Free Democrat party in 1981. Emilio Colombi of Italy subsequently collaborated with Genscher, and lent his name to a new campaign of negotiations and discussions with national governments. Presented in the form of a draft European Act and draft declaration on economic integration, what Genscher and Colombo argued for was not new: for example, more common policies, especially in foreign affairs, and greater cultural and legal cooperation. They further recommended that the European Council should report annually to the EP on progress towards European Union, and that the EP should be able to submit proposals on all aspects of European Union to the Council. The initiative was not particularly welcomed by the European Council, perhaps because at the heart of the Genscher–Colombo scheme lay the suggestion that the role of the EC institutions should be made more explicit, especially that of the European Council which had emerged outside the formal institutional framework of Rome. One further implication, an increase in the EC budget, aroused British opposition, while the hackles of several member states were raised by the idea of extending the use of majority voting. Greece and Denmark rejected out of hand any possibility of further restrictions on their own ability to formulate and apply national policies. France, too, was hesitant about any endorsement, to some extent perhaps because it had not been centrally involved in the initiative. But even Genscher's own premier, Helmut Schmidt, seemed to baulk at some of the consequences. He had already on several occasions hinted that West Germany could not continue indefinitely as the milch cow of the EC. In the end, the Genscher–Colombo Plan went the same way as its predecessors. Its ideas were to be diluted into a straightforward declaration of intent without any specific proposals, deadlines or timetable.

While the Genscher–Colombo Plan had little immediate impact, it was important in keeping the idea of union and political cooperation before the power centre of the EC. It contributed to the new round of discussions on political union upon which the national governments embarked in 1982, and in that context it was eventually discussed by the European Council at its Stuttgart meeting in June 1983. Though the proposals were rejected by the Council, the meeting concluded with the issuing of a general statement grandiosely entitled the Solemn Declaration on European Union. The Genscher–Colombo Plan had degenerated into what amounted to little more than an endorsement of current practices. On the other hand, the Solemn Declaration did perhaps clarify in writing what the purpose of the European Council was and its relationship to the EC. The Council declared itself responsible for providing 'a general political impetus to the construction of Europe', defining 'approaches to further the construction of Europe', issuing 'general political guidelines for the European Communities and European Political Co-operation', deliberating upon 'matters concerning European Union in its different aspects with due regard to consistency among them', and initiating 'co-operation in new areas of activity'. Furthermore, the document went on to state that 'when the European Council acts in matters within the scope of the European Communities, it does so in its capacity as the Council within the meaning of the Treaties'. This seemed to imply that the

European Council was accepting limitations on its freedom, that it could be regarded under certain circumstances as another version of the Council of Ministers. On the other hand, as long as the procedural requirements governing the actions of the Council of Ministers were met, decisions taken by the European Council would be binding under EC law. In re-emphasising its own political centrality, the European Council seemed to be effectively ruling out any radical overhaul of the EC institutions, including any enhancement of the Commission. But no schedule or details were set for political union: once again rhetoric had stopped short of meaningful action.

However, Genscher, Colombo and others who wished for some more decisive movement on the political front had a Community ally whose potential importance had increased. With its popular base now rooted in direct elections, the EP was anxious to demonstrate that its credentials were backed by some muscle. The EP had been kept informed of the discussions of the Genscher-Colombo Plan, and had strongly supported the initiative. On the other hand, with what it could regard as a popular mandate behind it, the EP would not be content with a secondary supportive role. Even before the Genscher-Colombo round had begun in 1981, a group of MEPs under the urging and leadership of the veteran Altiero Spinelli, now an independent member of the Communist group in the EP after serving between 1972 and 1976 as a Commissioner, had launched a thorough review of the EC with the aim of producing a new, forthright and specific blueprint for political union. Spinelli had never lost faith in the ideals of his youth, and a federal Europe was still his ambition.

The starting point, however, had to be the current institutions of the EC. Inevitably therefore, Spinelli sought enlarged powers for the Commission and EP, with a consequent downgrading of the Council of Ministers and the role of national governments. The working document listed Commission powers as being the ability to prepare and implement the budget, initiate policy, supervise the implementation of the treaty that would establish European Union, and represent that Union in its external relations. It would become the sole executive of the European Union. The Council of Ministers would become a Council of the Union, a legislative body sharing responsibility with the EP. The reformed EP would have an independent ability to raise revenue and would share powers over the adoption of the budget with the Council. To weaken the latter further and inhibit its ability to obstruct the passage of legislation, Spinelli and his co-authors suggested the introduction of majority voting and the placing of limits on the amount of time the Council of the Union would have to discuss any one measure. In short, in seeking to endow the EC with the supranational authority which had steadily dissipated over the previous decades, Spinelli's new venture was rather more than a simple revamping of Rome. It outlined a single institutional framework that would encompass all levels of cooperation, as well as making the institutions more efficient and democratically accountable.

The fruits of the exercise were brought together in a Draft Treaty on European Union which was submitted to the EP in February 1984, where it received an overwhelming endorsement. That, not perhaps unexpectedly, was the end of the matter: only a starry-eyed idealist, perhaps, could have believed that the Draft Treaty could be sold to the European Council as a finished and desirable product. It wanted too much too quickly, and in its general thrust it represented a direct challenge to the role of the European Council and hence also to national governments, most of whom still wished to hold the EP at arm's length. The only other resort available to the EP was to take its plans to the streets, and the opportunity to do so would be available in the next round of direct elections scheduled for later in 1984. Even by the standards of the 1979 elections, the 1984 experience was disappointing. In particular, the European dimension and the Draft Treaty did not figure prominently anywhere. The elections were fought as distinctive national campaigns on national issues by national political parties. The Draft Treaty would become another historical document.

On the other hand, this EP exercise was not perhaps entirely in vain. Its innovative and broad-ranging approach did present the choices to be made very clearly; in its depth of detail it went beyond much of the earlier discussions to indicate at least some of the possibilities that might reasonably be achieved; and it helped to keep the question of union on the agenda. If it did nothing else, it reconfirmed the EP's role as the conscience of the original EC ideal, worrying away around the edges of the existing system. In that respect the efforts of Spinelli and his supporters were one factor that persuaded the European Council itself to return to the question of political union and consider a revision of the original treaties.

The European Council returned to the theme of political union at the important Fontainebleau summit of June 1984. One reason for this was again the determination of François Mitterrand to reassert a decisive French leadership in the Community. For a number of years the Council had seemed to be marking time. Mitterrand, elected in 1981, and his West German counterpart, Helmut Kohl, had not been able to sustain the very close personal relationship that had been enjoyed by their predecessors. In addition, the EC had been weakened by the departure of Roy Jenkins in 1981. His successor as Commission president, Gaston Thorn of Luxembourg, proved less able to provide a decisive lead in a situation where, with the end of the Schmidt-Giscard d'Estaing era, a relative vacuum had emerged at the summit of the Community. Indeed, it could almost be said that the dominant personality of the EC was Mrs Thatcher; and her European credentials, not only because of her persistent attacks upon the CAP and the budget, were not regarded by the other nine states as being of the highest order.

At any rate, Fontainebleau was intended by Mitterrand to be an important monument to France's current occupancy of the Council presidency. Action was taken on a whole backlog of problems: Britain's complaints, the CAP, and further enlargement. As part of this clearing-up operation Mitterrand also urged action on political union. The 10 states agreed to launch yet another investigation into how they might try to condense the many and varied attitudes and views on integration into a set of proposals that would be politically manageable and acceptable. Two committees were established. The first, a Committee for a People's Europe, was charged with examining how the EC might develop practical symbols that would help nurture the growth of a European identity across the national populations, an area barely touched to date by the EC. Whatever symbolic gestures the EC might adopt to work for a common European identity could, however, come to fruition only in the very long term.

The second committee was to be an ad hoc group of 'personal representatives' of the heads of government, and was to be more directly concerned with political change. After Fontainebleau the presidency of the European Council passed to Ireland, and in July the Irish premier, Garret Fitzgerald, appointed as his personal representative James Dooge, leader of the Irish Senate and a former foreign minister, and announced, in his capacity as president of the European Council, that Dooge would be 'available' to serve as chairman of the ad hoc committee. The Irish move did not immediately meet with universal approval. Some doubts were raised in Belgium, while in Bonn Helmut Kohl voiced dissatisfaction about the status of some of the personal representatives, comments which were associated with a rather vague West German desire for Kohl's representative designate to be appointed chairman. Although these reservations were not pressed further, and Dooge did become chairman of the group, they did delay the launch of the committee.

The Dooge Committee was intended to conduct a preliminary exploration of the positions of the heads of government in order to determine the extent to which common ground might be possible. Inevitably, however, it went further than this in considering and proposing specific ideas for the future. It issued a preliminary report to the Dublin meeting of the European Council in December 1984, when national differences were already apparent: the representative from Denmark had insisted upon the inclusion of an annex to the report indicating that he 'was not convinced that the overall approach in the interim report was the right one'. In its deliberations and final report of the following year the Dooge Committee trod a familiar path. It declared that its overall aim was to turn the EC into a 'true political entity . . . with the power to take decisions in the name of all citizens by a democratic process'. It outlined four, by now commonplace, themes of institutional reform: strengthening both the Commission and the EP – the former to be made more independent and streamlined, with only one commissioner per country, the latter to be given joint decision-making authority with the Council of Ministers; simplifying decision making in the Council of Ministers by limiting the need for unanimity to only new areas of action and new applications for entry; and allotting a strategic role to the European Council which, meeting only twice a year, should concern itself with diplomatic and external affairs, and not the daily routine of the EC.

It was hardly likely, given past history, that these recommendations represented a consensus of opinion among the national leaders. And indeed, Britain, Denmark and Greece voiced strong reservations about the proposals on the Commission and the Council of Ministers. The task of convincing the heads of government about the virtues of the Dooge Report and of its final recommendation that a special intergovernmental conference should be organised to draw up a reform package on the basis of the proposals fell to Italy, which inherited the presidency of the European Council for the first half of 1985 and so would play host to the Council at its next session in Milan in June. Through bilateral discussions and a meeting of foreign ministers immediately before the summit, the Italian premier, Bettino Craxi, hoped to persuade his colleagues to accept the Dooge Committee's deliberations as the basis of the Milan agenda.

In that sense reform of the EC became a major subject of discussion at Milan, the first time that the European Council seemed to be prepared to sit down to discuss the details of reform. Yet perhaps because that was the core issue on the agenda, the Milan meeting was particularly ill-tempered; and so it was all the more surprising that the session was able to conclude with a decision. Craxi's bid to focus on the Dooge recommendations was complicated by the submission of two counter-proposals, both misleadingly labelled as dealing with European Union though they referred much more specifically to political cooperation and security. The first, known as the Howe Plan after the British foreign minister, Sir Geoffrey Howe, had been submitted at the preliminary meeting of foreign ministers at Stresa: it argued for little more than a code of good behaviour in decision making within EPC. At Milan Mrs Thatcher took this as the starting point of her arguments, as well as pushing for a more pragmatic approach on the establishment of a common economic and financial market. The proposals for European Union she dismissed as 'airy-fairy'. The other alternative submission was a surprise sprung on the eve of the summit by France and West Germany. Concentrating upon security cooperation and a strengthening of WEU, it might under other circumstances have been particularly welcomed as an important step in the reconciliation of France with the European branch of NATO. Yet in this context it added to the confusion. Paralleling as it did the British initiative, it further irritated rather than gratified Mrs Thatcher. It also, not surprisingly, perturbed Ireland. In addition, it seemed to indicate a reversal of the French and West German stand of recent years and a drawing back from the frontiers of European Union.

Mitterrand had made a powerful speech to the EP in Strasbourg the previous year in which he had raised expectations of a decisive push towards European Union under French leadership, if necessary by only some of the member states through a resurrection of Tindemans's 1975 idea of a two-speed Europe. His more muted stance in Milan suggested perhaps a reluctance to force the pace without the consent of all the member states. Domestic circumstances may also have played a role in that Mitterrand's personal popularity within France had declined substantially and the prospects were that his Socialist party would lose its legislative majority in the elections scheduled for 1986. With the Gaullists representing the major electoral challenge, it was not a time, perhaps, to be too closely identified with moves that might infringe upon national sovereignty. Similarly, in 1984 Helmut Kohl had ringingly declaimed in the West German parliament, 'Who is prepared to follow us on the way to European union with the stated objective of a United States of Europe?' Yet only a few days before the Milan summit was preparing to review the way forward, West German credibility was severely damaged when its government chose to exercise its veto in the Council of Ministers, for the first time in EC history, on the question of Commission proposals to raise cereal prices. The issue was reminiscent of the one in which Britain's use of the Luxembourg Compromise was rejected in 1982, though in this instance the West German decision stood: but it was another act that demonstrated how much domestic political concerns tended to contradict European rhetoric.

In the event the Milan session of the European Council did reach some decisions. Progress was made on the economic front, with agreement on a timetable for removing a great number of existing barriers to the internal market. In retrospect, the political decisions were equally satisfactory, though at the time this was not thought to be the case since each state came away from the meeting with a different interpretation of what had been achieved. The government leaders had differed on whether institutional reform should entail amendment of the treaties, on the extent to which the EP should be given additional powers, and on whether the right of veto in the Council of Ministers should be reduced and if so to what extent. What was important was that the major items put forward by the Dooge Committee by and large survived, as did its proposals for a mechanism under which the next step should occur. In an unprecedented move, the European Council actually voted on the issue of setting up an intergovernmental conference to construct a reform package out of all the reports and initiatives. Mrs Thatcher regarded such a conference as 'a waste of time', and Britain's opposition was supported by Denmark and Greece. However, the format of the decision to hold an intergovernmental conference did not preclude these three states from continuing to resist changes to the existing institutional arrangements. The brief for the conference enabled all sides in the Milan summit to provide their own interpretation of it, since it referred to the British and Franco–German documents as well as the Dooge Committee's report, and perhaps, more importantly, it did not refer, as Dooge had done, to a draft treaty of European Union as being the objective of the exercise. It was reasonable to assume that the national divisions at Milan would be reproduced at the intergovernmental conference, and also that if past history was any guide the end result would probably be only cosmetic change at the most, unless of course the protagonists of union were prepared to accept and create a two-speed Europe – something which would effectively negate European Union. In the end, the member states were to surprise everyone, including perhaps themselves, by agreeing to the most decisive changes in the structure of the EC since its inception.

CHAPTER SIXTEEN

Towards 1992

The European Council decision in Milan to invoke an intergovern-mental conference to consider the future of the EC and a possible revision of the founding treaties had been based, uniquely for the Council, upon a majority verdict. To some extent therefore, the degree to which the momentum for change, a momentum that steadily but surely had been building up steam throughout the 1980s, could be maintained would be dependent upon the three recalcitrants at Milan – Britain, Denmark and Greece. While disagreeing with the majority decision, all three nevertheless felt constrained to participate in the proposed conference, if only to continue their advocacy of a minimalist development. In fact, the terms of reference for the conference did not preclude that argument any more than it did those which argued full scale European Union. And in the end the three minority states could rest assured with the fact that any fruits that might emerge from the conference would have to be by unanimous agreement.

Other voices, almost invariably in favour of institutional reform and significant advances towards European Union, lent their weight to a positive result from the conference and against the three doubters. In particular, the EP demanded immediately after the Milan summit the right to collaborate in the work of the conference. It also argued, mindful of the past tendency for proposals on integration to be watered down by national governments whenever they got together, that if at the end of the day moves to Union were blocked by a minor-ity, then those states that wished European Union should go ahead by themselves. The minority states were therefore, in a sense, put on the defensive from the outset. Sir Geoffrey Howe eventually felt obliged to state that 'Britain is not afraid of European Union': however, he also took care to reiterate that in the British view European Union was 'a process of deepening and broadening the scope of European activities [that already] exists now'. Even so, Howe's speech sent a clear signal that Britain would be a willing partner in treaty amendments which it deemed pragmatic and valuable.

The formal proposal put forward by the new Luxembourg presidency of the European Council was that the conference should consider revision of the treaties 'with a view to improving Council's decision-making procedures, strengthening the Commission's executive power, increasing the powers of the European Parliament and extending common policies to new fields of activity'. This paralleled the brief from the European Council for a study of 'the institutional conditions in which the completion of the internal market could be achieved within the desired time limit', something which referred also to those changes that would require treaty amendment. There was some difference of opinion over whether EPC should be included in the province of the conference, or whether it should be made the topic of a separate exercise: in the end it was decided that EPC should also be incorporated in the discussions.

From the beginning of September onwards, two working parties met on a more or less weekly basis: one dealt with revisions to the treaties, the other with EPC. Both committees reported to the foreign ministers who themselves in their several meetings essentially constituted the Intergovernmental Conference. The deliberations were more or less completed by October, and a final conclave was held in December just before the scheduled meeting of the European Council in Luxembourg. The member states took up their well-ensconced positions on the broad issues, with disagreement over the level of integration desired (that is, on institutional reform), though with everyone being broadly in agreement on the reach of the EC, the Conference was able to construct a package of proposals for the heads of government to consider in Luxembourg.

THE SINGLE EUROPEAN ACT

On the basis of the proposals received from the Intergovernmental Conference, the European Council accepted in principle a number of texts referring to specific areas of projected action that were brought together into a Single European Act that with ratification by the member states would be written into the treaties. In essence the Single European Act (SEA) was an attempt to turn the EC towards the original goal of a common market set out in the Treaty of Rome and which had originally and optimistically been scheduled to be in place by 1970. In that sense the SEA was not a revolutionary document. On the other hand, in its proposals for institutional change it had potential for revolution, suggesting a shift in the existing balance of power away from the member states towards the Community institutions. The radical political implications of the economic target of a common market – the single internal market – were there for all to read in the document. In that sense the SEA target of a single internal market by 1992, something with which all states were broadly in favour, could be used as a lever by those who sought political union. In the years after 1986 the arguments would still rage over both questions: while the issues of political and economic integration are closely interlinked, the parallel debates tended to muddy the waters of each.

The agreements which formed the SEA covered the areas of the single market, EPC and institutional reform. In other words, as well as dealing with measures that were deemed necessary for completing the common market, it referred to new policy objectives, new forms of decision-making and legislative processes within the EC, and extending the scope of the EC to cover foreign policy and matters of defence and security.

At the heart of the SEA lay the commitment to a fully integrated internal market by the end of 1992, the objectives of which were summarised by the Commission draft which was the basis of discussion at Luxembourg as an area 'in which persons, goods, and capital shall move freely under conditions identical to those obtaining within a Member State'. The market was central in the sense of being fundamental to the initial logic of the treaties. Tactically, it was one of the few moves which would meet little resistance from more reluctant countries like Britain and Denmark. Establishing the market would entail the removal of all those barriers and factors which inhibited free movement. Inside the EC the benefits would, it was believed, go in the medium term to the consumer through the consequent greater specialisation of production at the company level and the economies of scale. Externally, the single market was meant to strengthen EC effectiveness in world markets, especially against the United States and Japan.

In retrospect, it is difficult perhaps to understand how there was a failure on the part of some to appreciate how far the significance of this would or could extend. It would inevitably focus attention not just on 'isolated' instances of national discrimination, but ultimately on the whole range of national systems of taxation and law, the plethora of national standards and regulations in a range of policy areas, and national social welfare and security systems. Indeed, the implications of the SEA, it could be said, would affect, and its success or otherwise would be affected by, factors far beyond the narrow field of economics, such as the linguistic diversity of the EC and the mosaic of national patterns of culture and traditions.

In setting the target the Luxembourg summit also incorporated into the document past developments which had stood at least partially outside the treaties, such as the advancement of cooperation in research and technology or the reduction of regional disparities. It also referred much more explicitly to the improvement of the quality of life, with references to environmental policy, the improvement of living and working conditions, and the raising of health standards. In short, in terms of policy objectives the SEA went far beyond the simple economic requirements of the single internal market. On the other hand, one element which would seem to be central to the market concept was barely covered by the document and the summit: while reference was made to a convergence of economic and monetary policy that should 'take account of the experience acquired in co-operation in the framework of the EMS and in developing the ECU, and shall respect existing powers in this field', the government leaders did not tackle the core issue of EMU. West Germany and Britain in particular had been doubtful of the virtues of including monetary questions in the package.

Potentially, the most significant element of the SEA was that relating to institutional reform, since it implied an important modification of the power structure of the EC. Most importantly, the summit agreed to an extension of the practice of qualified majority voting in the Council of Ministers. The criteria agreed upon were that unanimity should be retained only for the accession of new applicants to the club and for the enunciation of the general principles of new policies. Once a policy had been adopted in principle, the process of implementation would require only a qualified majority. With the accession of Spain and Portugal in 1986 the number of votes in the Council rose to 76: Britain, France, Italy and West Germany with ten votes each, Spain with eight votes, Belgium, Greece, the Netherlands and Portugal with five votes each, Denmark and Ireland with three votes each, and Luxembourg with two votes. A qualified majority demanded 54 of the 76 votes. The measure was designed to speed up the decision-making process in the EC by removing in a wide number of areas the ability of a single state to block progress. On the other hand, given the diversity of opinion across the member states, it meant that a minority of states – three or four at a minimum – could still, if their interests coincided, hold up developments.

For the proponents of European Union, the most disappointing element of the SEA was that which dealt with the EP. It fell far short of the proposals contained within the EP's own Draft Treaty or even those of the Dooge Committee. The reforms, however, were not perhaps insignificant in the way in which they marginally increased the legislative competence of the EP. The core of the reform lay in the proposal that where the Council of Ministers has decided upon an issue by a qualified majority, the EP would have the right to amend or reject the proposal: what could really give the EP more teeth, however, was the fact that where the EP rejected or modified such a Council proposal, the Council of Ministers could override the EP position only by unanimous agreement. At the time this proposal was regarded as a humiliating defeat by many MEPs, but it would force the Council of Ministers to take more note of and cooperate with the EP. In any case, given the structure of the EC and the distrust of the EP that could still be found in many national capitals, it was perhaps as much as could have been realistically hoped for.

Again, on the Commission the summit chose not to accept in full the recommendations of the Draft Treaty and Dooge. Instead, the states agreed only that the Council of Ministers may 'confer on the Commission, in the acts it adopts, powers for the implementation of the rules it lays down'. In addition, the Council of Ministers would retain the right to exercise implementing powers itself. It would be up to Jacques Delors and his Commission to exert their skills to maximise their influence within these parameters, an exercise at which in the late 1980s the Commission proved quite adept. Finally, the SEA agreed to an extension of the jurisdiction of the European Court, and to the setting up of a Court of First Instance to hear certain categories of cases and to ease the growing burden of the Court. It also conferred formal status, for the first time, upon the European Council, though without defining exactly what its role would be.

The final element of the SEA referred to EPC. It asserted that the member states should jointly formulate and implement a European foreign policy and that they should collaborate more closely on defence and security issues. The first part of these proposals was nothing more than a codification of EPC, though the second would represent a significant advance upon its current areas of operation. Moreover, the Act made the Commission fully associated with EPC, and the EP's views were also to be taken into consideration. To increase the coherence of EPC, the old idea of a permanent secretariat was resurrected as a body that would service both the foreign ministers and the Commission in this area of activity.

In short, the SEA was a comprehensive attempt to sweep away the logjam to which the EC was prone. It was, inevitably but perhaps also shrewdly, a package which contained something for everyone. It confirmed 1992 as the target date for the internal market, with the Commission being obligated to report on interim progress in 1988 and 1990, but in such a way that failure to meet the deadline would not automatically incur any legal penalties. But it also went beyond 1992 to incorporate matters relating more obviously to European Union. After 1985 the debate between how far these two objectives were desirable, or even compatible, would continue with all the old vigour. Given the great variety of national views, it was a matter of some achievement that the bargaining in Luxembourg resulted in a finished product. However, since the SEA involved a revision of the founding treaties, it would still have to be sent to the national parliaments for ratification. Several leaders had already entered reservations about some elements of the package. Britain was more than doubtful about the social dimension of 1992 and about European Union, while France disliked the extension of EPC. Italy thought the proposals relating to the EP to be totally inadequate. At the extreme, Denmark reserved its position on almost everything, mainly, however, because the minority government could not be certain of a parliamentary majority in Copenhagen. In the end, however, only nine states signed the Act. Italy refrained from signing because it thought the SEA insufficient, while also indicating that it was withholding signature as an act of displeasure over Denmark's hostility to the plan. Greece also refused to sign, ostensibly as a symbolic protest against the isolation of and pressure upon Denmark, although clearly, in terms of its previous opposition to encroachments upon its national sovereignty, Greece might well have also been unhappy about several aspects of the SEA. But it was Denmark upon which the fate of the whole scheme hinged.

Since the early 1970s Danish minority governments had found it exceedingly difficult to control the legislature: in particular, the Danish parliament had asserted its right to supervise and control Danish participation in the EC. While the minority government had accepted the SEA, it was rejected by the parliament. In exasperation, the Conservative premier, Poul Schlüter, sought to bypass his parliamentary opponents by calling a referendum, where he made it clear that what was at stake was not the Act, but Denmark's continuing membership of the EC. Bringing the old economic card into play, Schlüter said that a negative vote 'would be interpreted as our first step towards leaving the European Economic Community'. Yet even though the government argued that over one half of Denmark's exports went to the EC, and despite the leakage of a confidential report that estimated that withdrawal would cost Denmark at least 3,000 million dollars a year, Schlüter managed to gain only a slim majority in the February 1986 referendum. It was, however, sufficient, and the day after the referendum Denmark signed the SEA, along with Greece and Italy.

The SEA was due to come into force in January 1987. At the last moment, however, it had to be delayed because a court ruling in Ireland declared that the government should have held a referendum to amend the country's constitution before it could sign the Act. The offending item was the reference in the SEA to cooperation on European security, something which clashed with Ireland's constitutional position of neutrality. Little opposition, however, was expressed in the 1987 referendum: all the political parties were in favour of the amendment. With that hurdle overcome, the SEA finally came into force.

1992: SYMBOL AND REALITY

The SEA did not meet the EP's demands for a major overhaul of the EC, nor did it by and in itself advance European Union very far. It was, nevertheless, a significant step, and one which had been initiated and approved by the European Council, the body which in the 1980s ultimately held the key to any further integration. Even several years later, what the Act may bring in its wake still perhaps remains unclear. On paper, the details may not have seemed to amount to very much. Its direct effect upon the institutional balance of power within the EC was perhaps limited. The European Council would remain the main repository of power in the EC, and despite the continued rhetoric on European Union, a question mark would have to be placed against the willingness of national governments to relinquish in the last resort their grip on the determination of EC policy. But there was more to the SEA than this. Over and above its details 1992 became a symbol of something significant that all assumed would occur. What that something would be was a matter of interpretation, a single market or a greater European Union. The extent to which either goal was reached would depend not just on the European Council or the Council of Ministers. Much would rest first on the extent to which the EP could use its enhanced powers to push the Council of Ministers in the desired direction, and second on how effective the Commission would be in manoeuvring within the confines of the SEA to advance the causes of 1992.

Indeed, the Commission had already taken up the task with gusto. At the 1985 Brussels summit the European Council had asked the Commission to draw up a detailed timetable for completion of an internal market. Lord Cockfield, the British commissioner who had been given responsibility for the internal market, rapidly produced a long list of 300 separate measures relating to physical, fiscal and technical barriers that would need to be implemented. Astutely avoiding any attempt to rank these by priority, something which inevitably would have brought member states into conflict with each other, Cockfield simply produced a tight timetable for each measure that would have to be obeyed if the necessary directives were to be adopted by 1992. Moreover, his checklist was scrupulously restricted to practical measures, but carefully eschewing the potential political implications of each or all. The Commission had at least some lessons from past reversals.

The objective of 1992, according to the Commission, was the idea of a 'Europe without frontiers'. At the heart of this concept, something which perhaps tacitly implied something more than a mere economic community, lay frontier and customs controls – which themselves are but a matter of taxation. And it was the tax proposals which were central to Cockfield's checklist, and it was the one issue to which the document paid most attention. Basing his argument upon the American example of a spread of tax rates across the states of the union, Lord Cockfield suggested a harmonisation of the large range of national VAT rates by having only two permissible VAT brackets, a normal range where member states would be free to set their own national rates at anything between 14 and 20 per cent, and a reduced bracket where the permissible limits would be 4 and 9 per cent. It was the tax proposals which created the greatest dissension. Denmark, for example, with its high VAT rate, would lose considerable revenue: at the other extreme, Britain, with its zero VAT rate on several items, including books, children's clothes and food, feared a rise in the cost of living. The Commission did not envisage total harmonisation to be easily achieved. Acknowledging that some states would face hardship and severe problems of adjustment, the Commission was willing for states to apply for temporary 'derogations', or exemptions, to the directives. If the plan had been prosecuted, the number of derogations sought for may well have been so numerous as to defeat the purpose of the exercise. But the EC was unable to resolve the question of tax harmonisation, postponing it almost indefinitely. Simultaneously, progress became very slow on many other of the 300 measures.

Cockfield himself paid the penalty for his vigorous prosecution of harmonisation: Mrs Thatcher chose not to renominate him as a commissioner when his term of office ended in 1989. But Cockfield had been merely doing what was his responsibility under the SEA and his Commission portfolio. The taxation issue reflected the fundamental difficulties of establishing the internal market: albeit a practical and probably necessary measure, it struck directly at the jugular of sovereignty. In addition, the Commission's approach to the issue deviated from its general strategy of persuading the member states to accept a seemingly simple goal without drawing attention to the possible political consequences. This was simply not possible with taxation. The Commission instead reverted to straightforward harmonisation, perhaps precisely because the political consequences were so obvious and because it feared that in this sensitive area the national governments would not permit market-driven forces to decide the level of tax differences that could be sustained between states. Just how difficult the whole exercise could be may be deduced from the 1985 agreement by France, West Germany and the Benelux states to end all internal border controls by January 1990. While some progress was made, the deadline simply could not be met as the states discovered just how many national policies and practices needed to be changed.

The taxation issue may have been a defeat, temporary or otherwise, for the Commission, but it did not deter it from its overall approach to 1992. The Commission, under the vigorous leadership of Jacques Delors, utilised to the full its powers under the SEA to become perhaps the most activist Commission in the EC's history. And within the Commission Delors came to enjoy a predominance equalled in the past only, perhaps, by Hallstein. Delors used his powers and influence throughout the whole of the EC and beyond the narrow provisions of the SEA to become, in effect, the leading spokesman not just of 1992 but also of what will come after 1992. In 1989 he was re-elected as president for a term of office that will enable him, hopefully, to see the internal market completed in 1992. Delors' personal initiatives beyond the SEA were focused on three major areas: EMU, the budget, and the Social Charter. In each of these three areas the conflict was not between the Commission (and the EP) on the one hand and the two Councils on the other, but between those who wanted a maximisation of integration, for whom Delors became the principal advocate, and those who desired the economic single market, but beyond that only cooperation: the major proponent of that viewpoint was, not surprisingly, Margaret Thatcher.

At the same time as the EC was wrestling with the SEA and its consequences, it had to confront the continuous problem of budgeting and the demands upon its resources. As we have seen, the 1984 decisions on the budget were placed under further strain during the next two years. Delors took the initiative in constructing a package which proved on the whole to be acceptable to the European Council meeting in Brussels in June 1987. The Council endorsed the package, leaving the final details to be settled at its next meeting in Copenhagen. The only dissident voice was Mrs Thatcher's, but her dissatisfaction was over the potential effectiveness of the proposed constraints upon expenditure: in addition, she was concerned that any revision of budgetary contributions should not overturn the settlement of the British problem that had been reached at Fontainebleau.

On the other hand, Britain did agree with its 11 partners on a host of other measures: emergency provisions for balancing the 1987 budget, farm prices for 1987–1988, the phasing out of green currencies and MCAs by 1989. In short, Britain was not opposed in principle to the overall package, as long as more effective and binding discipline could be imposed upon the budget, and it agreed to cooperate on providing the finishing touches in time for the next European Council session. The communiqué issued at the end of the Brussels summit broadly endorsed the Delors package. It also confirmed the target of 1992 and accepted that certain decisions had to be taken 'before the end of 1988'. It accepted that the EC must have stable and guaranteed resources in order to undertake the tasks laid down for it by the European Council, but that the new level of resourcing must take account of 'the proportionality of contributions in accordance with the relative prosperity of member states'. Most importantly in the light of past battles and problems, the CAP was to be amended so that spending on it would be based upon a more realistic market balance between supply and demand, with any increase in EAGGF expenditure on guarantees to be pinned, at a maximum, to the rate of growth of the EC's own resources.

Mrs Thatcher's opposition was much more forthright when it came to two other of Delors' initiatives. The first was his argument for a Social Charter, a programme for a minimum set of workers' and citizens' rights which she labelled as 'Marxist'. For Delors, the internal market should be seen to benefit workers as well as businessmen and consumers. Fundamentally, the Social Charter was little more than a set of principles. After a series of consultations with governments, employers and trade unions, the Commission unveiled it as, formally, the Charter of Fundamental Social Rights in May 1989. It set out to codify in general terms what the EC had already begun to do in the social sector. It referred to living and working conditions, freedom of movement, training and opportunities, sex equality, and health and safety. In all of these areas, and in line with harmonisation, it wished to work for an upward approximation of working conditions throughout the Community. As such, much of the Social Charter appeared fairly anodyne; it did not, moreover, seek wholesale Commission intervention, but merely EC action where the necessary goals could more easily be achieved at the EC rather than the national level. What, however, particularly raised Mrs Thatcher's opposition was the suggestion for worker representation on the boards of industrial companies. If that proposal had been absent, then British protests, if any, may well have been only ritualistic.

The Social Charter eventually came up for European Council approval at Strasbourg in December 1989. The other 11 ignored Britain's objections, pointing out that in accepting the SEA Britain had also accepted a commitment to 'social justice', and that the Charter was nothing more than an essential equivalent of the package of commercial reforms that were currently progressing through the Community. Even so, the Commission had taken note of Mrs Thatcher's objections, and in order to appease Britain the final version that was approved in Strasbourg represented a considerable dilution from the original draft. That in turn led to complaints from other states. Belgium, Italy, Luxembourg, the Netherlands and West Germany accepted it only reluctantly as a pale version of what they had wanted, while the dissatisfaction within the Socialist party group in the EP was such as to lead to demands for the Commission to be censured.

The other area where Mrs Thatcher and Jacques Delors came into conflict was over monetary policy. This had, by and large, been a missing element from the SEA, yet the logic of 1992 demanded some harmonisation in the policy field. Delors took up again the quest for EMU, including those ingredients essential for it to be truly effective – a single central bank and a single European currency. Britain, still only a partial member of the EMS, rejected the idea of EMU as unnecessary for the creation of the single market, and steadfastly refused all the pressure to make it reconsider its position, though still insisting that it would eventually become a full member of the EMS when conditions were appropriate.

The point was that Delors was a committed Europeanist. For such people the SEA and the new opportunities it offered to the EC institutions were levers that could be used to push the EC beyond 1992 towards European Union. It was this belief that lay behind his initiatives of the late 1980s and his widely reported address to the EP in July 1988 when he declared that with the SEA some 80 per cent of economic legislation and most of that relating to social and fiscal affairs would, within 10 years, be passed at the European rather than the national level. The SEA might well lead to that, but it was not the direct intention of the Act. The statement was more a reflection of where Delors thought the EC ought to be going, and part of a strategy to create the right kind of psychological mood within the EC.

A riposte from Mrs Thatcher was not long in coming. Two months after Delors' address in Strasbourg, in a major speech in Bruges she attacked the speed with which Delors and others were trying to push the EC in areas where, under the SEA, the Community strictly speaking had no legal authority to act, and where she believed pragmatism was being sacrificed in a rush towards a political structure which she disliked and dismissed as unrealistic. Hence her comment that 'It is a matter of common sense that we cannot totally abolish frontier controls if we are to protect our citizens from crime and stop the movement of drugs, of terrorists, of illegal immigrants'. Mrs Thatcher took pains to stress that Britain was committed to the EC. What she was objecting to was not only the nature of the Europe that some wished to construct, but also that the drive was being led by a bureaucratic and unrepresentative Commission:

> I am the first to say that on many great issues the countries of Europe should try to speak with a single voice. But working more closely together does not require powers to be centralized in Brussels or decisions to be taken by an appointed bureaucracy . . . We have not successfully rolled back the frontiers of the state of Britain, only to see them recognised at a European level, with a European super-state exercising a new dominance from Brussels.

Both were perfectly legitimate views of Europe. The difference was that one was looking beyond 1992 to some kind of political union, while the other would be content with the internal market flanked by heightened cooperation among the member states on a host of other issues. It was a debate whose roots lay far back in the past, yet because the essential parameters of the debate had moved further away from intergovernmentalism towards supranationalism through the accumulation of the common practices of the past decades, Mrs Thatcher was, if for no other reason, on weaker ground than, for example, de Gaulle. While the European Council may have remained the ultimate repository of authority, after the SEA it was Jacques Delors and the Commission who seemed very much to have emerged as the driving force of the EC. And despite the complaints of the EP and others about the dilutions and delays, what counted was that all the member states had accepted that 1992 would mark the beginning of something new. It was precisely what the new world would or should look like that was in dispute, and the beliefs and behaviour of the member states were conditioned accordingly after 1986. At fault, if there was a fault, was the SEA itself, a document which essentially had been a compromise between several interests and which therefore was open to varying interpretations.

If any further evidence of the potential significance of 1992 was needed, it could be found in the reaction of those companies and West European states which still lay outside the Community. The former began anxiously to survey and launch possibilities of establishing industrial locations within the EC. The EFTA states all expressed grave concern over what exclusion from the internal market might mean for their own economies. The immediate reaction of individual EFTA states, however, were rather mixed. At one extreme stood Austria which, despite its neutral status and its previous interpretation of what that entailed, began in 1987 to discuss seriously the possibility of EC membership. In Norway too, voices were raised, for the first time since 1972, in favour of a reconsideration of membership as the only sure way of avoiding possible discrimination. At the other extreme, Sweden and Finland, their concern notwithstanding, reiterated that they would not consider membership.

During 1987 and 1988 the EFTA states, under the urging of the Scandinavian members, eventually agreed to pursue a collective line towards the EC in order to seek some form of collective agreement. This approach fitted well with the dominant prejudices within the EC which preferred not to consider Austria – or indeed any other country – for membership until after 1992, since any enlargement would inevitably delay the construction of the single market. Instead, the EC developed the concept of a European economic space to reassure the EFTA states that there would be a viable economic life outside the internal market. Responding to a Commission initiative, officials from the EC and EFTA began work in March 1989 on a joint agreement that would provide a framework for the economic space, with the aim of developing a draft treaty by the end of 1990.

Both sides were generally in agreement that EFTA would accept those EC laws that will govern the nucleus of the single market – the free movement of people, goods, services and capital – as well as those EC rules that were consequent upon the core of the programme, for example on the environment or competition and state aid. Exceptions, however, would be permitted where these conflicted with what any EFTA state considered to be of vital national interest. All of this still retained much scope for disagreement, although the fundamental dilemma the EFTA states had to face would relate to the institutional arrangements for the European economic space. Statements coming out of Brussels seemed to imply a two–pillar structure with some kind of joint body at the top. In other words, the EC was reflecting its own prejudices for some kind of institutional scheme in which there would be a form of supranational authority to ensure that both sides observed the rules of the economic space. This was a format which EFTA had resisted in the past. It also indicated that for the EC, EFTA should be allowed to participate in taking decisions, but without actually taking them, another position which EFTA rejected.

On the other hand, it was the EC which held most of the bargaining chips – on a collective agreement, or on considering applications for EC membership. The EC commissioner responsible for foreign affairs, Frans Andriessen, accepted that the EC position might be regarded rather unfair, but commented that that was simply part of 'the unevenness of life', that the EC simply could not give the privileges of club membership to those who were not willing to pay the entrance fee. That constituted the fundamental dilemma for EFTA. It did not want to be affected by the political implications which some in the Twelve had drawn from the SEA; on the other hand, it could not afford to be pushed totally to the sidelines after 1992. It created a problem too for the EC. For if the EC conditions were regarded by EFTA as being too severe, then some of its members in addition to Austria might decide that economic salvation lay only through seeking EC membership. While that would advance the long–term cause of European integration, it was not a course which the EC wished to contemplate before the single market was in position and operating.

In the second half of 1989 the EC along with the rest of the western world was shaken by the speed of events in Eastern Europe as one by one the Communist regimes saw their hegemony fatally weakened or were swept from power. The dramatic surge of Eastern Europe towards democratisation required an EC response, and for the first time since 1945 it raised possibilities of a genuine pan-European union. Eastern Europe, however, posed a serious dilemma for the EC – the same dilemma it faced with EFTA, but on a larger scale. The East European states wanted some kind of association with the EC. Some wanted more than this. Poland led the way by saying that it would shortly be seeking membership. Czechoslovakia followed suit by seeking a commitment from the EC to hold talks on membership within five years. After several hurried meetings, the Twelve eventually agreed as a first step to offer association agreements to the East European states along the lines negotiated with EFTA, but most did not wish these agreements, unlike those made with Greece and Turkey over 20 years earlier, to incorporate any explicit promise of eventual membership.

The one exception was East Germany. Because of the seeming headlong rush of the two Germanies towards reunification, the EC became resigned to East Germany becoming a member one way or another. Ever since the Ostpolitik agreements of the early 1970s East Germany had been linked to the EC through the bilateral German agreements. In any case, there was also a legal argument in that when the Treaty of Rome had been drawn up, West Germany had insisted upon the inclusion of a clause that would make membership of a reunited Germany possible. For some, however, this legal technicality was not a sufficient basis to discriminate between East Germany and the other states.

The events of 1989 led to a renewed debate within the EC between those who wanted first priority to be given to enlargement, and those that wanted first to push on with a tighter union. The wideners argued that the EC had to be more positive in sponsoring democratic developments in Eastern Europe, suggesting on the one hand that if East Germany was regarded as a special case, then much of the argument for delaying any consideration of Austria also disappeared, and on the other that it would be selfish and inappropriate not to offer a helping hand to Eastern Europe similar to that proffered earlier to the ex-dictatorships of Southern Europe. And beyond Eastern Europe lay the thorny problem of Turkey which in 1987 had renewed its application for membership. In addition, since the entry of East Germany seemed to have been accepted as being inevitable, some smaller states began to feel that enlargement would help to offset the even greater dominance a united Germany would have within the Europe of the Twelve. Those who wanted the EC to widen its horizons, reluctantly or gladly depending upon their views on European Union, were prepared to accept a slowing down of integration as the price of enlargement.

Their opponents argued that comparisons with the past were misleading, since conditions had changed because of the decision to introduce the internal market, and that all discussions on enlargement must be deferred until not only the single market but also, hopefully, European Union was in place. The member states most committed to this course seemed to be France and Italy, although the most powerful voice in favour was probably that of the Commission. For the medium term the Commission image of the continent was one of concentric rings, with the EC at the centre. The inner ring would be formed by the EFTA states which would have access to the single market, while Eastern Europe, as the outer ring, would receive some trade advantages and aid. Delors was prepared to accept East Germany into the epicentre more or less immediately, but in return wanted West Germany to support his plans for EMU.

It was the events in Eastern Europe which made Delors and others even more determined in 1990 to push harder for European Union as a necessary corollary of the internal market. As part of the campaign, speaking to the EP in Strasbourg, Delors called in January 1990 for institutional reform to supplement his demands for EMU and a Social Charter. He argued that the Commission must be given greater decision-making powers to become a 'real executive'; it would be answerable to and counterbalanced by 'the democratic institutions of the future Federation', especially an enhanced EP which he wanted also to have a say in choosing the Commission. Predictably, this federalist route was opposed by Britain, which commented that the proposal was 'premature'.

Delors' move was an attempt to make sure that the EC was not sidetracked by Eastern Europe. It was also intended to widen the brief of the intergovernmental conference which, scheduled to meet in late 1990, the European Council had agreed, in December 1989 in Strasbourg, to establish to consider EMU. The EP also weighed in to the campaign. Delors wanted the conference also to combine EMU with institutional reform in a package that the states would have to accept or reject as a whole. Most governments desired EMU, though only a few were, initially at least, in favour of the twin-track approach. What was clear was that as the EC moved into the final straight of its chase for the internal market, the events of 1989 had sharpened all the old debates that have plagued the EC over the decades: integration or enlargement, intergovernmental cooperation or supranationalism, national sovereignty or federalism. They are debates that cannot easily be resolved. The danger, ever present in the past, is that those like Delors who wished to advance towards European Union would themselves generate opposition with sufficient weight to block progress. This has been the European reality since 1957. On the other hand, the reality of 1992 in its most limited form, setting aside the symbolism, will involve a further loss of national sovereignty. This can only increase the democratic deficit within the EC. Because national parliaments already have little power within the EC, that perhaps will increase the pressure for a greater and more positive role for the EP. Several member governments, perhaps, underestimated the political consequences of the SEA, How the members will react to the post-1992 world will be decisive in determining the future direction of the EC.

But that the EC will remain central to the European firmament seems beyond dispute. Membership has locked the countries in a firm embrace, despite the innumerable squabbles. Even at the height of their disputes with the rest, neither Britain, Denmark nor Greece – at least at the governmental level – seriously raised the question of withdrawal. Even in her most strident critiques of the EC, Mrs Thatcher always stressed that Britain would remain an equal and loyal member of the Community. In that way the EC has become a fact of life, and like most lives it has developed through a layering of experiences, a series of accretions – some mutually reinforcing, some contradictory – which imperceptibly have bound its members ever more closely together, always pushing them towards closer and further collaboration. Despite the heartaches of the past, this slower and more erratic approach has over the long term perhaps been the better road to follow than the grand dramatic drives that have been suggested from time to time. Those drives, and the rhetoric which fuelled them, nevertheless had a useful role to play; they served to keep alive the debate over where the EC ought to be going.

For Western Europe the EC had by the 1990s become, more than ever, something which Helmut Schmidt had pointed to in 1983, 'the core of that part of Europe in which we live and which provides the political chance to shape the future of our societies'. On the eve of the first enlargement of the EC in 1973, there was a book published on the Community which had as its subtitle the phrase, 'Journey to an Unknown Destination'. By the 1990s, while the EC states might still not know exactly what they would find at the end of the road, they could not but be clearer in their minds about the direction of the journey and the destination for which they were aiming; and recent events suggest that the other European states might well be obliged, sooner or later, to follow along the same route. Despite the rise and continuing force of the European Council, the 1980s witnessed a further decay of nationalism and national sovereignty, if not of national identity. Short of a political cataclysm, it is probable that time can only bring the destination of the EC into sharper focus. Rhetoric may eventually be turned into reality.

Appendix 1

PRESIDENTS OF THE COMMISSION OF THE EUROPEAN COMMUNITY (UNTIL 1967 OF THE EUROPEAN ECONOMIC COMMUNITY)

1958	Walter Hallstein
1967	Jean Rey
1970	Franco-Maria Malfatti
1972	Sicco Mansholt
1973	François-Xavier Ortoli
1977	Roy Jenkins
1981	Gaston Thorn
1985	Jacques Delors

PRESIDENTS OF HIGH AUTHORITY OF THE EUROPEAN COAL AND STEEL COMMUNITY (MERGED WITH EEC COMMISSION IN 1967)

1952	Jean Monnet
1955	René Mayer
1958	Paul Finet
1959	Piero Malvestiti
1963	Dino Del Bo

PRESIDENTS OF THE COMMISSION OF EURATOM (MERGED WITH EEC COMMISSION IN 1967)

1958	Louis Armand
1959	Etienne Hirsch
1962	Pierre Chatenet

Appendix 2

DIRECTORATES-GENERAL AND SERVICES OF THE COMMISSION

Directorates-General as at September 1990

I   External Relations
II   Economic and Financial Affairs
III   Internal Market and Industrial Affairs; Small and Medium-Sized Enterprises
IV   Competition
V   Employment, Social Affairs and Education
VI   Agriculture
VII   Transport
VIII   Development
IX   Personnel and Administration
X   Information, Communication and Culture
XI   Environment and Nuclear Safety
XII   Science, Research and Development; Joint Research Centre
XIII   Telecommunications, Information Industries and Innovation
XIV   Fisheries
XV   Financial Institutions and Company Law
XVI   Regional Policy
XVII   Energy
XVIII   Credit and Investments
XIX   Budgets
XX   Financial Control
XXI   Customs Union and Indirect Taxation
XXII   Coordination of Structural Instruments
XXIII   Consumer Affairs

Services

Euratom Supply Agency
Joint Interpreting and Conference Service
Legal Service

248

Office for Official Publications of the European Communities
Secretariat-General of the Commission
Security Office
Spokesman's Service
Statistical Office (Eurostat)

Appendix 3

A POSTWAR CHRONOLOGY OF INTEGRATION

1947	March	Announcement of Truman Doctrine by USA; Signature of Treaty of Dunkirk
	June	Declaration of Marshall Plan by USA
	October	Establishment of General Agreement on Tariffs and Trade (GATT)
1948	January	Commencement of Benelux Customs Union
	March	Signature of Treaty of Brussels
	April	Establishment of Organisation for European Economic Cooperation (OEEC)
	May	Congress of Europe and formation of the European Movement
1949	April	Signature of Atlantic Pact and formation of North Atlantic Treaty Organisation (NATO)
	May	Signature of Treaty of Westminster and formation of Council of Europe
1950	May	Publication of Schuman Plan
	October	Publication of Pleven Plan
	November	European Convention for the Protection of Human Rights and Fundamental Freedoms
1951	April	Treaty of Paris and establishment of European Coal and Steel Community (ECSC)
1952	May	Signature of European Defence Community (EDC) treaty
	July	European Coal and Steel Community comes into operation
1953	March	Draft Treaty on European Political Community
1954	August	Rejection of EDC by France; collapse of EDC and European Political Community

250

	October	West European Union (WEU) treaty signed
	December	Association agreement between ECSC and the United Kingdom
1955	May	West European Union begins to operate
	June	Messina Conference on 'further European integration'
	July	Establishment of Spaak Committee
	December	United Kingdom proposal for a 'Grand Design' on European cooperation
1956	March	Completion of Spaak Report
1957	February	United Kingdom proposes a European free trade association
	March	Signature of Treaty of Rome
	October	Formation of Maudling Committee on free trade areas
1958	January	Commencement of European Economic Community (EEC) and European Atomic Energy Commission (Euratom)
	December	France terminates Maudling free trade area negotiations
1960	January	Signature of Stockholm Convention and establishment of European Free Trade Association (EFTA)
	December	Organisation for European Economic Cooperation (OEEC) reorganised into Organisation for Economic Cooperation and Development (OECD)
1961	July	Fouchet Plan for a 'union of states'; EEC agrees on associate membership for Greece; Ireland applies for EEC membership
	August	Denmark and the United Kingdom apply for EEC membership
	October	Negotiations begin between the EEC and the three applicant states
1962	January	EEC adopts basic regulations for a common agricultural policy
	May	Norway requests negotiations on membership

1963	January	President de Gaulle vetoes British membership of EEC; Signature of Franco–West German Treaty of Friendship
	July	Signature of Youndé Convention
	September	Agreement between EEC and Turkey on associate membership
1965	April	Agreement to establish unified executive for the three Communities
	June	France walks out of Council of Ministers: the empty chair crisis
	December	Signature of Free Trade Agreement between Ireland and the United Kingdom
1966	January	Luxembourg Compromise
	May/July	Agreement on a Common Agricultural Policy
1967	May	Denmark, Ireland and the United Kingdom apply for EC membership
	July	Unified Commission and Council of Ministers implemented; Norway applies for EC membership
	November	President de Gaulle vetoes British membership
1968	February	Draft treaty for a Nordek customs union
	July	Removal of EEC internal customs duties, establishment of a common external tariff, and acceptance of a Common Agricultural Policy (CAP)
1969	December	Hague summit agrees on principle of EEC enlargement; End of EEC transitional period, and acceptance of new financial regulations
1970	March	Abandonment by the Nordic states of NORDEK proposals
	April	Treaty of Luxembourg amends the Treaty of Rome to provide a new financial structure for the EC
	June	EC opens membership negotiations with Denmark, Ireland, Norway and the United Kingdom
	October	Publication of Werner Report on Economic and Monetary Union; Publication of Davignon Report on European Political Cooperation
	November	Launch of European Political Cooperation

1971	December	EC begins negotiations with non-applicant EFTA states; Smithsonian Agreement
1972	January	Conclusion of negotiations and signature of Treaty of Accession by Denmark, Ireland, Norway and the United Kingdom
	March	European states establish the Snake
	May	Irish referendum supports EC entry
	July	EC and the EFTA states conclude a series of Special Relations Agreement
	September	Norwegian referendum rejects EC membership
	October	Danish referendum accepts EC membership; Paris summit on guidelines for future Community development
	December	Denmark and the United Kingdom leave EFTA
1973	January	Accession of Denmark, Ireland and United Kingdom to EC
	February	Agreement on accession to Common Agricultural Policy and on a five-year transition period for the new members
	May	Signature of Special Relations Agreement with Norway
	July	Opening of Conference on Security and Cooperation in Europe; Second Davignon Report on European Political Cooperation
	December	Copenhagen summit deals with European identity
1974	April	United Kingdom demands renegotiation of terms of accession
	December	Paris summit agrees to establish a European Council
1975	March	Conclusion of renegotiations between EC and United Kingdom; First meeting of European Council in Dublin
	April	Signature of Lomé Convention
	June	Greece applies for EC membership; British referendum supports renegotiated terms and continued EC membership
	August	Conclusion of Conference on Security and Cooperation in Europe and signature of the Helsinki Final Act

1976	January	Publication of Tindemans Report
	July	Negotiations on membership begin with Greece
1977	March	Portugal applies for EC membership
	July	Spain applies for EC membership
1978	October	EC opens negotiations with Portugal
1979	February	EC opens negotiations with Spain
	March	Establishment of European Monetary System (EMS)
	May	Treaty of Accession between EC and Greece
	June	First direct elections to the European Parliament (EP); United Kingdom argues for a reduction of its budget contributions
1981	January	Accession of Greece to EC; Genscher–Colombo initiative on European integration
1982	February	Greenland referendum votes in favour of withdrawal from EC
1983	June	Signature of Solemn Declaration on European Union by EC heads of state and government
1984	January	EC and EFTA establish a free trade area
	February	European Parliament approves Draft Treaty on European Union
	March	Signature of agreement on withdrawal of Greenland from EC
	June	Second direct elections to European Parliament; Fontainebleau summit of European Council agrees on solutions to internal EC problems; Revival of West European Union as a European defence forum
1985	February	Greenland withdraws from EC
	March	European Council agrees on Integrated Mediterranean Programmes; European Council agrees on an internal single market by December 1992; Report of Dooge Committee on institutional reform
	June	Signature of Treaties of Accession with Portugal and Spain; Report of Adonnino Committee on a People's Europe; Milan summit of European Council agrees on reform of Treaty of Rome

	September	Opening of intergovernmental conference on EC reform
	December	European Council agrees on text for amending the Treaty of Rome and adopts the Single European Act (SEA)
1986	January	Accession of Spain and Portugal to Community
1987	July	Single European Act comes into effect
	August	Turkey applies for EC membership
1988	January	Introduction of Single Administrative Document
	February	European Council accepts Delors Package on budgetary reform
1989	May	Proposals for a EC Charter of Fundamental Social Rights
	June	Third direct elections to European Parliament
	July	Austria applies for EC membership
1990	February	Mrs Thatcher criticises EC centralisation in Bruges speech
	June	EC Commission calls for institutional reform

Appendix 4

ELECTIONS TO THE EUROPEAN PARLIAMENT

Since 1979 the European Parliament has been elected directly in all the member states. Since the accession of Spain and Portugal its membership is 518. Each member state receives an allocation of seats roughly proportional to its size. The lifespan of a Parliament is five years, with no provision for early dissolution. There is, as yet, no provision for a common electoral system, and each member state uses its own system. In the elections seats are contested by the national political parties. In the European Parliament, however, the elected representatives join in cross-national or European political groups. In the Parliament elected in 1989, there are ten such political groups.

Allocation of Seats

Belgium   24
Denmark   16
Federal Republic of Germany   81 (including 3 appointed members from West Berlin)
France   81
Greece   24
Ireland   15
Italy   81
Luxembourg   6
Netherlands   25
Portugal   24
Spain   60
United Kingdom   81

Electoral Systems

Belgium: Proportional Representation, regional party lists
Denmark: Proportional Representation, national party lists

Federal Republic of Germany: Proportional Representation, regional party lists

France: Proportional Representation, national party lists

Greece: Proportional Representation, national party lists

Ireland: Single Transferable Vote (STV)

Italy: Proportional Representation, regional party lists

Luxembourg: Proportional Representation, national party lists

Netherlands: Proportional Representation, national party lists

Portugal: Proportional Representation, national party lists

Spain: Proportional Representation, regional party lists

United Kingdom: Plurality (but Single Transferable Vote for 3 seats in Northern Ireland)

Political Groups

European Democratic Alliance (mainly Gaullists)

European Democratic Group (Conservatives)

European People's Party (Christian Democrats)

European Right

French Communists and Allies

Greens

Italian Communists and Allies

Liberal and Democratic Group

Rainbow Group (mainly Regionalist parties)

Appendix 5

The institutional structure of the European Communities

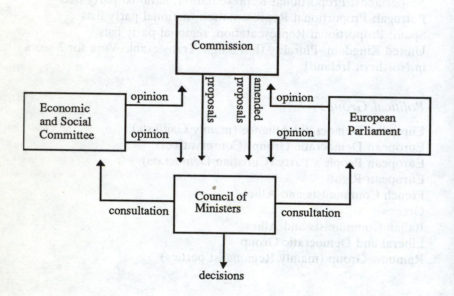

A Guide to Further Reading

There is a huge literature on European integration – and especially on the European Community – which is a complex mix of the dispassionate and the polemical. Apart from its daunting size, this literature poses two further problems for the general reader and those seeking more information on the subject: much of it is very specialised, even technical, and the speed of developments on the ground, especially over the past two decades or so, has been such that many books soon become dated. These points should be borne in mind by those who wish to use this introductory guide to further reading.

A comprehensive bibliographic guide to the earlier literature on the EC is provided by D. Overton, *Common Market Digest* (London 1983). For more recent EC developments, a useful source of information is the large number of pamphlets and other documents issued by the Commission in Brussels. These publications are available, many of them free of charge, from the information offices of the Community which are located in the national capitals and other major centres of the EC, as well as in several other large cities throughout the world.

The number of general introductions to the EC is immense. Among recent publications that offer a good overview of the situation are C. Archer, *Organising Western Europe* (London 1990), D. Leonard, *Pocket-Guide to the European Community* (London 1988), and W. Nicoll and T. Salmon, *Understanding the EC* (London 1990). Older texts which are still quite useful include S.A. Budd, *The EEC: A Guide to the Maze* (Edinburgh 1985), and A.J.C. Kerr, *The Common Market and How it Works* (Oxford 1986). Two recent reference works offer a guide to the multifarious bodies and policies of the Community. The

Directory of the European Community (London 1991) includes an extensive A–Z listing, with brief descriptions, of EC institutions, agencies, policies and practices, while A. Taylor, *Eurojargon* (Newcastle 1988) is a comprehensive listing of the acronyms and initials that pepper the EC structure.

Many useful insights into the operation of the Community are often provided by people who have participated in its activities. Two of the best, perceptive and informative, which nevertheless have different views of the organisation, are by an ex-commissioner, C. Tugendhat, *Making Sense of Europe* (London 1986), and a previous British Permanent Representative to the EC, Sir M. Butler, *Europe: More than a Continent* (London 1986).

The policy competences and activities of the EC are also the subject of a large literature: inevitably, perhaps, much of this literature is about economics as much as it is about politics. A standard introduction is D. Swann, *The Economics of the Common Market* (London 1988). Among others which adopt a general policy perspective, J. Harrop, *The Political Economy of Integration in the European Community* (Aldershot 1989) offers a useful and not too technical overview. Though somewhat dated, the chapters in H. Wallace, W. Wallace and C. Webb (eds), *Policy-Making in the European Community* (London 1983) are detailed analyses that, with a relevance beyond the 1970s, can still be read with profit. Also still of value is P. Coffey (ed.), *The Economic Policies of the Common Market* (London 1979). S. George, *Politics and Policy in the European Community* (London 1985) is a short textbook introduction to policy competences and applications. On more recent developments and their possible consequences, readers can consult the perspectives in J. Lodge (ed.), *The EC and the Challenge of the Future* (London 1989).

Studies of specific policy areas tend to be more technical. However, good accounts of monetary policy and the establishment of the European Monetary System can be found in D.C. Kruse, *Monetary Integration in Western Europe* (London 1980) and P. Ludlow, *The Making of the European Monetary System* (London 1982). The complexities of the Common Agricultural Policy are explained in detail in E. Neville-Rolfe, *The Politics of Agriculture in the European Community* (London 1984), B.E. Hill, *The Common Agricultural Policy: Past, Present and Future* (London 1984) and J.S. Marsh and P. Swanney, *Agriculture and the EC* (London 1980). Trade patterns and policies are discussed by R. Hine, *The Political Economy of European Trade* (Brighton 1985), while J. Drew, *Doing Business in the European Community* (London 1983) provides excellent background information. Despite the narrowness of its title, N. Haigh, *ECC Environmental Policy and Britain* (London 1987) is informative on Community thinking in an increasingly important policy area.

Most books on the Community refer in some detail to its institutional structures. In addition to the general references readers can turn to J. Fitzmaurice, *The European Parliament* (Farnborough 1978) and the more recent (and useful) A. Robinson, *The EP in the EC Policy Process* (London 1985). Albeit rather dully written, S. Bulmer and W. Wessels, *The European Council* (London 1987) is a wealth of information on its role and position within the Community.

The external political relations of the EC, attempts to develop a common foreign policy, and evaluations of the operation of European Political Cooperation have been dealt with by several authors. While no good integrated account as yet exists, good coverage is provided by C. Hill (ed.), *National Foreign Policies and European Political Cooperation* (London 1983); D. Allen et al., *European Political Cooperation* (London 1982); J.K. De Vrees, P. Coffey and R.H. Lauwaars (eds), *Towards a European Foreign Policy* (Dardrecht 1987); and P. Ifestos, *European Political Cooperation* (Aldershot 1987).

The EC's relationships with the Third World, especially with the signatories of the Lome Conventions, are adequately covered by C. Stevens (ed.), *The ECC and the Third World* (London 1981); C.C. Twitchett, *A Framework for Development* (London 1981); J. Ravenhill, *Collective Clientelism: The Lome Convention and North-South Relations* (London 1985).

The arguments about and efforts for closer political union within the Community have not as yet received any concise and systematic treatment. The contributions to R. Pryce (ed.), *The Dynamics of European Union* (London 1987) are informative, though of uneven quality. A more critical stance is adopted by P. Taylor, *The Limits of European Integration* (London 1983), while J. Lodge (ed.), *European Union* (London 1986) is an exhaustive dissection of the Draft Treaty on European Union and its implication. The arguments of the 1960s, focusing mainly upon the policies and attitudes of President De Gaulle, are treated in a lively manner by J. Pinder, *Europe Against de Gaulle* (London 1963), and more sombrely by S.J. Bodenheimer, *Political Union: A Microcosm of European Politics 1960–1966* (Leiden 1967), and L. Lindberg and S.A. Scheingold, *Europe's Would-Be Polity* (Englewood Cliffs 1970).

For an analysis of the recent roles of, and relationships between, France and West Germany, H. Simonian, *The Privileged Partnership: France–German Relations in the European Community* (Oxford 1985) is indispensable. Their interactions and roles in the first postwar decades are thoroughly covered in F.R. Willis, *France, Germany and the New Europe 1945–1967* (London 1969). Also useful are R. Morgan and C. Bray (eds), *Partners and Rivals in Western Europe: Britain, France and Germany* (London 1986), and S. Bulmer and W.E. Paterson, *The Federal Republic of Germany and the European Community* (London 1987).

Inevitably, Britain's 'problematic' position within the EC has attracted considerable attention. The most recent account which links Britain's behaviour in the Community with its domestic politics, is S. George, *An Awkward Partner: Britain in the European Community* (London 1990). Earlier studies which provide valuable analysis and comment include R. Jenkins (ed.), *Britain and the EEC* (London 1983); W. Wallace (ed.), *Britain in Europe* (London 1980); and K. Perry, *Britain and the European Community* (London 1984). The situation before and after the reversal of British policy towards Europe and the decision to apply for EEC membership is explained by M. Camps, *Britain and the European Community 1955–1963* (London 1964). The fate of the first British application is the theme of the brief but informative N. Beloff, *The General Says No* (London 1963), while U.W. Kitzinger (ed.), *The Second Try: Labour and the EEC* (London 1968) deals with the circumstances that led to the 1967 application for membership.

The historical background to and the wider European political and economic environment of the community are thoroughly covered by D.W. Urwin, *Western Europe Since 1945* (London 1989).

The tense international climate of the immediate postwar decade is well covered. Two useful introductions to the theme are L.W. Davis, *The Cold War Begins* (Princeton 1974) and A.W. Deporte, *Europe Between The Superpowers* (New Haven 1986). On American policy towards Europe during these years, students may consult M. Beloff, *The United States and the Unity of Europe* (London 1963) and F.S.C. Northrop, *European Union and United States Foreign Policy* (New York 1954). Marshall Aid is covered thoroughly by J. Gimbel, *The Origins of the Marshall Plan* (Stanford 1976); M.J. Hogan, *The Marshall Plan* (London 1987); and H.B. Price, *The Marshall Plan and its Meaning* (Ithaca 1955). The events that led up to the establishment of NATO are recounted in T.P. Ireland, *Creating The Entangling Alliance* (Westport 1981). A Grosser, *The Western Alliance: European American Relations since 1945* (London 1980) offers a broad postwar survey. The more uneasy relationship of the 1980s is the theme of J. Palmer, *Europe Without America?* (London 1987) and M. Smith, *Western Europe and the United States: The Uncertain Alliance* (London 1984). An earlier work by R.J. Schaetzch, *The Unhinged Alliance* (New York 1975), focuses more specifically on relationships between the USA and the Community.

There are several useful general introductions to the postwar efforts to achieve European integration prior to the Treaty of Rome. These broad surveys include R. Vaughan, *Twentieth Century Europe* (London 1979); A.J. Zurcher, *The Struggle to Unite Europe 1940–1958* (New York 1958); R. Morgan, *West European Politics since 1945: The Shaping of the EC* (London 1972). E.B. Haas, *The Uniting of Europe* (London 1958) is a more rigorous analysis within a neofunctionalist framework. For a fascinating account of the events of the first postwar decades by one of their prime movers, Jean Monnet's *Memoirs* (London 1978) is essential reading. Also of great interest is the book by the first president of the EEC Commission, W. Hallstein, *Europe in the Making* (London 1972).

A solid descriptive overview of the several organisations that emerged after 1945, from a rather legalistic perspective, is A.H. Robertson, *European Institutions* (London 1973). Other European institutions have not been as extensively researched as the EC. However, for the 1940s readers may consult J.E. Meade, *Negotiations for Benelux* (Princeton 1957) for the details of the first postwar experiment in integration, while the structure and first years of operation of Europe's first political association are reviewed in V.D. Hurd, *The Council of Europe* (New York 1958).

On the forerunners of the Community, W. Diebold, *The Schuman Plan* (New York 1959) and L. Lister, *Europe's Coal and Steel Community* (New York 1960) analyse the operation and problems of the ECSC. As for the ill-fated European Defence Community the passions it aroused, especially in France, are well portrayed in R. Aron and D. Lerner, *France Defeats EDC* (London 1957); E. Fursdon, *The European Defence Community* (London 1979) is a more clinical treatment.

For the split after the late 1950s between the Europes of the Six and the Seven, readers may consult F.V. Meyer, *The Seven* (London 1960) and E. Benoit, *Europe at Sixes and Sevens* (New York 1961). The developing relations between the EC and EFTA are covered in P. Coffey, *The External Economic Relations of the EEC* (London 1976), while the problems that the commitment of the EC to an internal market have posed for EFTA are discussed by T. Pedersen, *The Wider Western Europe* (London 1988).

Accounts of efforts at political and economic cooperation and integration in Scandinavia can be found in B. Cornelius, *Managing Transnationalism in Northern Europe* (Boulder 1978); and E. Solem, *The*

Nordic Council and Scandinavian Integration (New York 1971). The more suspicious and cautionary attitude of the Nordic states to integration is the theme of T. Miljan, *The Reluctant Europeans* (Montreal 1977). For a good account of the particular problems of and debates within Norway, reference can be made to H. Allen, *Norway and Europe in the 1970's* (Oslo 1979).

As for the future of the EC and European integration, much of the literature necessarily has a speculative content. A good starting point is P. Cecchini et al., *1992: The Benefits of a Single Market* (Aldershot 1988), the report of an exercise sponsored by the Commission on the value of a single market. A similar stocktaking can be found in J. Pelkman and A. Winters, *Europe's Domestic Market* (London 1988). Rather more of the potential political consequences is included in J. Lodge (ed.), *The European Community and the Challenge of the Future* (London 1989); J. Palmer, *Trading Places: The Future of the European Community* (London 1988); and N. Colchester and D. Buchan, *Europe Relaunched: Truths and Illusions On The Way to 1992* (London 1990). For a passionate and optimistic view by a leader of the International European Movement, see E. Wistrich, *After 1992: The United States of Europe* (London 1989).

Map

GREENLAND
(left EEC 1973)

The growth of the European Economic Community

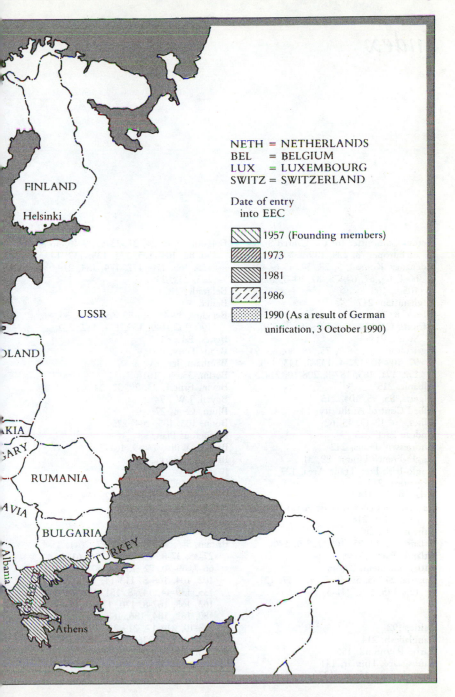

NETH = NETHERLANDS
BEL = BELGIUM
LUX = LUXEMBOURG
SWITZ = SWITZERLAND

Date of entry
 into EEC

1957 (Founding members)

1973

1981

1986

1990 (As a result of German
 unification, 3 October 1990)

FINLAND

Helsinki

USSR

OLAND

KIA

GARY

RUMANIA

AVIA

BULGARIA

TURKEY

Albania

GREECE

Athens

Index